Combat Over Korea

Combat Over Korea

Philip Chinnery

Pen & Sword
AVIATION

First published in Great Britain in 2011 by
Pen & Sword Aviation
an imprint of
Pen & Sword Books Ltd
47 Church Street
Barnsley
South Yorkshire
S70 2AS

ISBN 978-1-84884-477-3

A CIP catalogue record for this book is available from the British Library.

Typeset in 11pt Ehrhardt by
Mac Style, Beverley, E. Yorkshire

Printed and bound in the UK by CPI

Pen & Sword Books Ltd incorporates the Imprints of Pen & Sword
Aviation, Pen & Sword Family History, Pen & Sword Maritime, Pen &
Sword Military, Pen & Sword Discovery, Wharncliffe Local History,
Wharncliffe True Crime, Wharncliffe Transport, Pen & Sword Select,
Pen & Sword Military Classics, Leo Cooper, The Praetorian Press,
Remember When, Seaforth Publishing and Frontline Publishing.

For a complete list of Pen & Sword titles please contact
PEN & SWORD BOOKS LIMITED
47 Church Street, Barnsley, South Yorkshire, S70 2AS, England
E-mail: enquiries@pen-and-sword.co.uk
Website: www.pen-and-sword.co.uk

Contents

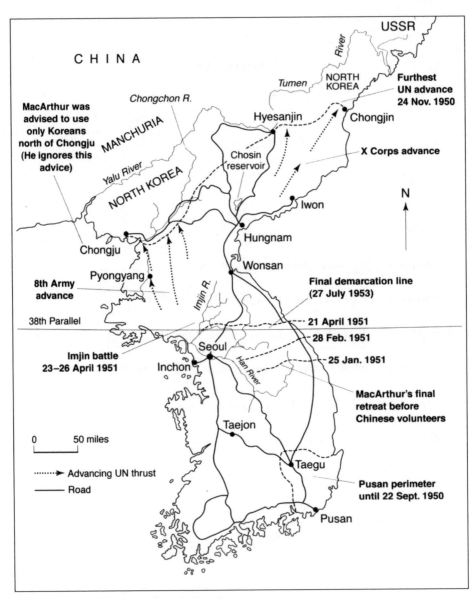

The movement of the battle lines during the war.

Combat Over Korea

Introduction

THIS IS a book about the reality of aerial warfare against a merciless enemy above the forbidding terrain of the Korean Peninsula. It will tell the story of a struggle by brave men to overcome not only enemy fighters and flak, but to prevail under horrendous flying conditions, often piloting aircraft that were outdated and using unreliable ordnance left over from the Second World War.

Generally speaking, most fighters or bombers return home at the end of their mission and their crews can look forward to a hot meal, a drink or two and a bed to sleep in. The unlucky few who have been shot down can expect terror, pain and the prospect of death before they hit the ground. Once on the ground in Korea, aircrew soon discovered that this was a different war to that fought over Europe in the Second World War. There would not be a brief interrogation, followed by a trip to the nearest Stalag or Oflag where one would exist on Red Cross food parcels, reading letters and books sent from home. There would be no camp theatrical groups to join and no escape committee producing false documents and altering uniforms to blend in with the civilian population.

Those unlucky enough to survive captivity under the Japanese in the Second World War claimed that the Korean guards were the worst of the lot. Aircrew shot down over Korea soon discovered what this meant – a complete lack of mercy and humanity, where captured aircrew would be tortured and killed, or forced to march bare foot through snow, without food or medical attention. Their interrogators would starve them or threaten them with death, before sending them to prison camps where they would slowly fade away due to the harsh conditions and poor diet.

When the Chinese entered the war things changed slightly in that captured aircrew had more of a chance of reaching a prison camp in one piece. Once there however, they would begin a process of indoctrination where the amount of food you had to eat was directly related to your willingness to embrace the communist cause. To incur their wrath however, would often result in severe punishment or death.

The stories in this book are told by aircrew who were lucky enough to return home after completing their tour of duty, as well as some taken prisoner and released at the end of the war. The final chapter will discuss the fate of those who did not make it back and the lessons to be learnt for the future. And the future may arrive sooner than we think.

Philip Chinnery, London 2011

Acknowledgements

I would like to thank the following for their kind assistance with the research for Combat over Korea; Spyros Andreopoulos, Peter Arbuthnot, Robert Arndt, John Baker, T.C. Crouson, Bob Dahlberg, Jim Flemming, Clarence Fry, Ron Guthrie, Lesley Gent, Martin Fick Henderson, Joseph Holden, Steve Kiba, Lyall Klaffer, Bill Latham, Walter Laute, Alan Leahy, Robert C. Mikesh, Dan Oldewage, Roland Parks, Leroy Pratt, Don Smith, David C. Swann, Howard Tanner, Joe Wosser and the Cold War Association. I hope they will enjoy the final product.

Chapter 1

Invaders from the North

Chapter Contents

The Shipwreck Party

ON THE morning that the Korean War began most of the pilots of 77 Squadron, Royal Australian Air Force, were either drunk or nursing hangovers. And why not? Their tour of duty in Japan was at an end and they were about to return home. Some of the ground crews had already left and many of their Mustangs were cocooned in plastic ready for the sea journey back to Australia. One of their pilots, Jim Flemming, recalled the day that war broke out on the Korean Peninsula:

'The final flight of 77 Squadrons Mustangs landed at Iwakuni on Friday 23 June 1950. The aircraft were then to be prepared for transportation back to Australia. Already the arrangements had been made for a weekend-long party for all members of the squadron, designed as a party to end all parties. The 77 hangar had been decked out as a venue where the airmen and other ranks could celebrate. The Sergeants Mess was transformed into a desert island and pirate's lair and many American guests, from as a far afield as Itazuke, Ashiya and Tokyo, had been invited to join the revelry.

'A "Shipwreck" party had been organised by the sergeants for all Mess members, and all officers and wives were invited to rendezvous at 8 pm on 24 June. To join the party was not without difficulty. Guests had to "walk the plank" to board a sailing ship model outside the Mess main door after disposing of a special pirate cocktail to gain entry. Geoff Thornton and me, dressed as skeletal looking pirates, had buckets of whisky and water pistols, and everyone who gained entry through the door had to open their mouths and a squirt of Scotch whisky was administered. This started at about 7 pm, so imagine how the party developed.

'Once inside, the guests were greeted by the sight of an island, rigged inside the Mess, surrounded by rubber dinghies in lieu of seats. Those found not imbibing at the required rate were thrown into a brig, where the piratical jailers would ply them with liquor until the recalcitrant ones were judged sufficiently respectably "sozzled" enough to be freed to mix with the island's "shipwrecked inhabitants".

'Everyone was required to wear suitable "castaway" attire. Those who were not suitably attired were given a "fair" trial and deposited in the fishpond outside the Mess as punishment. Most of the piratical members were clad in swimming trunks and shirts, shorts and nightshirts tied with neckties and all complimented by the required "snake bite remedy" under the arm. The CO Wing Commander Lou Spence and his wife had arrived in tennis shorts and shirts and were approved as they had been playing deck tennis when the ship was captured by the pirates.

'As etiquette required, the CO departed the festivities at about 1 am. The Japanese jazz band, in the tradition of that which played aboard the Titanic, performed until after 3 am on the morning of 25 June. Some had retired but the diehards were still at it at 5 am. The band was ordered back to start playing again at 8 am and the party regained its rather hectic pace and was progressing well until the fateful telephone call from Tokyo came in.

'Pilot 3 Ray Trebilco was acting Orderly Sergeant and had to stay reasonably sober so he answered the telephone at about 10.45 am on

25 June. The call was from the US 5th Air Force HQ in Tokyo and the caller, an American colonel, told Ray that 77 Squadron was to be on immediate standby as North Korea had invaded the South that morning. Ray laughed at this and replied, "Hey! Good try, but you can't take the mickey out of us. We are all packed up and ready to go back to Australia. We are having a great farewell party so come and join us" – and hung up the phone.

'Within twenty minutes another phone call came, this time from a rather angry American General at 5th Air Force HQ. Now Ray was a bit worried and reported by telephone to Squadron Leader Graham Strout, the squadron Operations Officer, at his home. Graham Strout drove to Wing Commander Spence's home and advised him of the situation. Spence and his wife were preparing for a skiing holiday, but it was never to be as he was shot down and killed a couple of months later.

'None of the pilots believed that the situation was genuine and many told Trebilco to "Bugger off and don't be ridiculous". However Spence ordered all drinking to cease and closed the bars. He arranged for all aircrew to be briefed in the Mess at 1.30 pm on Sunday, 25 June and by mid afternoon all ranks from the CO down to the cooks were actively engaged in the awful task of de-inhibiting the Mustangs which had been prepared for the sea voyage to Australia.

'The next week saw the drop tanks fitted, guns armed and all aircraft test flown. Under the expert guidance of Flight Sergeant Darby Freeman, the Squadron senior engineering NCO, all the pilots were trained in minimal aircraft maintenance and by 30 June the squadron was able to report 100 per cent serviceable craft. Bad weather prevented any flying until 1 July. The first squadron operational mission was flown at first light on 2 July 1950 and the first RAAF mission over North Korea on the afternoon of the same day.'

Dawn Attack

At 0500 hours on 25 June, as the 77 Squadron pilots were enjoying their farewell party and the early light of dawn was cresting the horizon, the North Korean gunners slammed the breeches shut on their Soviet supplied artillery pieces and began a short fifteen-minute barrage as the tanks of the 105th Armoured Division belched smoke from their exhausts and prepared to advance. At 0515 hours they crossed the line of departure, followed closely by infantry from the 3rd Division commanded by Major General Lee Yong Ho. With the 2nd Division on their left flank and the 4th Division on their right, they crossed the 38th Parallel and began their march on Seoul, the capital of South Korea. Seven infantry divisions were on the move, together with an armoured brigade and two more infantry divisions were following in reserve.

At first the 3rd Division made rapid progress as the surprised and outnumbered Republic of Korea (ROK) troops fell back, but as they reached the outskirts of Pochon they began to meet more determined resistance. That night the leading units dug in outside the town and when they moved forward in the morning they discovered that the defenders had withdrawn during the night.

The North Korean Air Force was also playing its part. Their fighters attacked the airfields at Seoul and Kimpo and destroyed a USAF C-54 on the ground at Kimpo. It was the first American aircraft loss of the conflict. Within hours John Muccio, US Ambassador to South Korea, relayed to President Truman a ROK request for US air assistance and ammunition.

To the east, the North Korean 5th Division lunged across the 38th Parallel and began to advance down the main road that paralleled Korea's rugged east coast. They were supported by the 766th Independent Unit, part of a large amphibious force under direct control of the North Korean Army's headquarters in P'yongyang. The 1,500 man strong unit had established bridgeheads along the east coast, in the rear of the ROK Army, in order to disrupt rear area communications and defences. Members of the unit had received extensive amphibious and guerrilla training, and after meeting up with the 5th Division they were to infiltrate through the mountains in the direction of Pusan, the southernmost city on the Korean Peninsula.

By the evening of the first day the division had reached Kangnung, where an all-night battle ensued. By the following morning they had won control of the town and the defenders joined the long lines of tired refugees heading south.

Back at Iwakuni the Australians had not been idle. The Wing Commander and his two flight commanders, Brick Bradford and Bay Adams, assembled the pilots in the Mess billiard room and told them to stop drinking and get out on the flight line. The aircraft were to be prepared for flight, armed and with drop tanks fitted to extend their range should they have to fly over Korea at short notice. Many of the ground crews had already left for Australia, so the pilots stripped to the waist and sweating profusely in the humid heat, began to ready their aircraft. One cracked the old Royal Australian Air Force joke, 'If I knew I'd be this thirsty now, I'd have had more to drink at the party.'

Samples of fuel were checked for water, glycol (the engine coolant) and oil levels were checked and the engines run. Next, the airframes were inspected for damage and flight controls checked for 'full and free' movement consistent with control column and rudder pedal movement. The pilots helped load the belts of 0.50-caliber ammunition into the ammunition bins and inspected and oiled the three Browning guns in each wing. Some planes needed their guns and gun-sights harmonising, so that they were most accurate at 300 yards.

. Eight planes and their pilots were put on immediate standby and they sat around the crew room until nightfall, discussing the best way to cope with the Russian-built Yak-9 fighter being flown by the North Korean Air Force. The Mustang was the best propeller-driven fighter of the Second World War, and easily outclassed its rivals with its top speed of over 700 kilometres per hour and range, with auxiliary fuel, of more than 2,500 kilometres. Its armament was varied and included six 0.50-caliber machine guns and a combination of standard bombs, high-explosive rockets, fragmentation bombs, napalm tanks and armour-piercing, high-velocity rockets.

Each inner gun carried 400 rounds of ammunition, while the middle and outers carried 270 rounds. This allowed about twenty-five seconds of firing with the middle and outers and the remaining time in the inners was often held for self-defence. So the guns could fire more than 1,000 rounds in twenty-five seconds and still have 800 rounds as a back-up.

Almost a full day passed before President Truman and his advisers in the White House began to stir themselves into action. The lack of action on the part of the Americans was only to be expected, after all, had they not recently made it clear that they would not fight for Korea?

Washington was half a world away and half a day behind in time when the news began to arrive. It was a summer Saturday and the President was out of town, visiting his family in Missouri. The weekend was always a good time to start a war; in the offices of government and the Pentagon only duty personnel were at their desks. As the evening came, press rumours of something happening in Korea began to reach the State Department. Then, at 2126 hours a dispatch was received from Ambassador John J Muccio in Seoul confirming that an invasion was underway. By midnight the Secretary of State had reached the President by telephone, and the Secretary General of the United Nations had been notified of the emergency.

Sunday in Washington would be a day of frenzied activity. At 0200 hours Secretary Acheson spoke with the President again and the decision was made to ask the Security Council to convene at the United Nations. The Council met at 1500 hours, but with the notable absence of the Soviet delegate. The United States proposed a resolution which called upon the North Korean

Peoples Republic to desist from aggression. It was passed by nine votes to nil, with Yugoslavia abstaining.

While the politicians were discussing the breach of the peace at the United Nations, the Secretary of State, the Secretary of the Army and the military chiefs were in conference at the Pentagon. In the meantime, President Truman boarded his plane for the flight back to the Capital. The Russians who had backed the invasion, and the North Koreans themselves, were in for a surprise; despite earlier statements to the contrary, President Truman had decided that the United States would oppose the invasion.

On Monday 26 June, President Truman announced the decision to send arms to the Rhee government under the Mutual Defence Aid Pact, but no mention was made of the movements of US armed forces. In the evening a second conference of military and civilian chiefs took place and the decisions taken at the end of it were far-reaching. The Secretary of State recommended that air and naval support be given to the Republic of Korea under sanction of the Security Council resolution of the day before; that increased military aid be extended to the Philippines and Indochina and that Formosa be neutralized to prevent invasion by the Chinese. At that time there was little belief that the Soviets or Chinese would intervene, and in the mistaken belief that the ROK Army could hold its own against the invaders, little thought was given to committing US ground forces. The recommendations were accepted by the President and a directive was sent to General MacArthur, authorizing him to use his air and naval forces against the invading army south of the 38th Parallel and instructing him to neutralize Formosa by use of the Seventh Fleet to prevent either an attack on Formosa from the mainland or an invasion of China by the forces of Chiang Kai-shek.

While these decisions were being made, the ground offensive was gathering pace. The day after the start of the invasion, the North Koreans captured Chunchon, Pochon and Tongduchon. On the ground the ROK infantry slowly retreated, with no means of stopping the enemy tanks and no air cover to try to even the odds. The South Korean Air Force was outclassed by the Soviet equipped North Korean Air Force and sent an urgent request to the US Air Force for the loan of ten F-51D Mustangs. A composite unit of USAF and South Korean airmen was to be organised at Taegu airfield, to fly the aircraft.

Although American advisers had been training and equipping the Republic of Korea (ROK) Army, they were in no condition to take on the North Koreans. They had no aircraft or tanks, nor any means of destroying the enemy T-34's. As they began to retreat, the US Far East Air Force headquarters in Japan despatched transport aircraft to evacuate the Americans and other western civilians in South Korea. In the Philippines the US Seventh Fleet began to raise its anchors and start to steam steadily towards the war zone.

The initial evacuation of US citizens began in freighters from the west coast port of Inchon, with air cover provided by F-82G Twin Mustangs of the 68th Fighter All Weather Squadron. Plans were in hand for air evacuation too, once Far East Air Force had traded in its larger, heavier C-54s for C-47s that could land on the smaller airfields.

On the afternoon of Tuesday 27 June, the United Nations Security Council met again in New York. The Soviet Union was not represented at the meeting, having decided to boycott the council, as a member of which they had veto power over action by the international body. It was a great mistake on their part. In the evening, the Security Council passed a resolution that called on member nations to assist South Korea to repel the North Korean attack. It could not come quick enough. Although the nations of the western world were heartened to see the leadership of the United States in standing fast against communist aggression, the news on the ground was getting worse by the hour. The invaders were advancing virtually unopposed and Seoul, the capital of South Korea, was about to fall.

General MacArthur ordered the 5th Air Force to establish air superiority over South Korea, partially to prevent the North Korean Air Force from attacking ROK forces, but also to protect the evacuation forces. The 374th Troop Carrier Wing at Tachikawa Air Base in Japan was the only air transport unit in the Far East. Colonel Troy W. 'Swampy' Crawford, the Wing Commander, called a meeting of all flying personnel to explain the situation and sent them away to bring out the American civilians, diplomats, missionaries and military advisory personnel. They were warned that enemy fighters might try to interfere with the evacuation, so they carried loaded weapons, wore helmets, and had filled canteens and first aid kits strapped on. By the time they were finished they had managed to evacuate 748 persons from Kimpo airfield near Seoul and Suwon airfield, some twenty miles south of the capital.

When North Korean aircraft appeared over Kimpo and Suwon airfields, the USAF aircraft flying air cover engaged the enemy in the first air battle of the war. Major James W. Little, commander of the 339th FAWS fired the first shot. Lieutenant William G. Hudson, 68th FAWS, flying an F-82, with Lieutenant Carl Fraser as his radar observer, scored the first aerial victory. In all, six pilots shot down over Kimpo seven North Korean propeller-driven fighters, the highest number of USAF aerial victories in one day for all of 1950.

Far East Air Force had not been idle and orders went to the 20th Air Force to send all combat ready B-29s in the 19th Bomb Group to Kadena Air Base on Okinawa and prepare to attack targets in Korea the next day. They would manage to put four bombers in air which flew north along the railway from Seoul and dropped their loads on any likely targets.

Yaks on the Horizon?
Wednesday 28 June 1950. Air Force Lieutenant Bill Bailey squinted through the windscreen of his aircraft at the four dots fast approaching from the north. Were they the Air Force F-82s that were supposed to be escorting their supply mission to Suwon? The F-82 was a twin tail two-propeller fighter, but the approaching aircraft were clearly single prop types. They came nearer and then, to Bailey's surprise, they broke into two pairs, the first pair diving towards the airstrip below and the cargo plane unloading on the ground. The second pair headed directly for Bailey's C-54 aircraft.

Instinctively, Bailey turned his aircraft away and ordered his navigator, Lieutenant Ahokas, to climb up on a stool and look out of the astrodome towards the rear of the plane to try to see what was happening. The fast approaching aircraft were North Korean Yak fighters and they were right on their tail. As the navigator peered through the glass dome, their wings sparkled and a burst of tracer fire flew by his head. Startled, he dived backwards into the plane as the pilot dived towards the paddy fields below. For the next thirteen minutes Bailey threw the big cargo plane around the sky, trying to keep one step ahead of the attackers.

Suddenly a bullet exploded with a bright flash and a cloud of smoke in the rear of the cargo compartment. They were carrying 14,000 pounds of 105mm howitzer ammunition and the bullet struck close to the powder canisters stored in the rear of the plane. Bailey increased his speed as the Yaks came round again, their guns hammering out a cloud of bullets towards the large target below them. Holes appeared in the hydraulic system, the radio operator's station, the fuselage and the wings, and much of the engine instrumentation to two of the four engines was knocked out. Eventually, their ammunition exhausted, the Yaks drew level with the plane and stayed there, observing for twenty or thirty seconds. Finally they broke away, towards the north.

Bailey climbed into cloud cover and turned his plane towards Japan and home. Air-Sea Rescue sent an SB-17 Flying Fortress to escort them to Ashiya Air Base, where ground crew later counted 292 holes in their aircraft.

Back at Suwon airfield, the C-54 unloading on the ground was a sitting duck. The two Yaks could not miss and they peppered the plane with fire as the crew ran as fast as they could to shelter in the nearby rice paddy. One of the crew was hit by a machine gun bullet and became Combat Cargo's first Purple Heart winner. Eventually the right wing and cockpit began to burn, slowly at first, but taking hold as the sun sank lower towards the horizon. Two Air Force cameramen hurriedly descended the steps at the rear of the aircraft, carrying blankets, thermos flasks and a five gallon can of fuel. As the fire inside glowed brighter, they emerged again, carrying several cases of 105mm shells which they figured might make a mess of the airstrip if they went off. Within minutes the fuel tanks in the wing exploded, transforming the plane into a burning wreck, lighting up the area as the sun was finally extinguished and another cool, dark night began.

On the ground the situation was deteriorating fast. Enemy forces had occupied Kimpo airfield and on the east coast, Mukho naval base below Kangnung. Their Yak fighters strafed Suwon airfield, destroying one B-26 light bomber and one F-82. As T-34 tanks approached Seoul the order went out to the American advisers at the Korean Military Advisory Group headquarters to 'leave immediately and head for Suwon'. A short time afterwards *Time-Life* correspondent Frank Gibney and Burton Crane of the *New York Times* found themselves in a jeep stuck in a traffic jam on the bridge over the Han River. The streets were full of refugees carrying their worldly belongings on their back, and the traffic was moving at a walking pace. In front of the jeep was a huge six-by-six truck full of South Korean soldiers.

Halfway across the bridge the sky was suddenly lit by a huge sheet of amber flame, followed by a tremendous explosion immediately in front of them. Their jeep was thrown back fifteen feet by the blast and two spans of the bridge began to crumble thirty feet into the river. Gibney's glasses were smashed and blood began pouring down from his head over his hands and clothing. Crane was in a similar state and the two shaken men raced for cover, thinking that an air raid was underway. They were wrong; the bridge had been dynamited on the orders of the Korean chief of staff, who panicked and ordered the bridge to be blown too soon. The six-by-six truck was now burning brightly and its occupants were all dead. Bodies of the dead and dying were strewn all over the bridge; both civilians and soldiers. The two reporters were lucky, having been shielded from the blast by the truck in front of them, but now they had no choice other than to join the crowds of refugees searching for a way to cross the river.

Apparently half of the South Korean troops had been killed or cut off during the first day of attack. Nearly all their field guns had been lost or abandoned, out-ranged by the heavier North Korean guns. Command and control had broken down and the priority of the soldiers and civilians now was to get as far away from the invaders as quickly as possible.

On the morning of 28 June, the weather was still good and American planes went into action. Flying from bases in Japan, B-26 and B-29 bombers began to bomb roads and railway lines north of Seoul, while F-80 and F-82 fighters strafed troop concentrations and columns on the road. Unfortunately, with the poor ground to air communications that existed in those early days, South Korean troops were also liable to be strafed by the over-zealous American pilots.

More than twenty B-26 Invaders of the 3rd Bombardment Group attacked the Munsan railway yards near the 38th Parallel and rail and road traffic between Seoul and the North Korean border. One, heavily damaged by enemy anti-aircraft fire, crashed on its return to Ashiya, killing all aboard. Flying from Kadena air base on Okinawa, the 19th Bombardment Group, in the first B-29 bomber strikes of the war, attacked a railroad bridge and targets of opportunity such as tanks, trucks, and supply columns along the North Korean invasion routes.

During the early days of the war most of the USAF aircraft employed over Korea were propeller-driven types such as the F-82, originally built as a long range escort fighter. With standard 110-gallon drop tanks under the wing, the F-82G had a range of 2,400 miles and could loiter over a target for hours. Because of its firepower, endurance and radar capability it remained in service for much of the war, until the arrival of Lockheeds F-94 Starfire. Night missions with F-82s began on the third day of hostilities and were very successful, eventually totalling 1,868 sorties and claiming twenty-four victories, four of them in air-to-air combat.

There were also plenty of WWII vintage P-51 Mustangs available and they found a new role as F-51s, changing from the ultimate long range escort fighter to a close support fighter-bomber which carried a typical load of two bombs and four rockets. At the time, they were slowly being replaced by the Lockheed F-80C Shooting Star jet fighter, which would go on to fly 98,500 combat missions in which they dropped 41,500 tons of bombs and fired over 81,000 rockets. This was not without loss however, and 150 of them would

be destroyed in operational accidents, with another 113 shot down by anti-aircraft fire and fourteen more lost in air-to-air combat. One of the drawbacks of the F-80 though, compared to its predecessor, was that it was limited to a 100-mile combat radius unless it was fitted with external fuel tanks. However, with external tanks fitted it could not carry bombs. They also required sizeable modern airstrips, a rarity in Korea at that time.

Back in Washington the news from the other side of the world was far from encouraging. The ROK Army was proving weaker than anyone had expected, and that of the North Koreans, stronger. The threat of US air and naval action was not very effective and the discussion inevitably turned to the question of committing American ground troops. War on the mainland of Asia was the last thing the military experts wanted, although North Korea should be an easier opponent than say China. The decision would be made following advice from General MacArthur who was about to fly to Korea for a personal reconnaissance of the battle front.

Thursday, 29 June. The fifth day of the war and North Korean forces were massing on the north shore of the Han River. The weather was clear and dry – perfect tank weather, but also good for the American fighters who were now ranging far and wide looking for the enemy. While B-26s attacked the Han River bridges and F-82s from the 86th FAWS attacked the enemy with the first use of napalm of the war, the F-80s patrolled the Han River area. Lieutenant Bob Wayne from Garden City, New York returned home that day with two kills under his belt; Russian-built Yak fighters that he had shot down with his F-80C near Seoul. The F-80s also caught an enemy convoy halted at a bombed-out bridge near Pyongtaek. Along with B-26s and F-82s they claimed the destruction of 117 trucks, thirty-eight tanks and seven half-tracks.

On the airfield at Suwon, Brigadier General John Huston Church, the newly-appointed field commander of US forces in Korea, walked over to an observation plane that had just landed. Out climbed the US Ambassador and Syngman Rhee, President of South Korea, who had just had the flight of their lives. On their way up from the temporary capital at Taejon they had been jumped by a lone Yak. By staying at treetop level they managed to out-manoeuvre and shake off their pursuer.

Within minutes another C-54 landed on the airstrip, bearing the name 'Bataan' painted on its nose. General MacArthur stepped down, his trademark corncob pipe clutched in his hand, followed by his chief of staff, Major General Almond. A staff car came to a halt nearby and the officers climbed in, followed by Church. They drove away northwards, passing streams of refugees and dejected soldiers, and came to a halt at a crossroads near Youndungpo. From there, they could see enemy artillery fire landing south of the river less than a mile away. After a few minutes of discussion with his staff he returned to his car and began the journey back to the airfield. Back at his headquarters in Japan, he put a call through to the President and recommended that two American divisions be sent without delay. President Truman agreed and directed the Pentagon to set the wheels in motion. America was at war again.

MacArthur also authorized FEAF attacks on airfields in North Korea, and in the first USAF attack on North Korea, eighteen B-26s of the 3rd Bomb Group attacked Heijo airfield near P'yongyang, the North Korean capital, claiming up to twenty-five aircraft destroyed on the ground. The 8th Tactical Reconnaissance Squadron began photographic reconnaissance of the North Korean airfields and the 31st Strategic Reconnaissance Squadron (Photographic) also started operations with their RB-29s from Yokota, Japan.

The Aussies Join the Battle

The four 77 Squadron Mustangs took off at night on 2 July and climbed through the clouds, heading for Korea. They were not proficient in night flying, but they were now flying under wartime conditions and much had to be learnt as they went along. They were supposed to escort some C-47s flying wounded out of Taejon airfield, but they could not contact Taejon by radio, nor find the airfield on their poor quality maps and had to return home. One of the pilots described the Korean landscape as, 'grim and dirty, with a monotonous sameness in the colouring. Normally it was reddy-brown with sparsely-wooded hills and cultivated valleys. The torrential rains filled streams and rivulets with muddy water, and turned the red surface to a dirty-chocolate colour. The whole country looked like a dirty piece of parchment on which had been scrabbled a thousand little water courses and meandering streams … a chaotic patchwork.'

The second mission of the day saw eight Mustangs take to the air to rendezvous with seventeen USAF B-26 Invaders on a bombing raid. They rendezvoused near Pusan at the peninsula's southern tip and escorted them to Seoul where they attacked the railway bridges crossing the Han River. On the way two USAF F-80 jets mistook the Mustangs for the enemy and opened fire before realizing they were friendly. Fortunately, the attackers' marksmanship was as bad as their aircraft recognition and they missed. There would be other instances until the American pilots learned to tell the difference between a Mustang and a Yak-9.

The last mission of the day was to escort USAF B-29 Superfortress bombers from Guam, in the Mariana Islands, to attack Yonpo airfield, well inside North Korea. Despite heavy flak they all dropped their bombs within the airfield perimeter, causing extensive damage. They were in the air for almost five hours, much longer than any jet fighter could have managed.

Within days, 77 Squadron was joined at Iwakuni by a B-26 squadron from the US 3rd Bombardment Group. Unfortunately, the Americans tried to take over the base and began commandeering offices and hangars. Military Police went into the local village where the Australians had lived for three years and tacked 'Off limits' signs on shops and other buildings. They were soon followed by a jeep load of Aussies who pulled the signs down. A group of airmen went into the swimming pool and were told by a guard that it was off limits. They threw him in the pool and then had to pull him out again as he could not swim. Squadron Leader Lou Spence was arrested trying to return to his home at night, as the Americans had imposed a curfew without telling anyone. Eventually, these misunderstandings were sorted out and relations remained excellent until the end of the war.

Lyall Klaffer was with some reinforcements who joined the squadron shortly afterwards and he takes up the story:

'We arrived at Iwakuni on 8 July. I was greeted by Milt Cottee and Ray Trebilco who gave me the news that Squadron Leader Graham Strout, who had been one of the flight commanders, had been killed the previous day. The news had a very sobering effect indeed on the group.

'77 Squadron had a full complement of pilots before the twelve of us arrived, so the flying was slow until some of the pilots were sent home after fifty combat missions. Those of us who remained flew 100 missions, 300 operational flying hours, or remained there for nine months. My first operational mission was as wing man to Flight Lieutenant "Bay" Adams a very experienced fighter pilot who had flown in Europe in WWII. His pre-flight briefing was, "Go in low and hit them hard!" We were to carry two 500-pound bombs and a full load of ammunition for our six machine guns embedded in our wings. Our target was located near Konju.

'We found our forward air controller circling near the target area. He identified the target for us and then we rolled into our attack and released two bombs each, circled back and strafed the enemy troops we could see in the target area. The FAC confirmed we had hit the target with great results and we climbed back through the clouds and headed back to Iwakuni. The round trip took four hours and forty-five minutes.

'On my third mission a week later, we attacked an enemy unit near Hamhung in North Korea. We found the target and I followed the leader into the first attack. I selected a tank as my target. I fired six armour piercing rockets, and then pulled up and took evasive action, trying to look over my shoulder to see if I had hit my target. The pilot in the third aircraft confirmed a direct hit and stated that the tank was burning. We strafed the troops that we could see and returned to Iwakuni where congratulations were in order from the CO.

'By the end of July we were able to fly out of Taegu in South Korea and would remain there for two or three days at a time. We could fly ten missions during that time and could take off, contact our controller, deliver our ordnance and be back on the ground in twenty-five minutes! On one of these missions my aircraft sustained some damage from ground fire. A bullet passed through the air intake for the glycol radiator for the engine, which is located under the aircraft. If the round had continued it would have gone through the bottom of the cockpit, through the bucket seat and into my dinghy and parachute! I reported the leaking radiator to the US engineering officer, who immediately ordered another radiator from Japan. He was quite a character who always wandered around with two pearl-handled Colt 45 revolvers strapped to his waist! For the next couple of days I lounged around in his tent.

'He had a make-shift desk, which consisted of a huge crate with some boards nailed across the top. On the second day I asked him to tell me the nomenclature of the radiator for the Mustang. He looked through his records and read out the title. It tallied with the sign on the side of the crate which he was using as his desk. He laughed and said that "it was impossible." But we tore the boards off his desk and opened the crate. Yep, it contained a brand new radiator! In a few hours I was back in the air. I caught up with the next flight coming over from Iwakuni and flew a few more missions before finally going back to the squadron.

'On 3 September four of us were returning from a B–29 escort mission and descended near Taegu to attack a target which was only about twenty miles from the airfield. We encountered quite a bit of ground fire and when Bill Harrop called up and stated he only had twenty gallons of fuel remaining, we called off the attack and headed towards Taegu. Then Bill reported that he had been hit, his engine was losing power, and he would have to force land. He landed safely, wheels up, on the banks of the River Naktong near an orchard. I watched him get out of the cockpit unharmed. He waved to me as I flew down over him. Michelson told me to cover Bill, while he headed to Taegu to organize the rescue. I circled the area looking for, and strafing, enemy troops until four US Mustangs arrived on the scene and began to strafe the area around the orchard. By then I was down to about twenty gallons of fuel, so I left the area and landed at Taegu.

'The rescue helicopter had to come up from Pusan and did not arrive until much later in the afternoon. The pilot descended into the orchard and hovered right outside the building, but was advised not to land or leave the aircraft to go into the building, because the area was teeming with enemy soldiers. After hovering for some time, he then searched the area for another hour before landing at Taegu. There was no sign of Bill, so we assumed that he had been captured. Some months later, after the enemy troops had been pushed back above the 38th Parallel, the area was searched and Bill's body was found in a shallow grave near the orchard. He had been tortured and shot several times. It came as a dreadful shock when we heard the news, which confirmed our worst fears.

'Then, on 9 September, tragedy struck again. We were sitting in the crew room at Iwakuni when we heard the news that our CO, Wing Commander Lou Spence, one of the finest officers I have ever met, had been killed carrying out an attack with two 100-gallon drop tanks of napalm. Apparently, he dived through a hole in the cloud to press home his attack, and did not have sufficient altitude in which to recover from the dive. By all reports, he almost made it, but the aircraft hit a stone wall and exploded. He was killed instantly.'

Shooting Stars
When the war began on 25 June, the 36th Fighter Bomber Squadron of the 8th Fighter Bomber Group had been flying the F-80 Shooting Star at Itazuke for seven months, since it turned in its F-51 Mustangs at the end of 1949. The following day they flew combat air patrols over Kimpo Air Base while American personnel were being evacuated by Transport aircraft. Three North Korean aircraft were sighted, but the Americans held their fire. Things changed the next day when the F-80s attacked the advancing North Korean forces, hitting tanks, trucks, artillery and troops.

On 30 June, the 36th recorded its first enemy kill of the Korean War when First Lieutenant John B. Thomas shot down a North Korean Yak fighter. The same day First Lieutenant Edwin T. Johnson narrowly escaped death in his F-80 which had been damaged by anti-aircraft fire, and then hit overhead cables following an attack against the rail marshalling yards near Suwon. At

13,000 feet, with the entire tail section moving back and forth as though it was about to fall off, Lieutenant Johnson bailed out, hitting the right horizontal stabilizer and breaking it free from the plane. He landed near Suwon and was picked up and airlifted back to Itazuke that same afternoon, with one tremendous headache.

In August, the squadron converted back to the Mustang in order to make use of their longer range. They would move across to Kimpo airfield in Korea in October.

The North Koreans were not the only danger the pilots faced. The weather could be fatal at times. Colonel Howard N. Tanner recalled:

'In September, during the Inchon Invasion, my flight "Cousin Willy" was assigned the mission of making diversionary attacks around the Pohang area on the east coast of Korea. The weather was marginal, but flying F-51s we did not worry. On the way to Pohang we flew through two lines of thunderstorms, one over Japan and one over the Sea of Japan. Flying very tight formation we penetrated both thunderstorms and completed our mission in the Pohang area. During the return flight to Tsuiki we made it through the first thunderstorm OK, but the second thunderstorm had become so violent it broke up the flight. Flying at different altitudes we headed back for different bases in Japan. I flew back to Tsuiki only to learn the ceiling was 400 feet with limited visibility. The tower radar was able to position me over the end of the runway where I began a Bad Weather Procedure. All went well until I touched down on the runway. There was so much water on the runway the F-51 stopped in so short a distance it was like a carrier landing. The tower told me to shut down and I would be towed to the parking area. An inspection of the aircraft revealed no damage and soon it was ready to fly the next day.

'Following the enemy counter-offensive we moved back to Japan and converted back to the F-80. As the Chinese Divisions were moving south in December our intelligence reported that the Chinese Generals were using the North Korean school houses for their headquarters. When our squadron was ordered to fly armed reconnaissance missions into North Korea, our squadron commander would take the mission and assign me as his wingman. In North Korea we would search for a school house. They were all alike with a door in the centre of a long building with a window on each side of the door. When we located a school house we would arm our napalm bombs. The squadron commander would fly at the right window and I the left window. We put the napalm bombs through the windows and destroyed everything.

'When the Chinese captured Seoul they had to build a new bridge across the Han River because all the original bridges had been destroyed. After they had completed their new bridge and were moving troops and supplies across the Han River, my flight was assigned the mission to knock out the bridge. Our aircraft were loaded with two 1,000 pound bombs. On my first run my bomb barely missed the bridge. On my second run-in the bomb landed dead centre and knocked out a span. After my flight's attack it would be several days before the Chinese could cross the Han River again.

'Probably the most dangerous mission I ever flew was on a "last light armed reconnaissance" just south of the Yalu River. Our aircraft were armed with two 500-pound bombs, six HVAR rockets and six machine guns. As the sun was setting I spotted smoke coming out of a tunnel which indicated a locomotive was getting ready to move supplies south. I attacked and placed a bomb on the railroad tracks about one hundred feet in front of the tunnel. Then I thought "That's no good because the workmen will have the track repaired in no time." I had to place the bomb *in* the tunnel. I knew the risk because if the bomb did not go in the tunnel it would skip back up under the aircraft, explode and destroy the aircraft. This type of accident had happened in the past. Happily my bomb went into the tunnel before exploding, so the delivery of those supplies would be delayed.

'After completing my first tour of combat, I began a second tour as the Squadron Operations Officer. The 4th Fighter Group was given the mission of Combat Air Patrol along the Yalu River and our squadron returned to Ground Support missions. On one of the ground support missions the only time my aircraft was struck by enemy fire, a 23mm shell went into the engine destroying twenty-eight turbine blades. I was fortunate to be flying an F-80 powered by a centrifugal engine. If I had been flying an axial flow engine it would have been destroyed.'

Into the Breach – Task Force Smith

Air attacks alone could not prevent the fall of the South Korean capital, or stop the tide of North Koreans sweeping all before them. On 30 June President Truman ordered the immediate despatch of a regimental combat team to Korea and a naval blockade of North Korean ports. The British already had ten ships in the area, and the Australians two, and they began to steam towards Korea as plans were being made to commit American ground troops.

The 24th US Infantry Division was not the best of the four infantry divisions then stationed in Japan, with the lowest combat efficiency rating of sixty-four per cent. However, they were the nearest, and while the bulk of the division embarked on ships bound for Pusan, a port on the south east corner of Korea, a small combat team from 1st Battalion, 21st Infantry Regiment was flown in ready to fight. By the time Task Force Smith had arrived at Pusan airfield and boarded trucks for the drive northwards, the North Koreans had crossed the Han River and taken Suwon, and were already on the way toward their next objective: Taejon.

Many of the men were airlifted to Korea by C-47 Skytrains of the 21st Troop Carrier Squadron, which originally shared the air base at Ashiya. They were then moved due to overcrowding to Brady Field, about ten air minutes distant. 'We're just a bunch of Gypsies. Kyushu Gypsies,' grumbled one pilot. The name stuck and since that time the squadron has retained the nickname. The C-47s were better suited to the poor conditions found at the airstrips in Korea. The terrain in Japan and Korea was extremely rugged, with mountains rising to 13,000 feet in Japan and 7,500 feet in Korea, with unbelievable variations in altitude over a distance of a few miles, and with clouds frequently hiding the mountains from sight on an unpredictable basis. Most of the early flying to Korea was done by seat of the pants navigation, since there were few landing aids or radio controls. Pilots would fly out across the Japan Sea in the proper direction, fly in low near the Korean coast and then pick up a major river near Pusan by spotting discolored sea water, fly up river until they hit a railroad track and then follow the track into Taegu, the most forward strip of the Pusan Perimeter. As long as visibility was good, this system worked well, but there were major navigational problems when darkness came or clouds obscured both the sea and the land.

There was one additional problem common to both Korea and the Berlin Airlift. Many of the pilots had not flown for years and were on desk jobs when the Korean War broke out. Hastily restored to flying status, they were rusty on technique and had much to learn. They had to learn quickly or perish in the process.

Lieutenant Colonel Charles Smith and his 400 men moved into positions about eight miles south of Suwon, where the road ran through a saddle of hills. Supported by six 105mm howitzers they dug in and waited with trepidation for the enemy to appear. At 0730 hours on 5 July, the North Korean column came in sight, led by thirty-three T-34 tanks. They were engaged by the howitzers, then the recoilless rifles and bazookas of the infantry. However, none of them managed to penetrate the armour on the tanks, and by 0900 hours they had driven down the road and past the defenders. Now the main column came into view, led by three more tanks, and when they got closer Smith ordered his men to open fire with mortars and machine guns. The North Koreans quickly disembarked and instead of attacking the defenders head on, began to outflank them. The artillery managed to destroy two of the tanks with anti-tank rounds, but as they only had six of them they did not last long. The normal high-explosive rounds simply ricocheted off the sides of the tanks. Anti-tank mines would have stopped the T-34s, but there none in Korea at that time. It would be another week before the first large 3.5-inch bazookas and their shaped charges arrived from the United States.

At 1430 hours Smith ordered his men to withdraw, but only half of them made it back to safety, the rest were either dead or prisoners of war. In the meantime Major-General Dean, the commander of the division, had arrived at Pusan and sent the 34th Infantry Regiment up to Pyongtaek with orders to hold the line. Unfortunately the regiment was a third under strength and the two battalions were ill-equipped and poorly trained for the battles ahead. The blame for this went right to the top, from the division's officers, to General Dean and the commander of the US Eighth Army, General Walton Walker. Ultimately the buck stopped at the desk of General MacArthur whose primary concern at that time was the rehabilitation of Japanese society and that country's economy.

Lieutenant Colonel Loveless had only been in command of the 34th for a month. He had been brought in to replace the previous commander, who had failed to improve the fighting qualities of the regiment. Not only were the companies under strength, with about 140 officers and men each, but their weapons were inadequate as well. Each man had either an M1 or a carbine with 80 or 100 rounds of ammunition each – enough for about ten minutes of firing. There were no hand grenades either, essential items for close-quarter fighting.

The men of the 1st Battalion stood in their waterlogged trenches until dawn broke. They had earlier been told that Task Force Smith had been defeated, and in the early hours they had heard the sound of the bridge behind them being destroyed, to prevent its use by tanks. It was bad for morale and when dawn broke and they saw a line of tanks and trucks extending as far as the eye could see, they were ready to run. They were also without artillery support and when the first tank shells began to explode around them, they climbed out of their foxholes and began to retreat back to

Pyongtaek. When the frightened survivors reached the town, one of the platoon sergeants examined his men's rifles and discovered that twelve out of thirty-one of them were either broken, dirty or had been incorrectly assembled.

This uneven fight, representing what later would be called military 'speed bumps' in the path of an enemy advance, marked the start of a long ordeal for the US soldier; a fight not just with armed enemies, but against the Korean environment. For three years, he contended with rugged terrain, hot summers, brutally cold winters, particularly aromatic growing seasons, and abundant mud, dust, rain and snow.

Mosquitos

In order to integrate the efforts of the Air Force and their Army 'customers', a Joint Operations Centre (JOC) was established at Taejon on 5 July. The Air Force combat operations section was manned by officers from the advanced echelon of 5th Air Force headquarters and airmen from the 8th Communications Squadron; ten officers and thirty-five airmen in all, commanded by a Colonel Murphy. However, since the Army did not man its air-ground operations section side of the establishment it was not exactly a joint operations centre. Situated at 24th Infantry Divisions headquarters in an office adjoining the division G-3 intelligence department, the Air Force intelligence officers scouted around the headquarters building picking up targets for their fighters and bombers.

Designed to operate in close association with the JOC was the Tactical Air Control Centre (TACC), a communications organization which was the focal point of aircraft control and warning activities for the tactical air force.

At that time the state of the war was so confused that the 24th Infantry Divisions Operations Officer was frequently unable to confirm the accurate location of friendly troops. Even when Colonel Murphy's section obtained worthwhile targets, communicating them back to the advanced echelon of the 5th Air Force in Itazuke proved to be a difficult to impossible matter. The section had a very high-frequency radio for air-control work and a land-line telephone and teletype to Itazuke, but the wire circuit back to Japan was said to have been out of order approximately seventy-five percent of the time. Understanding this lack of communications, General Timberlake at FEAF Headquarter's scheduled F-80 flights from Itazuke and Ashiya at twenty-minute intervals during the daylight hours, and these flights checked in over Taejon with Colonel Murphy's control station 'Angelo'. When 'Angelo' had supporting targets, it gave them to the pilots; when 'Angelo' had no targets, the fighter pilots proceeded up the roads between Osan and Seoul and looked for targets of opportunity.

According to the existing doctrine on air-ground operations, the tactical air force furnished tactical air control parties (TACPs) to serve as the most forward element of the tactical control system and to control supporting aircraft strikes from forward observation posts co-located with the front line fighting units. Each TACP was composed of an experienced pilot officer, who served as forward air controller, and the airmen needed to operate and maintain the party's jeep-mounted communications equipment. Each of the parties was equipped with an AN/ARC-1 radio jeep and another jeep which served as a personnel carrier. All this equipment was old. Most of it had been in use or in storage in the theatre since the Second World War.

Two TACP parties under Lieutenants Chermak and Duerksen had been at Suwon before they retreated to Taejon and they joined the 24th Division advanced command post on 3 July. Both parties were from Detachment 1, 620th Aircraft Control and Warning Squadron, and Colonel Murphy brought the other four control parties of this detachment with him from Itazuke. Since Detachment 1 had been formed for the purpose of cooperative training with Eighth Army troops, the control parties had had some manoeuvre experience in directing close-support strikes.

As the forward elements of the 24th Division advanced northward from Taejon to engage the enemy, the two lieutenants and their TACPs went with them. However, the weather was very bad and the ceiling was too low for the fighters to operate. Also one of the radios broke down and they had to get a replacement jeep from Taejon. On 8 July, the weather cleared up as Chermak was working with the 21st Infantry Regiment at Chonui and he finally got the chance to control his first flight of F-80's onto a target. However, the radio could not be removed from the jeep and in order to see the target and operate the radio, the jeep had to be moved up in sight of the enemy. Needless to say the enemy would soon target the jeep and the forward observer with mortars or artillery.

Within a few days attrition began to take a toll of the men and equipment of Detachment 1. The AN/ARC-1 was heavy and fragile, and it was quickly put out of action by travel over the rough roads. Because of the lack of replacement parts and test equipment, only three radio-control jeeps were operational on 11 July. On this day, Lieutenant Arnold Rivedal – a young officer who was described as 'very willing and eager … a very fine example' – was hit by a burst of hostile fire while reconnoitering along the front lines. His radio operator and mechanic survived and evaded capture, but

Lieutenant Rivedal was lost in action, with his radio jeep. Later that day, while moving north from a regimental command post at Chochiwon toward the front lines, Lieutenant Philip J. Pugliese and his party were cut off by a North Korean road block. They destroyed their equipment and dispersed to walk out, but two of the airmen – S/Sgt. Bird Hensley and Pfc. Edward R. Logston – never returned to friendly territory.

As the first week of American air-ground operations ended, certain facts were becoming evident. The rough roads of Korea were quickly battering the old AN/ARC-1 jeeps out of commission. The unarmored jeeps, moreover, could not be exposed to enemy fire, and thus the TACPs could seldom get far enough forward for maximum effectiveness. Under normal circumstances, Army units were supposed to request air-support missions against specific targets through the air-ground operations section of the JOC. But the 24th Division was retreating, and, more often than not, its battalions were unable to identify points of enemy strength on their front lines. American ground troops badly needed close support, yet the jet fighters, limited to short time at lower altitudes over the front lines, had to have an immediate target for air attack in order to give effective ground support.

The answer lay in the deployment of airborne tactical air coordinators, as used in some of the theatres during the Second World War. Colonel Murphy asked 5th Air Force to provide an operations officer and five pilots to fly reconnaissance and control missions, and on 9 July Lieutenants Bryant and Mitchell arrived at Taejon with two L-5G liaison planes, modified with four-channel very high frequency radios. However, they were unable to get their equipment to work in the L-5s and borrowed two L-17s for the day. They managed to direct about ten flights of F-80s, despite some confusion as the fighter pilots had not been expecting airborne controllers.

Bryant had been bounced by two Yaks and it became obvious that the liaison planes were too slow to evade enemy air attacks. However, the next day Lieutenant Morris arrived in a faster T-6 two-seat trainer aircraft, and it was soon equipped with eight-channel AN/ARC-3 and proved ideal for the job. The airborne controllers reconnoitered the front lines, located worthwhile targets and 'talked' fighter-bombers in on them. Afterwards they would go into Taejon city and brief the combat operations officers, so they could keep their situation maps up to date with the current location of friendly and enemy forces.

On 13 July the operation was moved back to Taegu airfield, and the next day the 6132nd Tactical Air Control Squadron was activated and more T-6 aircraft arrived. They would establish a Tactical Air Control Centre adjacent to the 5th Air Force – Eighth Army Joint Operations Centre at Taegu – and work with both Air Force and Navy aircraft. Two days later the airborne controllers were given radio call signs, 'Mosquito Able, Baker, Charlie etc'. Thereafter the airborne controllers and their planes were called 'Mosquitos'. They also shared the airfield with the 51st Fighter Squadron (Provisional) who flew the first USAF Mustang combat missions in Korea. There would be no shortage of the type as the aircraft carrier USS *Boxer* was on its way with 145 F-51s aboard.

The Navy Arrives

On the day the war began, only one of the seventeen active United States aircraft carriers was in the Western Pacific; USS *Valley Forge* (CV-45), was more than a thousand miles away in the South China Sea. Two days later, following a quick replenishment at Subic Bay, Rear Admiral John M. Hoskins led *Valley Forge* and her group north to the war zone. Admiral Struble's Seventh Fleet Striking Force, Task Force 77, was made up of a carrier 'group' containing one carrier, a support 'group' containing one cruiser, and a screening 'group' of eight destroyers.

The duty carrier in the summer of 1950 was *Valley Forge*, an improved postwar version of the *Essex* class, completed in 1946, with a standard displacement of 27,100 tons, a length of 876 feet, and a speed of 33 knots. *Valley Forge* had reported in to the Western Pacific in May, at which time her predecessor, *Boxer*, had been returned to the west coast for navy yard availability.

Fortunately there were other carriers in the two reserve fleets, located at ports on both coasts of the United States. However, budget cuts had meant that there were five times as many 'mothballed' carriers as there were on active service. Thousands of Navy aircraft were also in storage at Cherry Point, Pensacola, San Diego, Alameda and the huge naval aircraft storage centre at Litchfield Park, near Phoenix, Arizona. Within days, 500 planes were being prepared to return to service.

Great carriers such as the *Essex* and the *Wasp* were slated for service, as well as cruisers, destroyers and submarines. The first of the carriers to be de-mothballed was the *Cabot* (CVL-28) which had been put into a preserved state two years previously. All exposed surfaces had been protected and corrodible parts below deck sprayed with plastic paint. Topside strippable hoods covered special gear and gun mounts. Three dehumidifying machines kept the air at thirty per cent humidity in the three sealed zones of the ship.

Although recommissioning a carrier was much quicker than building a new one, it would still take a while to bring it back into service. The instructions of the things to be done on the *Cabot* filled seven books; the engineering book alone was 1,000 pages and six inches thick.

The 13,000 ton British light aircraft carrier HMS *Triumph* had just left Japan and was on its way home when the North Koreans invaded. On board was the 13th Carrier Air Group, consisting of 800 Naval Air Squadron equipped with the Supermarine Seafire FR.47 and 827 Naval Air Squadron equipped with the Fairey Firefly FR.1. The twenty-four aircraft were old and were due for retirement, but the order came to turn the aircraft carrier around and return to Japan.

HMS *Triumph* was accompanied by the cruiser HMS *Belfast* and the aircraft carrier HMS *Unicorn*, which was only configured as a repair carrier, but would play a vital role by providing replacement aircraft and shuttle between the British fleet forwarding operating base at Sasebo in Japan and the main Royal Navy aircraft maintenance yard in the Far East at Sembawang in Singapore. The three ships comprised the 1st Aircraft Carrier Squadron, Far East, but when they arrived in Japanese waters they were placed under the control of Vice Admiral C. Turner Joy, the American Commander in charge of operations in Korean waters. After reaching Okinawa the British ships joined up with their American allies to form Task Force 77 which included the American aircraft carrier USS *Valley Forge*, carrying up to eighty Grumman Panther jets, Douglas Skyraiders and Vought Corsairs. On the way to Korea the British Fireflies flew anti-submarine sorties while both British types flew around the US Navy ships to allow the anti-aircraft gunners to familiarize themselves with them, and hopefully avoid any friendly fire incidents.

At 0545 hours on 3 July 1950, the *Triumph* launched all twelve of its Seafires and nine of its Fireflies and carried out a rocket attack on the North Korean airfield at Kaishu, destroying hangars and buildings. There were no enemy aircraft there at the time and one Seafire returned home damaged after flying through debris thrown up by its own rockets.

The designated launching point, in the middle of the Yellow Sea, was some 150 miles from the target area, but only 100 miles from Chinese Communist airfields on the Shantung Peninsula and less than 200 miles from the Soviet air garrison at Port Arthur. Just in case the North Korean Air Force or any of its Communist allies decided to join the party, the *Valley Forge* launched combat and anti-submarine patrols at 0500 hours. One hour later the *Valley Forge* launched its aircraft against the airfield at Heiju.

Sixteen Corsairs loaded with eight 5-inch rockets each, and twelve Skyraiders carrying heavy bomb loads, were launched against the P'yongyang airfield. When the propeller-driven attack planes had gained a suitable head start, *Valley Forge* catapulted eight Panthers, whose higher cruising speed would bring them in first over the target area. No serious opposition was encountered by the American jets as they swept in over the North Korean capital. Two Yak-9s were destroyed in the air, another was damaged, and nine aircraft were reported destroyed on the ground. The two Yaks were shot down by Panthers from Navy Fighter Squadron VF-51 who were flying top cover for the strike, and were the first kills to be scored by US Navy jets. All of the attacking aircraft returned safely, but one of the CAP Corsairs had to ditch when its engine caught fire.

More strikes took place the next day, with some of the Royal Navy aircraft returning with minor damage. However, the *Valley Forge* fared much worse with nine aircraft destroyed when a damaged Skyraider missed the barrier on landing and careered into the aircraft parked on deck. They also lost their Sikorsky HO3S-1 rescue helicopter which had to ditch when its engine failed.

These attacks, the Navy's first jet aircraft combat operations, added to the already ongoing US Air Force effort to eliminate the enemy's air capabilities. Further attacks, targeting railroads and other transportation facilities, followed later on 3 July and on 4 July. Both the USS *Valley Forge* and HMS *Triumph* provided air cover for the unopposed amphibious landing of the 1st Cavalry Division at Pohang on the east coast on 18 July. A strike by propeller driven aircraft that afternoon caused considerable damage to the Wonsan Oil Refinery.

It soon became obvious that the American aircraft had longer range and were more suitable for operations over Korea. The British carriers had to sail nearer to the coast to launch their aircraft and it was agreed that the Seafires would mount CAPs over the fleet while the Fireflies flew anti-submarine patrols. The round-the-clock protection of the fleet eventually took its toll on the Royal Navy planes and four Seafires were lost to landing accidents. The heavy landings also caused the rear of the fuselage to wrinkle, and eventually all Seafires would be grounded due to this damage. One was also shot down by a 'friendly' United States Air Force B-29 on 28 July. A flight of Seafires on CAP were sent to investigate a formation of unidentified aircraft on their radar screens. As the British aircraft flew alongside them, Seafire VP473, flown by Commissioned Pilot White, was hit by gunfire from one of the B-29s and its rear fuselage fuel tank burst into flames. By the time White managed to roll his Seafire onto its back and bail out, he had been badly burned on his face, arms and shoulders. He spent an hour in the heavy sea before a US destroyer picked him up.

The *Valley Forge* was the first aircraft carrier in the Navy to attempt the sustained shipboard operation of jet aircraft. On board was Carrier Air Group 5 with four fighter squadrons; VF–51 and VF–52 with thirty F9F–3 Panthers between them, and VF–53 and VF–54 with twenty F4U–4B Corsairs between them. Attack Squadron VA–55 had fourteen AD Skyraiders with them; the night flying detachment from VC–3 had two F4U–5N Corsairs and three AD–3N Skyraiders, and the ASP (Anti Submarine Patrol) detachment from VC–11 had three AD–3W Skyraiders. Last, but not least, was a detachment of Marine pilots from Marine Air Group 12 with two F4U–5P Corsairs and three pilots. There were usually fifty per cent more pilots than planes, so that the workload could be shared around.

In general, the remainder of the flights and sweeps throughout July were 'armed reconnaissance' and covered an area inland from Phong to north of Hamhung on the east coast, and on the west coast ranged from Kwangju north to Kaesong, going inland as far as Namwon. Targets attacked and damaged were airfield installations, railroad facilities, locomotives and rolling stock, bridges, power stations, oil tanks, small boats, factories, troops and vehicles. On 26, 28 and 29 July, close support operations were conducted under control of Air Force Tactical Air Coordinators in the critical southwest sector of Korea, in an area along the front line from Hadong, north to Hamchang. Targets were mainly troops, armour and transportation facilities. HMS *Triumph* worked with the *Valley Forge* at all times, providing CAP (Combat Air Patrol) and ASP (Anti-submarine Patrols).

During the two-week period, Carrier Air Group 5 on USS *Valley Forge* flew almost six hundred sorties over Korean targets, with two-thirds of them flown by props rather than jets. However, they lost two Corsairs to enemy anti-aircraft fire, and a Skyraider flown by Ensign Stevens was lost on 22 July when it dragged its wing on a hillock during a strafing run and crashed and exploded in enemy territory. Two Panthers were lost at sea, having experienced a partial loss of power after take-off from the carrier and forced to ditch.

The first Navy jet to ditch in the sea was a Panther, which went down on the first day of Navy carrier operations. The best way to ditch a jet was the same as the procedure used during the Second World War; wheels up, flaps down and nose-high. In this first instance the pilot had his wheels up and flaps down, but hit the water with one wing low and cartwheeled, knocking out the pilot. Fortunately, he came to, was able to free himself, and was picked up by a rescue helicopter from the carrier. The second ditching came on 18 July. The Panther lost power after leaving the catapult and ditched with its wheels down. It flipped over on its back, but the pilot was saved. The third came on 22 July after catapulting. The pilot was able to get his gear up and made an easy water landing.

During the first couple of months of the war a dozen Navy planes ditched safely, with one exception, a TO-1 Shooting Star which hit the water in a nose-down attitude. The plane flipped over on its back and sank rapidly, killing the pilot, who may have been knocked out and unable to save himself.

Contrary to popular opinion, having the wheels down did not automatically invite disaster, as only six of the twelve crashes studied had the wheels retracted. Out of the six that landed with the wheels down, only one flipped over. When an FJ-1 was forced to ditch, the plane was in the optimum attitude, with flaps down, wheels up and nose-high. The impact with the water, in that case, was reported to be no worse than a carrier landing. The nose of the plane remained high throughout the landing run, and no appreciable water or spray hitting the cockpit or upper fuselage. The plane floated high and level and the pilot had a minute and a half to get out.

During August the British ships sailed away to join the Commonwealth Task Force which would be responsible for blockading the enemy ports and attacking shipping on the west coast of Korea. The Americans would be responsible for the east coast with similar objectives. The month ended on a sad note with the loss of the Commanding Officer of 800 Naval Air Squadron on 29 July. He was inside the operations room in the carrier's island when a Firefly crashed into the barrier outside on the deck and fragments of its wooden propeller detached and flew through an open porthole striking him as he stood inside. He was the only aircrew fatality of *Triumph's* entire Korean tour and was buried at sea with full military honours.

Taking the Fight to the Enemy
On 6 July the Chief of Naval Operations ordered the Bureau of Ordnance to develop a new rocket which would stop the North Korean tanks. The first T-34 tank destroyed in the war was credited to Jim Flemming, one of the Australian Mustang pilots on 9 July. The tank crew had forgotten to close the rear radiator doors and Jim directed a stream of 0.50-caliber bullets into the engine compartment and the tank exploded. However, a new rocket was what was really needed until plentiful supplies of the 3.5-inch infantry bazooka arrived for the ground troops.

Other rockets in use for the close air support work of Corsairs, Panthers and Skyraiders at that time, were the huge 11.75-inch 'Tiny Tim', the conventional 5-inch HVAR rocket and the 3.5-inch aircraft rocket. The new ATAR (anti-tank aircraft rocket) would be the first to use shaped charges. Essentially it was a 6.5-inch head filled with a shaped charge powered by the same 5-inch rocket motor on the HVAR Holy Moses projectile. It had far greater penetration power than the 3.5-inch bazooka rocket which could penetrate 11-inches of armour plate. Unlike an explosive charge, the shaped charge squirts a stream of hot gasses and molten steel through steel plate. After it reaches the inside of a tank it ignites inflammable materials, burns out the oxygen and scatters red-hot metal around the interior.

The first supplies of the new rocket were shipped to the war zone by air on 29 July, and it was used by the Air Force for the first time on 16 August. The first use of the Tiny Tim 11.75-inch aircraft rockets took place two days earlier, when carrier based planes destroyed thirteen locomotives, damaged twenty-three others, blew up eight ammunition cars, set fire to two fuel oil trains and strafed seven cars loaded with troops. The rockets destroyed the highly important temporary bridge that the North Koreans had built to span the Han River. The Tiny Tim rocket weighed 1173 pounds and was 114 inches long. Packed with 152 pounds of TNT in its warhead, the rockets business end was essentially a 500-pound bomb with a rocket motor and fins attached to it for driving power.

Around this time the Kyushu Gypsy squadron was tasked with providing a Special Air Missions detachment as a part of the Eighth Army's psychological warfare programme. The programme was outstandingly successful in persuading enemy troops that they would get better care, medical treatment, food and accommodation if they surrendered than if they continued to fight. A large number of the Korean, and later Chinese, in South Korean prisoner of war camps surrendered as a direct result of successful psychological warfare operations.

The first psy-war mission of the war was flown by a 374th Troop Carrier Wing C-46 piloted by Captain Howard Secor. Shortly after the war broke out, the plane was loaded at Tachikawa with small cartons containing cargo and Secor was directed to deliver them as ordered by the Army at Ashiya. He was briefed to fly low over enemy occupied cities in northern South Korea and drop his cargo of leaflets urging residents to remain calm, telling them that American troops would be soon helping fight North Korean aggression. Secor had two fighter escort planes on his low level sweep over the west coast of Korea up to and including Seoul, already firmly in North Korean hands.

Flying at 500 feet, with enemy troops shooting at him from the ground, Secor and his men dropped thousands of leaflets, scattering them widely over Seoul, Suwon, Taejon and three other cities. Crew members wearing parachutes and firmly tied in with ropes, leaned out the wide open door of the C-46 to throw out leaflet bundles, cutting the cords as they did so, the leaflets scattering far and wide in the wind.

During the summer of 1950 there were only five leaflet drops, requiring from one to four C-47s each time, delivering surrender or propaganda leaflets to North Korean troops. In the Pusan Perimeter days there was not much point in encouraging victorious North Korean army troops to surrender, for at that time the enemy soldiers honestly believed they would soon push the Americans into the sea. The main objective of early propaganda was to convince the North Koreans that substantial American and United Nations aid was on the way and they could not hope to win in the long run.

General Walker's advance party established the headquarters of the US Eighth Army at Taegu on 8 July, and the next day the 25th Infantry Division began to arrive. To the east of the country the South Koreans were carrying out a fighting retreat to prevent the enemy from outflanking the American forces. By 25 July, most of the North Korean Air Force and their airfields were out of action. As the North Korean 3rd and 4th Divisions prepared to cross the Kum River and advance on Taejon, General Dean marshaled his forces to oppose them. The 4th Division was at half strength with 6,000 fighting men, but they also had fifty tanks. The 3rd Division had no tanks, but was up to full strength. The US 24th Infantry Division had 11,000 men on its strength, but there were only 5,300 at the sharp end. It would be a hard fought battle.

On 14 July, under cover of an artillery barrage, the North Koreans began to cross the Kum River in barges and drove the US 34th Infantry Regiment back in disorder. The 19th Infantry Regiment was engaged in heavy fighting on the flank of the 34th and then began to retreat as they found themselves encircled and casualties mounted. Forty of their wounded men were left behind with the chaplain and the medical officer. When the North Koreans reached them they shot them all. It would be a very dirty war and American soldiers and pilots falling into enemy hands could expect no mercy.

On 19 July, General Dean and the three regiments of the 24th Division prepared to defend Taejon. General Walker told him that he had to hold the town for at least two days to allow the 25th Division and the 1st Cavalry Division to reach the front. It was easier said than done. The enemy had rebuilt the bridge over the Kum River, ten miles north of Taejon and started to move tanks and artillery across. By midnight the two enemy divisions had encircled the town and were establishing roadblocks to the south and east. General Dean and his aide had spent the night in Taejon and awoke to the sound of small arms fire. Amazingly, considering his heavy responsibilities, the General found a pair of bazooka teams and went out tank hunting.

By the afternoon of 20 July, General Dean realized that the battle was lost and ordered the withdrawal of the remaining units. Towards evening the main convoy tried to leave the town but came under enemy fire. Most of the men abandoned their vehicles and tried to make it out of the town on foot. Some made it home but many others were killed or captured.

General Dean's jeep took a wrong turning and soon came under fire. After sheltering for a while in a ditch, Dean and his party made it to the banks of the Taejon River. They hid there until dark and then tried to climb the mountain north of the village of Nangwol. During a pause for rest, Dean decided to go off on his own to look for water for the wounded. He fell down a steep slope and was knocked out. When he came to, he discovered he had a broken shoulder and was disoriented. Up above, the rest of the party waited for two more hours for Dean to reappear, then set off for the American lines. General Dean spent thirty-six long days wandering the countryside before he was betrayed by two civilians and captured. His weight had dropped from 190 to 130 pounds, and he was to spend the rest of the war in solitary confinement. If that was not bad enough, almost 1,200 of his men had become casualties.

While the US 24th Division was being broken up by the North Koreans at Taejon, the 1st Battalion 'Wolfhounds' of the 27th Infantry Regiment, 25th Infantry Division, was taking up positions on an important road running north out of Okchon, a few miles east of Taejon and south of the Kum River. Here the road ran through a valley, surrounded by high hills, and the companies began to dig in and prepare to engage the North Koreans. High on one of the hills, Lieutenant Addision Terry and his team of forward observers sat in their foxholes and watched the retreat of the 24th Division in the distance. Suddenly, they saw a column of eight North Korean tanks around five thousand yards away, heading in their direction at full speed. Frantically Terry cranked the handle of his radio and passed on their coordinates to the 8th Field Artillery Battalion. However, hitting moving tanks with artillery based miles away is not an easy thing to do, and by the time the bursting artillery rounds got anywhere near the tanks, Terry and the battalion were also under attack and the communications wire to the battalion command post was cut by mortar fire.

The eight tanks were soon inside the battalion perimeter, cutting down the bazooka teams sent forward to intercept them. They could now bring their main 85mm gun and machine guns into action against the rear of the American positions up on the hillsides. The first two tanks drove down the road to the schoolhouse where the CP and aid station were located and began pumping shells into the building. Terry later recalled:

'Then, a miracle happened. Out of the blue came four angels in the form of Australian F-51 Mustangs. They swooped down over the hill, so close that I could see the pilots, and made a strafing run on the first two tanks with their 0.50s blazing. The 0.50s did not knock the tanks out, of course, but they did cause some damage. Then the planes made a wide circle and came in over us again for their second run, this time with rockets. They knocked the track off the second tank with a near miss and a direct hit was scored on the first tank, which was set on fire.

'While this attack was going on, the third and fourth tanks pulled a tricky manoeuvre. They backed off the road into a field on the east side of the road and thus blended in with the terrain. The other four tanks foolishly tried to turn around or back up to the north. They were silhouetted perfectly in the dusty road and were easy pickings for the Aussies, who rocketed them most skillfully. They were all set on fire. When the rockets were gone, the planes came back and strafed the second tank, whose track was off and lay prostrate in the road. Then they flew away to their base for more ammo and gas. After they had gone, the two tanks that had pulled into the field cranked up and pulled into the road and bugged for the Red lines. They had had enough. A recoilless rifle got a hit on the rear of the last one as it ran for its lines and crippled it. Both tanks made it out however, leaving six behind; five burning and one hopelessly crippled.'

The rest of the day passed uneventfully, except for a strafing by two ROK 'jackasses' in Mustang fighters, and as night fell the battalion pulled out, fighting their way down 'Heartbreak Highway' towards Taegu, with the North Koreans in hot pursuit.

Air Rescue
This would be an appropriate point to introduce the Air Rescue Service, which first came to the country on 7 July, and to mention that the airfields were now allocated 'K' numbers to identify them, in addition to their Korean

place name. Known as Mercy Mission #1, the two L-5 liaison planes and the single SC-47 arrived at K-1 Pusan West airfield, but the rice paddy runway was not suitable for them and they returned to Japan on 16 July. A week later, the commander of the Air Rescue Service, Colonel Richard T. Kight, flew an SC-47 in to K-2 Taegu #1, escorting the first H-5 helicopter of Detachment F of the 3rd Air Rescue Service. They relocated on 1 August to Pusan as the North Korean offensive threatened the Pusan Perimeter. Four days later they recorded the first evacuation using an H-5 of a wounded soldier from the Sendang-ni area to an Army hospital. Thousands more soldiers would be evacuated over the next three years of fighting which lay ahead.

In the September, when the allies broke out of the perimeter, Detachment F with its six H-5s moved back to Taegu. Advance elements, usually one L-5 and one or two H-5s would be co-located with Mobile Army Surgical Hospitals (MASH) in order to be closer to their area of operations and to provide a quicker response time.

Although the original plan called for a strip alert helicopter to be on standby to rescue downed pilots, they were also on call so front line organizations could call them up for evacuation of seriously wounded casualties. These requests were routed through the Eighth Army Surgeons Office, which would prioritize the evacuation flights and then contact the pilot by telephone. The surgeon's medical staff would also be on the ground to determine the best approach and evacuation, in order to minimize the risk to the pilots.

For rescue of fliers, the T-6 Mosquito spotter plane, which had contact with all fighters and bombers in its area and who received reports of distress or damage, maintained close contact with his base of operations. When the T-6 pilot received the report of a flier down, he would immediately relay it to the nearest rescue strip alert helicopter. However, these calls were not very frequent so there was plenty of time for evacuation missions.

In late August, an air rescue liaison officer from the 3rd Air Rescue Squadron was sent to the Joint Operations Centre at Taegu, to act as JOC Rescue Coordinator or Controller. Thereafter, the T-6 calls for rescue would be coordinated through the Tactical Air Control Centre and the JOC Rescue Coordinator. Sometimes though, time constraints meant that the rescue helicopter would be launched without waiting for official approval from the JOC. Three months later the Rescue Control Centre was increased to three personnel, to provide round-the-clock cover. The control centre was renamed Headquarters, 3rd Air Rescue Squadron in Korea, and the senior officer had the title of deputy commander, 3rd ARS, responsible for all rescue activities in Korea.

During the month of August, the H-5s carried 110 critically injured soldiers between the front line aid stations, MASH units and other hospitals. And on 4 September a new era began with the first rescue of a downed pilot, Captain Robert E. Wayne of the 35th Fighter Bomber Squadron, when he abandoned his damaged F-51 after a strafing run behind enemy lines just north of Pohang. The pilot, Captain Paul Van Boven, had no established doctrine to follow, so he just crossed the front line on his own initiative near the east coast and picked up the pilot. Wayne's wingman strafed the area around the helicopter, killing one soldier who had almost reached the downed pilot. As he hovered above the pilot, his medic, Corporal John Fuentes, reached down and pulled Wayne into the cabin. For the rescue Boven was awarded the Silver Star, the first of forty to be awarded to Air Rescue Personnel during the Korean War.

Two months earlier, on the first day of aerial combat of the war and flying the F-80, Wayne became the first USAF pilot to shoot down two enemy aircraft in a single day.

The Superfortress Arrives
As the build up of US air power continued, there was an urgent requirement for reconnaissance photographs and the mission fell to the Superfortresses of the 91st Strategic Reconnaissance Squadron. Earl Myers, one of the RB-29 crewmen later recalled:

'Our Combat Crews operated RB-29s prior to the Korean Conflict from Kadena Air Base, Okinawa. We were accomplishing border surveillance flights both electronic and visual photography of sensitive areas with some over-flights of targets of concern to the defense of the United States. Unfortunately our equipment, aircraft, photo and electronic capabilities, were antiquated and derelict. The RB-29s had been in the theater almost since the end of WWII and suffered from extreme corrosion due to the salt air environment of the Pacific.

'The determination of the ground and flight crews to "AIM HI" never wavered. We accomplished the impossible, fighting the elements with the equipment at hand. At the excellent direction of our maintenance officer Captain Mike Moffett and his maintenance personnel, the mission was accomplished with a lot of sweat, blood and tears working around the clock to complete the assigned mission.

'June of 1950 was not a magic month that all aircraft were in commission when the Korean outbreak occurred. We were immediately reassigned to Yokota Air Base, Japan, for our assigned mission of armed reconnaissance over Korea. We did pre- and post-bomb damage assessment of dams, power plants, airfields, bridges and targets of military importance along the Yalu River and entirety of North Korea. Targets of opportunity from the ground up to 30,000 ft. Targets included military convoys, trains, tank farms and moving tanks scurrying from the open area to cover.

'One tank farm consisting of approximately eighty-six tanks was spotted and we called in fighter-bombers to work them over while we flew top cover for them. Then we worked them over with everything we had while the fighters covered for us. Munitions trains were prime targets and there were ample amounts of them. Raking a target of that type from the rear to the locomotives in front was especially inviting. Soldiers would be firing at us on board the trains with rifles and machine guns as we passed. When the steam engine was hit by 50 cal. armored piercing bullets, they would penetrate all the way through and it almost looked like Old Faithful erupting. Of course, when the munitions cars were hit it looked like a Fourth of July display that you've never seen.

'They would scramble for a tunnel and we would seal both ends off and call Navy dive bombers in to lob 500-pound bombs inside. In Wonsan and Hamhung Harbor's when Sampans were spotted and rather than to shoot them up we would blow them over by coming in at deck level and pull up just before passing over. They were loaded with munitions. That was ample and at least they would have a chance of survival.'

On 24 July, 5th Air Force moved its advance headquarters from Japan to Taegu, locating it next to the Eighth Army Headquarters for ease of communication and coordination. The UN Command was formally established in Tokyo, Japan, commanded by General MacArthur, who assigned responsibility for ground action in Korea to Lieutenant General Walton H. Walker, commander of the Eighth Army; naval action to Vice Admiral C. Turner Joy, commander Far East Naval Forces, and air action to General Stratemeyer, Commander, Far East Air Forces.

As July came to an end, the USAF was finally able to use its B-29 bombers in the role for which they were intended – strategic bombing. There were a total of eighteen strategic targets nominated by the JCS in North Korea, and five B-29 bomb groups were now in the Far East theatre and available to carry out combat missions north of the 38th Parallel. Most of the targets were concentrated in five industrial centres and targeted due to their war-making potential; Wonsan, P'yongyang, Hungnam (Konan), Chongjin (Seishin) and Rashin (Najin). They included sea ports and harbours, railway industries, POL production and refining, arsenals manufacturing weapons, vehicles and aircraft, chemical production for use in explosives, metal production from aircraft aluminium to locomotive iron, and hydro–electric plants. On 30 July, the B–29 strategic bombing campaign began with the first of the 'Nannie' missions. Nannie 'Able, Baker and Charlie' were carried out over five days and resulted in the destruction of the Hungnam chemical complex, including the Chosen Nitrogen Explosives Factory which was flattened by forty-seven B–29s on 30 July.

Interdiction Campaign Number 1 commenced on 4 August with the granting of permission to destroy North Korea's supply lines and transportation routes. On 8 August, the newly arrived 307th Bomb Group flew its first mission against P'yongyang's marshalling yards, and two days later a major effort by the 22nd, 92nd and 98th Bomb Groups struck the marshalling yards and refinery at the North Korean port of Wonsan. The 98th had only just arrived too, moving into Yokota Air Base in Japan with its 343rd, 344th and 345th Bomb Squadrons.

Walter Laute was a tail gunner on a B–29 in the 343rd Bomb Squadron. He told the author:

'I joined the 98th Bomb Group in the Fall of 1949. I was assigned to the 343rd Bomb Squadron at Spokane, Washington. I was told I would be the new tail gunner on Captain Louis H. Breinger's crew. I learned my job quite quickly and started to feel like part of the team. I was the youngest crew member and the rest of 1949 and the first part of 1950 went by rather fast as we flew training and gunnery flights. The rumour was the 98th was headed to Ramey AFB, Puerto Rico, but that changed in June 1950 when North Korea attacked South Korea.

'Orders came down from Strategic Air Command Headquarters that the 98th was going to Yokota AFB, Japan. All three squadrons were to go; the 343rd, 344th and 345th Bomb Squadrons. We took off from Spokane and after touching down at various islands, we landed at Yokota AFB on a Sunday afternoon. We started to unload our plane, B–29 6335 which wore the "Square H" group identifier on its tail and the nose art "TDY Widow" on one side and "Miss Tampa" on the other. After we unloaded the plane, our crew was assigned our new quarters and then we went to the mess hall. Straight afterwards we went back to the flight line to load up with bombs; twenty 500-pound bombs in the front bomb bay and twenty more in the rear bay. The next day, 10 August, we were up at dawn's early light and attended our first bombing mission briefing where we were told the location of the primary target. If, for some reason we could not make the primary, we were given a secondary. If that did not work out we had a target of opportunity. The primary target today was the oil refinery and railroad shops at Wonsan, North Korea. Forty-six B-29s from the 22nd, 92nd and 98th Bomb Groups would be taking part.

'We gunners checked our weapons and ammunition and the gun sights. In my case, since I was the tail gunner I would go into my position about one hundred miles from the Korean coast. After reporting in, the Central Fire Control would have us fire a short burst to make sure the guns operated OK.

'The target at Wonsan was clear and when the lead aircraft dropped his bombs the other planes dropped theirs also. We encountered light anti-aircraft fire. We could see the explosions and smoke up to and above 5,000 feet and as we headed back to Japan, we could see the smoke 400–500 miles away. After we landed at Yokota we attended de-briefing. After our gunners report, we returned to our planes and cleaned and checked our guns and ammunition ready for the next day's mission.

'I was of course scared of getting shot down and at that time we had no idea how long we would be there and how many missions we would have to fly. Most of the crew felt tired, hungry and cold. Myself, I wore fatigues, heated suit, plus leather jacket. It depended on the altitude how cold it was.

'We also flew support missions, including marshalling yards and barrack areas. I am sure we also flew during the breakout from Pusan and over the Chosin Reservoir when the Marines were trapped there. On flare missions we were assigned targets, mostly railway tunnels. The North Koreans hid their supply trains in rail tunnels and we left about dusk, so that when we reached the target area it would be dark. We would drop the flares and the fighters would attack their targets.

'The first several of the bombing missions went smoothly, but in the latter part of October we started to encounter heavy flak, plus MiG fighters. We did have fighter cover on many of our missions, when they flew alongside the formation. When the Sabres dropped their wing tanks it meant MiGs in the area. The MiGs made their attacks during the bomb run. As tail-gunner I never hit one of them, but I did get the chance to fire at them. The 98th was the last group to fly daylight missions. Heavy losses meant a change of tactics to night operations.

'We flew 56 combat missions, and when our replacement crew arrived in March 1951 we flew home by civilian airliners. The new replacement crew 6335 "JACKIE", and the last crew had the SAC symbol on it, as well as the 343rd Bomb Squadron logo. It flew 136 missions before returning to the US in 1952 where it was scrapped. We reported to March AFB in California where we reactivated the 44th Bomb Group and began to train replacement crews for Korea.'

Within six weeks the campaign was over and all targets had been eliminated. However, the campaign was not decisive for two reasons. The first is that the US planners had incorrectly believed that the North Koreans were dependent on transportation, as the US Army was, whereas the Communists generally moved on foot without a long logistical tail. The second reason was that the North Koreans were receiving much of their supplies from the Chinese and Soviets, driven across the Yalu River bridges into North Korea. As the border area was out-of-bounds to the Far East Air Force, for fear of antagonizing the Chinese and Soviets, the supplies had to be targeted as they were making their way south. This interdiction campaign would be known as Operation Strangle and involved bombing the roads, although the planners soon realized that most of the supplies were being shipped south by train and attention was turned to the railway network.

Before long though, the operation was put on hold as Close Air Support missions began to take priority.

Marine Close Air Support
In early August, more flight decks arrived, in the form of the fleet carrier USS *Philippine Sea* (CV-47) and the escort carriers USS *Badoeng Strait* (CVE-116) and *Sicily* (CVE-118), the latter two with US Marine air groups. That, plus the addition of more underway replenishment ships, allowed a much increased tempo of carrier combat air operations, which were urgently needed to support the beleaguered defenders of the Pusan Perimeter and to continue the reduction of the enemy's rear areas. This work went on steadily through August and into September. Sadly, its potential effectiveness was constantly hampered by inadequate capabilities for controlling close air support of the ground forces, who were thus deprived of badly needed help. For a three day period from 5 August the *Valley Forge* supplied Target Air Controllers to Taegu Air Force Base to direct both Navy and Air Force aircraft on the north-south bomb line from Chinju to Hamchang.

During eleven days of action in August, the aircraft from USS *Valley Forge* and USS *Philippine Sea* fired 214,000 rounds of 20mm ammunition, as most target sorties involved strafing. This usage began to wear out the guns and, with insufficient spares available, soon led to more frequent gun failures during flight. The 20mm gun however, proved to be a devastating attack weapon, and the more experienced pilots who had flown during WWII were unanimous in their preference for four 20mms instead of the six 0.50-caliber gun installations.

Another complaint was that the Mark 9, Mod 2 and 3 rocket launchers were not strong enough to withstand the rigors of arrested landing on the carriers with a hung-up 5-inch HVAR rocket or 100-pound bomb. Either the locking latch shear pin would shear, allowing the projectile to drop on to the deck, or the rear part of the launcher would start pulling away from its base plate due to the overhanging rocket tail. An improved bomb-rocket pylon was sorely needed that would be strong enough to withstand bringing ordnance back on board and fitted with a manual and electrical means of jettisoning hung ordnance.

Another recommendation was to reduce the number of squadrons in the CAG to three, VF Jet, VF Prop and VA Prop, plus the specialized detachments. This would reduce administrative work and the confusion of having the same type of aircraft in two different squadrons, and two separate squadrons in one ready room would be eliminated.

Though more US Army divisions came into action during July, the North Koreans pushed steadily south. They had not achieved Kim Il-Sung's promised quick victory, but they were still winning. US and South Korean casualties were severe. The defenders retreated into the Pusan Perimeter, an area in the southeast corner of the country, about eighty miles by fifty and anchored on the vital seaport at Pusan. In early August, the situation along this Pusan Perimeter was critical, and remained so for more than a month, as the North Koreans tried relentlessly to shatter the defenses.

However, also in early August, the First Provisional Marine Brigade arrived on the *Badoeng Strait* (CVE116), three weeks after sailing from California. It was an air-ground team built around the 5th Marine Regiment and Marine Aircraft Group 33 (MAG-33). General Edward A Craig, with Brigadier General Thomas J. Cushman, a renowned and experienced Marine aviator, assigned as his deputy commander, commanded the brigade. They brought with them Marine Fighter Squadrons VMF-214 and -323 flying the Corsair and Marine Night Fighter Squadron VMF(N)-513 with its Grumman F7F Tigercat and Douglas F3D Skyknights. They also brought an observation squadron VMO-6 with its eight Consolidated OY Sentinel light observation planes and four Sikorsky HO3S-1 helicopters. It was the first time that the United States Armed Services had actually deployed helicopters in a unit mounting out for combat service overseas.

The tough Marines, though few in numbers, bested the enemy every time they met, taking back his hard-won advances and generally serving as the Pusan Perimeter's fire brigade. The Marines were assisted by an invaluable asset, one not then generally available to the US and South Korean soldiers – their own close air support that was really close, and fully integrated with the ground effort. The Korean War would decisively prove the tactical superiority of this ground-air teamwork over the competing concept that all air power should be centrally directed from afar.

The brigade disembarked on 2 August and departed Pusan for the front line the following day. Their own close air support was on hand with VMF-323 flying from the *Badoeng Strait* and the 'Black Sheep' of VMF-214 from the *Sicily*. The night-flying aircraft of VMF(N)-513 were based at Itazuke Airfield on the southern Japanese island of Kyushu and flew night 'heckler' operations over the brigade combat area. The helicopters of VMO-6 would operate out of Pusan, so they could respond as soon as possible to requests for air evacuation.

The first Marine air offensive of the war took place on 3 August when eight Corsairs of VMF-214 took off at 1630 hours for a strike against Chinju and the communist held village of Sinbanni. Using incendiary bombs, rockets, and numerous strafing runs, it was an impressive show for the previously unopposed North Korean troops. On the following day twenty-one more sorties were flown to help relieve pressure on the Eighth Army southern flank, striking at bridges, railroads and troop concentrations.

On 6 August, VMF-323 joined the fray with strikes west of Chinju along the Nam River, hitting large buildings and railroad lines with rockets and 500-pound bombs. Because the carriers were so close to the front lines of the perimeter the strikes could reach their targets in a matter of minutes at any point where air support was required. Each of the Marine battalions had their own Tactical Air Control Parties (TACP) in direct control with Marine Tactical Air Control Squadron 2 and VMO-6 at brigade headquarters. Each party consisted of one aviation officer, an experienced and fully qualified pilot, and six enlisted technicians, equipped with a radio jeep, portable radios and remote communications gear.

One of the first helicopter rescues by marine aircrews occurred on 10 August 1950, when an HO3S of VMO-6 flown by First Lieutenant

Gustave F. Lueddeke picked up Captain Vivian M. Moses of VMF-323. Moses Corsair had been hit by enemy ground fire and lost engine oil pressure and had to ditch. He volunteered for another mission the next day, only to be shot down again. Sadly, he was thrown from his aircraft after crashing into a rice paddy and drowned. He was MAG-33's first combat fatality. VMO-6 also flew several OY Sentinel artillery spotting aircraft nicknamed 'Grasshoppers'. They were unarmed, but some pilots carried hand grenades to throw at groups of enemy soldiers as they flew low over their positions.

On 11 August, the Corsairs of VMF-323 teamed up with USAF Mustangs in what became known as the 'Kosong Turkey Shoot'. They caught a convoy of over a hundred vehicles from a North Korean motorized regiment, a mixed bag of troop-carrying trucks, jeeps and motorcycles near Kosong, and after destroying the vehicles at both ends of the convoy, proceeded to hit everyone in between.

The operations in the Pusan Perimeter were basically divided during the six-week period into three major actions. The first was the counter attack in the extreme southwest which ran from 3 to 15 August and was known as the Sachon Offensive; the second was the First Naktong counter offensive from 16 to 19 August, and the third was the Second Naktong counter offensive from 3 to 5 September. All three resulted in defeats for the Communist forces, but cost the Marines 170 killed and 730 wounded. Enemy casualties were estimated at around 10,000 killed and wounded.

It was during this time that the Americans realized what kind of men were facing them. The mortar platoon of H Company, 5th Cavalry Regiment, allowed the enemy to infiltrate their positions on 15 August and were all taken prisoner without a fight. The following day the North Koreans executed all thirty-four of the men, prior to retreating across the Naktong River. On 17 August, a company from the 3rd North Korean Division shot dead forty-five American prisoners of war who were standing in a trench with their hands tied.

On the night of 31 August, the 23rd Infantry Regiment from the US 2nd Infantry Division was overrun by the North Koreans. Private Jimmy Montoya found himself one of only five survivors out of a group of 200 Americans. He later related; 'It was sad to see all those brave Americans dead and strewn all over the rice paddy. Nobody to bury them, to put them in body bags, to take their ID tags and to tell the story of their heroism. The only consolation we had was that they had died valiantly helping their fellow GIs by taking as many North Koreans with them as possible.'

Fortunately, Montoya was amongst eighty prisoners of war liberated at Namwon by advancing American tanks a month later.

Night Fighting Tigercats

Robert Dahlberg was one of the reserve pilots recalled to duty to fly the Grumman F7F Tigercat night fighter:

'I was activated for Korea in Mid-August, 1950. I had mixed emotions. I had a contract to teach maths in a West St. Paul high school and had been married less than two years, but, on the other hand, I had been training for such an eventuality and looked forward to active duty. The thought of avoiding active call up never entered my mind; it was just, "Got my orders, so I go." That was the feeling of all the pilots. I never heard any Marine pilot grumble about unfairness, or unwillingness to go.

'I was assigned to Marine Night Fighter Squadron VMF(N)-542 and we left San Diego near the end of August 1950 on a "baby" flat top aircraft carrier named the USS *Cape Esperance*. Our aircraft was the Grumman F7F Tigercat, a twin engined heavy fighter with four 20mm cannon mounted in the wing root. It could carry two 500-pound bombs, eight 5-inch rockets and a 300 US gallon fuel tank slung under its belly.

'The F7s were lifted aboard in port, and lifted off again when we got to Japan. The trip was very slow, and included two days just drifting when the ship's engines broke down. Our sister night fighter squadron VMF (N)-513 had Corsairs, but 542 preceded them into combat. After the Inchon invasion we flew over from Japan and set up a squadron parking area at Kimpo Airport, just southwest of Seoul. The Marines recaptured the airfield on 17 September and 542 was the first fighter squadron to occupy Kimpo known as "K-14".

'We liked the F7F. Most of us were seasoned F4U Corsair pilots and found the F7 faster by 30–40 knots, but not as agile, and the cockpit was extremely narrow. It was not as control sensitive as the F4U, but seemed more stable as a gun platform and the knowledge of having that second engine was comforting. Back inbetween wars it was found that the F7 was not to be used on aircraft carriers, as the hard landings developed cracks in the wing roots between the engines and the fuselage. That was no problem for us, as we were land-based in Korea.

'My transition to F7Fs was one familiarization flight in the daytime, when I met my new RO (radar operator), Byron Hall, a seasoned, old (had five years on me) REGULAR Sergeant, who I am sure was not too pleased with his assignment. My second hop in the F7 was a night convoy interdiction flight, searching and shooting up truck convoys. Training? It was "just do what you've been trained to do in the Reserves – only at night."

'I was over there from August 1950 to July 1951. We never flew escort for the B-29s; that activity for the squadron came much later, after I had gone home. While I was there, my job was primarily night interdiction of truck and train traffic, with occasional flights of close air support of troops.

'The F7 radar was no good against ground targets. The primary value, then, was to keep navigational track of where we were. We pilots were given a geographical area to snoop around in and find trucks, trains, etc and we didn't keep good track of where we were most of the time – the ROs were a great help in finding our way home. Oh, the radar was always searching for AIR targets, but during the early part of the war there were none – and when they did start, rarely would there be any night enemies.

'The F7 was a good basic night fighter, with no frills. During the winter, it was extremely cold and the heaters weren't worth a damn – what heat was produced came mainly in the front cockpit – the poor ROs got almost none at all.

'I don't think it had any weaknesses, that is if you compare them to the somewhat "antique" technology of World War II. Because the equipment was so old the F7 didn't have tone generators on its radio. When a pilot needed to call for a steer home, the home station asked for a one-minute tone in order to get a vector fix. Lacking a tone generator, the pilot held down the microphone button and said a long "AAAAAAAAAAH!" interspersed with gasps and choking noises most of the time. Very humorous. Back in Itazuke in Japan, on R and R, at the Air Force bar one night, I was surrounded by Air Force blue types who flew more modern night-fighters. During the conversation, I was asked what our squadron call sign was. When I responded "Night Train" I was greeted with a loud chorus, "AAAAAAAAAAH!"

'I heard that we lost twenty-seven Tigercats in Korea, but we never knew what most of the losses were caused by, as we went alone at night and some were never heard from again. My guess, based on my own experience, was that the pilots got so engrossed in their work, they just flew into the trees. I remember one night getting a convoy stopped on a mountain pass with some of the trucks on fire. I got pretty excited and made quite a few lower and lower strafing passes until my RO said "Knock it off, let's get out of here." We did see some anti-aircraft fire, but my plane only sustained one hit from that end. It took about a foot off my wing tip. I don't think they had good radar control firing until early 1951; probably the Chinese started equipping them.

'On 24 September we lost our first aircrew to hostile fire. Major J.W. Beebe, the squadron intelligence officer, and his radar operator were shot down and killed by heavy ground fire on a close air support mission northwest of Seoul. I nearly followed them a few days later. I was green as grass about flying the F7F. I'd been a Corsair pilot all my career and this was my third hop in an F7F. It was 3 October and we were flying a night combat air support mission over Seoul and a forward air controller called me in to knock out a fortified bunker located on high ground in a strategic area at Uijongbu that was holding up the 7th Marine Regiment. I located the general area and the FAC gave me instructions as to the direction of approach, direction of pull out, altitude of terrain features and how the target would be marked. We were going to make a dummy run and use my navigation lights so the FAC could get a visual on our approach.

'The dummy run went well and we lined up for the strafing run, using our 20mm cannon while we dropped a napalm tank, which was being carried in lieu of a 300 gallon fuel drop tank. We came in, strafed and dropped our napalm, only to find that it had not ignited. We pulled up and circled while the FAC reported that the troops were still taking incoming fire from the bunker. The Marines on the ground were asked by the FAC to mark the position of the bunker again with a mortar star shell, but when they did so I was not in position, but decided to make the run while I still had the target identified. I kept steepening the dive in order to stay on target and decided to fire four of my eight rockets. However I screwed up as I had the rocket switch on "Salvo" a definite no-no, and when I fired the rockets my radar operator's canopy blew off. I also had both eyes open when I fired and went totally blind. I was completely disoriented and somehow rolled the aircraft over on its back at about seventy knots airspeed! It seemed an eternity before I could see the instruments again and get the plane righted. I never did figure out why we didn't auger in; I was really fouled up. Then when I got back to Kimpo, it was socked in and I had to make a GCA approach. Was so shook, that I made two over speed passes at the strip and had to go around with Byron Hall sitting out in the cold under a flailing canopy.

'My RO, Sergeant Byron Hall who was about five years my senior, climbed out on the wing of the plane after we landed, threw up and said to me, "I'll be Goddamned if I ever fly with you again!" But we did and logged eighty-two missions together.

'The next morning word came down from the 1st Marine Division that two of the rockets had been direct hits on the bunker and that, combined with the napalm which was ignited by the rockets, the bunker was completely destroyed.

'One day around October 1950 a B-29 hit our flight line at K-14 Kimpo airfield, just outside of Seoul. The B-29 had been hit by AA fire and lost most of its hydraulic power, landed on the runway, but veered off into our area and its wing travelled down our flight line and neatly bent over the tails of four F7Fs which had been foolishly parked in a row. The North Korean gunner probably never knew what a hero he was; he got five aircraft with one shell. I guess that qualified him as an Ace!

'In October, 1950 I was scheduled for a daytime mission to fly fighter escort to a F7F photo plane but was not told the exact destination, just that it would be north of the "bomb line" and a long flight, so belly tanks were rigged. We flew right up into the northeast corner of North Korea, and I thought, right over the border at Vladivostok. The purpose, it turned out, was to see the extent of MiG strength parked at the airfields. This was early in the war, before the Russian-made jets were real active in the North Korean skies, but the sphincter muscles were still tight. Then, after pictures were finished, we turned east out over the water, then south, and headed home at minimum altitude right over the water. An uneventful flight, but some MiG pilot could have had two lonely F7s very easily.'

Major Leroy Pratt was a control tower operator at K-14 and recalled receiving an emergency call from an F7:

'It was after sunset and he declared an emergency for landing and requested a straight in approach. I cleared him for that and called out the crash crew. He reported that his port engine was out and he was able to maintain only partial power on the starboard engine. He also reported that he had snared a cable trap north of us.

'The Chinese and North Koreans used heavy steel cable to string across narrow valley-type road cuts. This was anchored on the hill above the road and on the ground on the opposite side of the road. This was repeated on the high side to low side from the other side of the "cut" creating an "X" of cable across the road. A burned-out or otherwise tank or truck was then placed in the roadway. Our night interdiction strikes depended on radar imaging and you could not see the trap. Since the run to the target was made along the road it was almost impossible to avoid flying into the cable. We lost several aircraft in that fashion. The cable had jammed the port engine, was wrapped around the wing, and trailed about 125 feet behind the plane, causing a shower of sparks on the landing roll out. The pilot turned off the runway after slowing and completed an engine run up prior to shutdown.

'I talked with the crash crew and the Marine Radar Operator that was in the backseat of the F7 that night and again the next day. I was informed that there was cable wrapped around the prop on the starboard engine and that it was striking the cockpit with every revolution and the pilot was pretty beat up from that.

'The RO said that he was afraid that the pilot was going to bail out and when he opened his canopy the RO would be trapped. Obviously he didn't and it turned out as well as could be expected. As an aside the flaps were jammed in addition to other damage and the pilot made a no-flap landing. I was very impressed by the Marine pilot's dedication by bringing his aircraft and especially his crew member home!'

While the situation around the Pusan Perimeter was stabilizing with the arrival of more American ground troops and air support, General MacArthur was far from idle. After studying the map of the Korean peninsula at his headquarters in Japan, he pointed with the end of his corn cob pipe at the west coast port of Inchon, far behind enemy lines; 'That's our next move gentleman – we will put the Marines ashore there.'

It was to be the first amphibious landing on enemy soil since the Second World War.

Chapter 2

Counter Attack: Sept 1950–July 1951

Chapter Contents

The Landing at Inchon

INTENSE fighting took place around the Pusan perimeter during August and early September 1950 as the Americans continued their build up of ground forces. With only one or two airfields within the perimeter, all of their air support had to come from Japan or the Navy carriers offshore. During the UN's air campaign in the Yellow Sea, USS *Badoeng Strait*, USS *Boxer* with Carrier Fighter Group CVG-2 embarked, USS *Philippine Sea* with CVG-11, USS *Valley Forge* with CVG-5, USS *Sicily* and HMS *Triumph*, plastered North Korean positions with pinpoint precision. Alarms were a daily occurrence, but only once were the carriers themselves seriously threatened.

On 4 September, *Valley Forge's* combat air patrol, comprising four F4U-4B Corsairs from VF-53, was stationed twenty miles from the carrier at 10,000 feet. At 1329 hours radar detected 'bogeys' closing from sixty miles away, not showing 'identification friend or foe'. A minute later the CAP was ordered to intercept just as the raid split, with one part retiring north toward Kaiyo To Island, the other part closing on the task force at a ground speed of 180 knots at 12–13,000 feet.

At 1336 hours the Corsairs intercepted a bomber marked with Soviet red stars. The bomber's rear gunner fired on them, whereupon permission was given to open up. Ensign Edward Velora Laney, Jr. riddled the enemy aircraft with his guns, hitting the engine and exploding the fuel tank, as well as shooting off the tail section. Later identified as an Ilyushin IL-l0, the intruder spun into the sea in flames. One of the bodies retrieved from the wreckage was Russian, and it was surmised that the aircraft had been delivered to a Manchurian field for North Korea. The bomber's actions confirmed the depth of Soviet involvement in the Korean War.

General MacArthur realized that the enemy supply lines were over-extended and proposed an amphibious landing at Inchon, a port on the west coast near Seoul and deep behind enemy lines. 'Operation Chromite' would see the landing of X Corps under Major General Edward Almond with the 1st Marine Division leading the way, followed by 7th US Infantry Division. Once ashore they would cut the enemy supply lines through Seoul and recapture Kimpo and Suwon airfields.

On 14 September – D minus 1 – the four 'Death Rattlers' of VMF-323, took off from the USS *Badoeng Strait* at 1145 hours, each Corsair carrying two belly tanks of extra fuel for a rendezvous with the Navy four miles off Inchon. It was the first time that American forward air controllers would be used to adjust the aim of the guns of British war ships. Two of the aircraft worked with two US Navy Cruisers and First Lieutenant Joseph Wosser, Junior, and his wingman Sid Fisher worked with two British Cruisers. The first targets that Wosser started firing on were two anti-aircraft guns next to a baseball park right in the city. He relayed the coordinates to the British and soon their shells knocked out the guns, as well as a tank that was hiding under some trees. Then he spotted six more anti-aircraft emplacements on the top of a hill and called in two more adjustments before a broadside of nine six-inch shells landed on top of them.

The following day, 15 September, the 'Death Rattlers' were airborne at dawn, heading for the port of Inchon. As the Corsairs arrived in the area a three-hour naval bombardment began, while offshore the men of the 1st Marine Division waited in their landing craft for the tide to rise. One area of resistance was around the lighthouse on Wolmi-do Island, but the Corsairs soon removed that obstacle with their 500-pound bombs and napalm. The strategic location of the island, bordering Inchon harbour, made seizing the peninsula crucial to the success of the invasion. The peninsula was blasted so intensely that following a pass over the island, one *Valley Forge* pilot remarked that 'the whole island looked like it had been shaved.'

At 1432 hours on 15 September, *Boxer's* CVG-2 – comprising VFs 23, 24, 63 and 64, Attack Squadron (VA) 65, and detachments from Composite Squadrons 3, 11, 33 and 61, and Helicopter Utility Squadron (HU) 1, began plastering Inchon. With Skyraiders acting as target coordinators, a dozen Corsairs and five Skyraiders attacked the Inchon beach with 500- and 1,000-pound general-purpose bombs, five-inch high-velocity aircraft rockets, HVAR and three-and-a-half-inch target-spotting rockets, and also conducted strafing runs. This strike was immediately followed by two more Corsairs flying as target coordinators for another seven Skyraiders and ten Corsairs, which pummeled buildings throughout the area, hitting factories and oil tanks and starting intense fires in the area. Again, only light flak was encountered.

The enemy defenders were not the only problem facing the Marines. The harbour approaches were plagued by a treacherous tidal range, of up to thirty-five feet, one of the most extreme in Korea. Landing craft could cross the wide mud flats only at flood tide, and if enemy fire could not be suppressed it would be a blood bath. The narrow islands and channels of the approaches were also a navigational nightmare. To offset these problems and to prevent the North Koreans from strengthening their defenses, Kunsan, 105 miles south of Inchon, was chosen as a decoy to convince the North Koreans that the landings would occur there and not at Inchon. When a relieved MacArthur learned that the outer harbour had been secured at the cost of only seventeen wounded, he had Rear Admiral Doyle signal the task force commander, 'The Navy and Marines have never shone more brightly than this morning.'

More was yet to come.

The support given by VMF-323 continued, from before the first wave of landing craft hit the beach and through the day, in support of Major General Oliver P. Smith's 1st Marine Division, as they secured the beachhead and began to move inland. The 'Blue Knights' of the Navy's fighter squadron VF-53 also joined in the fray, and Ensign Eldon W. Brown, Jr., in his Corsair, caused what looked like an atomic explosion when he hit a long line of boxes seven feet high by three boxes wide near a machine gun emplacement. The peculiar orange flame of burning ammunition made him leave the area in a hurry. He later recalled: 'I grabbed the stick and throttle tightly, leveled my wings and held on. "Wham!" The explosion was terrific. A big red cloud of dust mushroomed up past me and by that time I was up to almost 4,000 feet.'

The next day, the strikes moved further inland to keep pace with the advancing troops on the ground. In the face of heavier and more accurate ground fire, four strikes delivered bombs, HVARs and napalm. Six CVG-2 Skyraiders on deep support hit a railroad yard adjacent to Yongduri and a railway at Suishokiri with HVARs, setting rolling stock and warehouses afire. The final strike consisted of eighteen Corsairs and eight Skyraiders flying offensive sorties, supported by eight F4U-4s on CAP. Concentrating on communications targets and infrastructure, they hit the railroad yard at Eitoho five to ten miles southwest of Seoul, as well as targets around the capital, including railroad yards, an oil storage depot and an ammunition dump. All of the strikes recovered by 1200 hours.

During a counterattack early on 16 September, a column of six North Korean T-34 tanks rumbled toward the 5th Marines' positions, whose lighter weapons were useless against them. Just as the tanks were practically on top of the Marines, Corsairs from the Marine Fighter Squadron 214 'Blacksheep' operating from USS *Sicily* swooped in and blasted the column apart. When the column lost its cohesion, the surviving tanks were then picked off by Marine M-26 Pershing tanks. During the attack, enemy fire shot down Captain William F. Simpson, whose Corsair struck the ground and exploded.

The 7th Infantry Division would begin to land at Inchon the following day as the 5th Marines began its drive towards Kimpo airfield. Lieutenant Wosser and the Corsairs of VMF-323 were back in the air again and he later wrote:

'Well our boys are really moving. They secured Inchon today and are moving out on the roads to Seoul and Suwon with tank columns leading the way. I took off at 0945 hours and reported in to the target controller who assigned us a road patrol between Inchon and Suwon. Just then I spotted an enemy jeep doing about fifty miles an hour! I peeled off with my wingman and caught it dead centre with a burst of 20mm. It swerved off the road and stopped and then my wingman caught him solid. Then we returned to our assigned target in Seoul and really had a field day. We put six 500-pound bombs, one napalm and fifty-five rockets into a yard full of truck trailers and fuel supplies. It was leveled, along with a locomotive and two tank cars we attacked next.'

The following day, 17 September, Lieutenant Wosser was in the thick of the fighting again: 'At 1430 hours dispatch requested all planes we could supply immediately to hit targets in Seoul. Inside one hour we had twenty-four planes fully armed, loaded and in the air – some kind of record! The Admiral was very pleased. I hit a railroad yard east of Seoul with napalm, some vehicles on the road with rockets, and 20mm and some more rockets hit some anti-aircraft guns. Our troops were just assaulting Kimpo airfield as we were returning, so I imagine we'll have planes flying off it in a day or two.'

Kimpo airfield was back in Marine hands by the end of the day and the first Marine aircraft began to fly sorties from the field on the 21st. VMF-212 with its Corsairs, VMF(N)-542 with its night-fighting F7F Tigercats, and F3D SkyKnights, moved in straight away and VMF-312 with its Corsairs was due to follow shortly. The enemy suffered heavy losses on 21 September, trying to cross the Han River into Seoul. They were caught in the open with nowhere to hide and the 'Death Rattlers' made run after run on them, with napalm, bombs, rockets and 20mm. Even though the Corsairs had over fifty guns that were worn out and not working, they earned their flying pay that day. Lieutenant Wosser later recorded in his diary:

'When we were finished, there were so many dead lying on the beach we couldn't count them. It really makes you feel funny to be shooting at them when they have no place to hide. Usually we never see troops, or if we do, just a few because they are always camouflaged, but that white sand made them really stand out. Two of our planes were hit, but not seriously. VMF-214 had a plane shot down, but they got the pilot back after a little trouble. He had a broken leg and the pilot of the helicopter (God bless 'em) got out and was helping his mech get the pilot out of the plane leaving his copter running, and just as they got back to it, it took off with no one in it and crashed. They had to send another copter out to get all three of them. Boy, those copters are really wonderful for rescue – in fact, for just about everything except fighting.'

The 22nd was a busy day for CVG-2 as aircraft from *Boxer* broke up a column of 1,500 NKPA troops while they were crossing the Han River, killing an estimated two hundred. Not to be outdone, the deep support group hit a railroad tunnel two miles east of Yongyu by dropping a 500-pounder inside the tunnel – no easy feat under any circumstances, but an even more remarkable achievement considering the heavy ground fire.

Meanwhile, General Walker's Eighth Army pushed out of the Pusan Perimeter, helped considerably by B–29s making a carpet bombing attack at Waegwan. At first, the enemy resisted vigorously but then their lines collapsed and what started as an orderly retreat turned into a rout. Eighth Army would link up with the 7th Division near Suwon early on 27 September and by the end of that day Seoul was back in UN hands. By the end of September, what was left of the North Korean Peoples Army was scurrying back across the 38th Parallel. South Korean troops crossed the Parallel on 1 October, followed by the Eighth Army on 7 October.

The Breakout from Pusan

The Eighth Army had been reorganized into I Corps and IX Corps. The most reliable units were allocated to I Corps; the 5th Regimental Combat Team, the 1st Cavalry Division, the rebuilt 24th Division, the 27th British Commonwealth Brigade and the South Korean's best division, the 1st ROK Division. They were to break out of the Pusan Perimeter and spearhead the 180-mile drive north to meet up with X Corps which was coming ashore at Inchon. IX Corps and its 2nd and 25th US Divisions would follow on a week later. On the east side of the country the ROK I and II Corps were to engage the enemy the best they could.

The Air Force's contribution to the invasion was Air Interdiction Campaign 2, the first objective of which was to limit the flow of reinforcements to the landing zone at Inchon. Intelligence was reporting a build up of Chinese Communist forces in Manchuria and interdiction of North Korean transport routes might help delay these forces if they should decide to intervene in the war. The FEAF B–29s would also have to hit the rail yard at Seoul in the days before the landing, and MacArthur made it clear that he would require heavy air support for Eighth Army as it broke out of the Pusan Perimeter in pursuit of the North Koreans. On 9 September the bombing missions began, with one of the five groups flying daily against rail yards and two of the other groups sending eight planes at a time to cut the railway lines. A maximum effort on 13 September saw sixty B–29s flying missions against the North Korean railway network.

The breakout of Eighth Army was to begin on 16 September with a force of eighty-two B–29s bombing a pathway along the line Taegu-Taejon-Suwon. However, the weather delayed the attacks until the 18th when forty-two B–29s started to clear a path for the 38th Infantry Regiment to cross the Naktong River. This was followed by 286 close air support sorties from F–51s, F–80s and B–26s. A further 361 were flown the next day, halting

North Korean counter attacks and weakening their defenses until, on 22 September, the North Korean Army collapsed, leaving the door open for a race to the 38th Parallel.

The advance would not be all one sided though. The 25th US Division was hampered by the performance of one of its infantry regiments. The 24th was an all-black outfit that had performed so badly during the summer that the divisional commander asked that the unit be disbanded. His request was refused and it was left to the 27th and 35th Regiments to get the division moving.

Bomber Command pursued the retreating North Koreans and attacked them by day and night. The B-29s had been practising dropping flares at night, so that B-26s could attack the targets illuminated by the flares. On 22 September, the roving B-26s bombed and strafed a long North Korean ammunition train south of Suwon and the explosions went on for an hour. Other B-29s flew psychological warfare missions, dropping leaflets over retreating North Korean columns. Many prisoners surrendered with these leaflets in their hands.

As the bombing effort switched from the south to the north, the B-29s ranged far and wide looking for new targets. On 22 September, a B-29 from the 98th Bomb Group spotted a town with a rail marshalling yard and bombed it. Several days passed before the Air Force managed to identify the town and discovered that it was actually Antung, across the Yalu River in Chinese Manchuria. The warning to stay clear of the Chinese border went out to the bomber crews, and four days later attacks began against the North Korean hydro-electric plants, the first target for the 92nd Bomb Group being the electric plant at Hungnam. On the same day, UN forces fought their way into Seoul and began three days of street to street fighting to evict the North Koreans. When Seoul fell to the 1st Marines on 22 September the total US Marine casualties for the Inchon-Seoul operations had reached 2,301.

It is a sad fact that the North Korean People's Army slaughtered more South Korean civilians in September 1950 than in any other month of the war. Almost fifteen thousand were killed in the last four days of that month alone. It was quite clear that the murders were as a result of policy dictated by the North Korean leaders. By the end of September the US forces driving north were capturing up to two thousand North Korean prisoners every day. Many were South Koreans, conscripted at gunpoint, with the choice of a painful death as the alternative. Sometimes captured enemy personnel would readily admit to participating in the most heinous crimes, such as the Taejon

Massacre which saw the slaughter of between 5,000 and 7,500 civilians, as well as forty-three American and seventeen ROK Army prisoners. The 3rd North Korean Division was responsible for the killings, between 23 and 26 September. The American prisoners had been held in the jail at Taejon and were taken out half a dozen at a time, shot and thrown into a ditch. There was only one survivor who lived despite being wounded and buried with his comrades. He was recovered when the 24th US Infantry Division took the town on 28 September.

As the US Marines fought their way from Inchon to Seoul, the North Koreans were making arrangements to march all American prisoners of war up to the North Korean capital at P'yongyang. Three hundred and seventy-six American prisoners began the march on 26 September, but only 296 were still alive when the column reached P'yongyang on 10 October. Once, an American plane flew over the hapless prisoners and dropped supplies for them, but the North Koreans immediately collected the items and kept them for themselves. Any Americans dropping out of the column were shot or bayoneted and left for dead.

North Korean Communists often escaped pursuing United Nations forces by dressing in the white clothing of refugees. The wearing of white, usually a dress for mourning, became popular after the Japanese occupied Korea in 1905. However, the flowing white robes can often conceal guns and ammunition and pilots were expected to target such groups or risk being sent home for 'lack of moral fibre'. On this occasion pilots of the Death Rattler and Black Sheep squadrons were pouring fire into the village of Yongdun Po, a suburb of Seoul, until the enemy troops had to evacuate the area. On the way out they began to change their clothes for the white garb of a Korean peasant. However, a sharp-eyed Marine forward air controller spotted them and called in Corsairs from the *Badoeng Strait* to attack them. Shortly afterwards US troops moved into the area unopposed.

Two Marine pilots found themselves grateful to the *Badoeng Strait* when they got into trouble on the way home one day. Fortunately all Marine fliers were carrier-qualified. If they had not been, Captain Irving J. Barney and T/Sgt Charles L. Radford would have had to ditch in the snow-swept peaks of North Korea or the icy sea of Japan. Heading back to their airfield after hitting enemy targets near Apungsan, the two ran into heavy weather among 6,000 feet peaks. Radford's gyros were out and his pitot tube frozen. He had two hung rockets that wouldn't shake off. The pair let down through the clouds until they sighted the *Badoeng Strait*. The emergency alarm brought Marine pilots aboard to the flight deck to taxi the planes forward so the two could land before their fuel ran out. With only a minute's fuel left, Captain Barney landed aboard after Radford had to take a wave-off. Coming in a second time Radford ran out of fuel before he landed, but he made it by catching one of the last wires and nicking one barrier with his prop. It was his first carrier landing accident in 120 tries.

Hiding in tall, wet grass near his downed fighter plane in deep North Korean territory while patrols of the enemy searched for him, was the unpleasant experience of Captain Wilbur D. Wilcox. Together with another Marine, Major Charles McClain, he had flown in during the day to give aerial cover to a downed Air Force pilot north of P'yongyang. They stayed too long and ran out of fuel, with McClain coming down inside friendly lines, but Wilcox landed in a dry river bed behind enemy lines.

As soon as he landed, he climbed out of his Corsair and hid in tall grass 200 yards away. Soon ten North Korean soldiers appeared, piled tree branches over his plane to hide it from search planes, and then fanned out to find Wilcox. After dark, unable to locate him, the Communists settled down for the night. They departed the next morning and Wilcox signaled to villagers carrying South Korean flags. Two planes flew overhead, one piloted by McClain. Wilcox set off some smoke flares and used his pistol to hold off the Koreans until one of them said: 'Say, American soldier, I want to talk to you'. It turned out the man had lived in Los Angeles years ago. He refused a gift of Wilcox's wrist watch, but brought him some boiled water, chestnuts and three apples. Overhead, McClain pointed out his buddy's position to a Marine helicopter which came down and rescued him after twenty-six hours in enemy territory. The pilot of the pinwheel was Lieutenant Lloyd J Englehardt.

On 27 September, MacArthur received authorization from the Joint Chiefs to send his forces across the border into North Korea, and on 1 October all bombing in South Korea ceased. The same day the first South Koreans crossed the 38th Parallel, heading north. By now there were four US Army Divisions and a Marine Division in action. The first major Allied contingent had arrived in the shape of the 27th British Commonwealth Brigade, and the 90,000 ROK troops were now receiving the weapons and training they sorely needed two months earlier.

On 7 October, the UN General Assembly approved a US-sponsored motion that stability be restored on the Korean Peninsula, by defeating the North Korean forces and restoring democracy to both sides of the border. MacArthur met President Truman at Wake Island a week later and informed him, that although there were intelligence reports of Chinese forces massing across the border, he considered it safe to pursue the North Koreans right up to the Yalu River.

After a couple more days chasing North Korean trucks as they tried to flee north from Seoul, the pilots of VMF–323 aboard the aircraft carrier *Badoeng Strait*, returned to Japan for ten days leave and resupply. On 16 October they were back, sailing off the east coast and flying missions against targets north of the 38th Parallel. The news from the radio was that there will be a battle for the North Korean capital P'yongyang and then they should be on their way home. The pilots had a drawing for possible arrival dates in the UK and Joe Wosser got 17 November.

A second seaborne landing had been planned at Wonsan on the east coast of Korea, but enemy mine fields had to be cleared first by the Navy and by the time this was done, the ground forces had advanced past Wonsan. While the Marines of X Corps sat in their ships in Wonsan harbor, the race for the North Korean capital of P'yongyang was under way. Three ROK divisions were driving northwards, together with the US 1st Cavalry Division, the 24th Division and the 27th British Commonwealth Brigade. On 19 October, units of the 5th Cavalry entered P'yongyang, just minutes ahead of the ROK 1st Division. With the fall of their capital, North Korean resistance began to increase. At the same time, 5th Air Force began reporting increased air attacks along the border. MacArthur wanted bombing missions against the bridges crossing the Yalu River, as long as no aircraft actually crossed the border, but at the time the Air Force was prohibited from flying within five miles of the Manchurian border.

On 20 October, the Air Force conducted the largest airborne drop of the war when 110 Far East Air Force cargo aircraft dropped 2,800 paratroopers from the 187th Airborne Regiment thirty miles north of the capital, to secure the vital crossroads of Sukchon and Sunchon. One of their aims was to intercept a large number of American prisoners of war being taken northwards by their captors.

Shortly before the fall of P'yongyang the North Koreans packed four train boxcars with American prisoners and steamed out of the city heading north. The Americans were aware that they were being moved and tried desperately to overtake the train. After what seemed to be an eternity, the train was halted inside a tunnel. The prisoners were told that the North Koreans did not want to travel in daylight because of the fighter–bombers. They said that they would wait until dark and then start moving again. In the meantime they would feed the men, one boxcar at a time. The men thought that they might be better off now; they were no longer walking and a train would get them to one of the permanent prisoner of war camps situated in the extreme north of the country. How wrong could they be?

The last boxcar was unloaded and the men were told to go to the mouth of the tunnel where they would be fed. They were told to sit down in groups and then, without warning, they were machine-gunned. In the scramble a few men actually managed to get away, but for the most part they were all murdered. The next morning the train slowly left the shelter of the tunnel, with the remaining prisoners still locked in their boxcars. There were two small windows at each end of the cars and the nearest prisoners suddenly exclaimed that the guards were running back into the tunnel. Then they screamed that planes were coming. One of the survivors, Ed Slater, told the author: '"They are ours! They are ours!" they yelled. Then they were silent and a rocket tore into the train. I still don't know if the prisoners tore the door off the car or if the rockets blew it off, but in any case people started jumping off the train. The guards had set up machine guns and the prisoners the planes didn't hit were shot by the guards. The plane made another pass strafing the train. Another rocket hit in the middle of our group and exploded just as I reached the door. The planes made one more pass and this time didn't fire a shot. Perhaps they recognized us as prisoners?'

The survivors were herded back on to the train, including several wounded who had body parts missing. The guards shot some of the wounded where they lay, and then the train was moved back inside the tunnel. That night the train moved out of the tunnel again and continued its journey until it halted once more and the prisoners were told to get out and walk. Many refused or were unable to move and were shot where they lay. The prisoners realized that it was now or never and tried to run from the guards. Ed Slater recalled, 'I just fell out and rolled down a fifteen-foot embankment. The guards were throwing bodies from the train which were landing on me. Some guards were dragging more bodies to the growing pile. They shot fifteen or twenty who were still standing and added them to the pile. Then they poured diesel fuel over us all. The man on top of me had been shot and his blood was dripping on to me. I smeared it all over my face and told him to be quiet and lie still. Then something hit my head, a tremendous blow, and I passed out.'

When Slater came to he found that he was pinned under a pile of dead bodies and felt a bayonet stuck into his head. He pulled it out and fought his way out of the carnage. The boxcars were now burning and the guards had all gone. He stumbled away, following the railway tracks to the south. The following day he was found by the advance guard of the task force that had been trying in vain to catch up with them.

Originally, the Joint Chiefs only approved the use of South Korean units north of the 38th Parallel, but MacArthur ordered all of his forces to advance with all possible speed. He was taking a considerable risk and did not fully appreciate the possible reaction of the Soviets and Chinese as the UN forces approached their borders. By 24 October, the Eighth Army was crossing the Chongchon River and on 26 October, advance units of the 6th Division of the ROK III Corps reached the Yalu River near Ch'osan. Over the radio came the first reports that they had killed a small number of Chinese troops. At the same time the ROK 1st Division captured Chinese prisoners at Sudong. As the reports began to filter in, MacArthur's intelligence experts began to realise that the possibility had turned into reality; Chinese troops were now inside North Korea. What they did not know was that a quarter of a million other Chinese were hidden in the mountains, waiting for the order to attack.

The Chinese Intervene

The 1st Marine Division moved its command post to Hungnam on 4 November, while the 5th and 7th Marines continued their march north towards the Yalu River. The airfield at Yonpo was in the centre of the Hungnam-Hamhung area and was ideal for the 1st Marine Air Wing to set up shop there and provide close air support to the Division. On 6 November, MAG-33 was ordered to Yonpo from Japan and four days later it received VMF-212 from Wonsan. On 15 November, VMF-214 was ordered ashore from USS *Sicily* and set up at Wonsan with MAG-12 in support.

The 1st Marine Division continued its progress northwest from Hungnam to the Chosin Reservoir. Elements of the division reached Hagaru at the southern tip of the reservoir on 15 November. The following day Joe Wosser and VMF-323 on the *Badoeng Strait* returned to Japan again, but there would be no quick return to the States. Unknown to the Marines, Chinese divisions were massing on the border and the war was about to take a turn for the worst. Joe recalled, 'On the 23rd we got underway again and were issued winter flying gear which consisted of long underwear, heavy knee-length socks, one piece rubber exposure suit, special gloves and special boots. We were going to relieve Task Force 77 with its three Essex Class carriers with four squadrons apiece aboard.'

On 27 October, Chinese troops moving into Korea attacked the ROK 6th Infantry Division near the Yalu River. The Chinese also hit the Eighth Army and other ROK units, halting their advance. In the X Corps zone to the east, smaller Chinese attacks only blunted the advance. The 1st Marine Division continued toward the Chosin Reservoir, while the 7th US Infantry Division and the ROK Capital Division continued north. A regiment of the 7th US Infantry Division reached the Yalu at Hyesanjin on 21 November.

Within a few days the enemy counterattacks ceased and the Chinese seemingly vanished. Most intelligence reports considered these actions to have been little more than spoiling attacks by a few 'volunteers'. MacArthur, too, believed the Chinese would not enter Korea in force. To ensure they would not, on 5 November, he ordered a series of air strikes on Yalu River bridges, especially in the region near Sinuiju. However, he also ordered that the Manchurian border was to remain inviolate. Naturally, this restriction served to limit the effectiveness of the air attacks. After all, it is hard to bomb a bridge when half of it is untouchable. It probably would not have mattered because the Chinese supplemented the permanent bridges with easily repairable pontoon bridges. The Yalu River was also beginning to freeze, making it an easy matter for men and supplies to cross directly over the ice.

Unknown to MacArthur and his intelligence experts, 300,000 Chinese had already crossed the border into North Korea and on the evening of 25 November, they launched a massive surprise offensive against the UN forces. Ironically, the previous day Walker had renewed his own offensive toward the Yalu only to be brought up short by the Chinese counteroffensive. The shock of the immense Chinese assault brought the UN advance to a halt and split Eighth Army and X Corps apart with the enemy pouring down the middle.

By 27 November, the 1st Marine Division was concentrated in the area of the Chosin Reservoir, with its command post at Hagaru, the 5th and 7th Marines at Yudam-ni and the 1st Marines along the main supply route, with a battalion each at Hagaru, Koto-ri and Chinhung-ni. That morning the Division began its attack from Yudam-ni, but had only advanced 2,000 yards when it was stopped by stiff resistance. Opposing them was the Chinese 9th Army Group, 3rd Field Army totalling more than 100,000 seasoned infantry and by the evening they were in contact with all units of the 1st Marine Division. The strength of the Marines, plus attached Army and Royal Marine units, was just over 20,000, so they were outnumbered by five to one.

On 28 November, General MacArthur called Generals Walker and Almond to Tokyo for a conference and decided to immediately abandon the drive north and pull back instead to a line further south that was easier to defend. The Marines' advance had been halted by the Chinese at Yudam-ni on the Chosin Reservoir's western shore on the 27th. At the same time, on the opposite side of the reservoir, three battalions of the 7th Division had been destroyed. General Smith ordered the 5th and 7th Marines to retreat from Yudam-ni to Hagaru and rejoin the 1st Marine Division for a move back to Hungnam. It would be the first leg of a sixty-eight-mile fighting withdrawal through the Chinese 9th Army Group and frantic requests went out for close air support.

Joe Wosser continues, 'On the 28th we finally flew again after four days of snow. We were assigned to support the ROK Capital Division in their drive up the east coast to the Soviet border. Flew the early morning CAP and was up for 3.6 hours and then flew a strike in the afternoon for 3.4 hours and practically had to fight our way to the beach, it was snowing so hard. We worked over a couple of ridge lines, a road block, a small village and some dug in emplacements. I was leading the hop and they wanted us to drop our bombs and rockets 500 yards ahead of them, which we did and strafed 200 yards ahead of them as they moved up to take the ridge line. A Korean interpreter thanked us very profusely.'

By the end of November, the 1st MAW was established at Yonpo with five Marine Fighter Squadrons, while a sixth, VMF-323, was still operating from the *Badoeng Strait*. They also had VMO-6 with them, with its OY and H helicopters. They were given the job of supporting the Division as well as the rest of X Corps, while the Navy and 5th Air Force tactical squadrons attacked the advancing enemy formations as they chased Eighth Army and X Corps southwards. They flew over a hundred sorties each day in support of the 1st Marine Division and the three battalions of the 7th Division which had been hit heavily to the east of the Chosin Reservoir. The Marine pilots in the Tactical Air Control Parties were responsible for directing the air support against the Chinese troops massing around them. The napalm, bombs, rockets and 20mm strafing runs kept the Chinese at bay during the hours of daylight, but at night the Marines were largely on their own.

Joe Wosser noted in his diary on 1 December:

'Our afternoon hop was in support of the Marines in the Chosin Reservoir. We supported a couple of battalions which are cut off and trying to fight their way back. The controller was so frantic, he couldn't talk fast enough or clear enough but it made little difference because we could drop our bombs, napalm or strafe in any direction and hit enemy troops. He wanted us to make strafing runs closer than fifty feet in front of our men because the Commies were pulling the pins from grenades and rolling them down the hill into our lines. When we had expended all our ammo, the next flight was not on station so the controller requested that we make dummy runs anyway.

The next day we worked over the Reservoir again and I am happy to report that some of the men we were helping yesterday broke out of the trap and made it across the ice to comparative safety. Today our flight burned out a little village about three miles south of the airstrip which the Reds had taken over. The Commies had infiltrated so far south that they had the entire 1st Marine Division cut off and isolated, except by air. The weather over the target was very poor; I had been flying in weather which normally I wouldn't even walk in!

'We did not just have the enemy to contend with. On 4 December I watched one of the pilots bring his plane in on one wheel because of battle damage, a dangerous maneuver at any time. I took off on a CAP and sprung an oil leak so it was difficult to see the LSO as I was coming aboard. In the second plane the heater didn't work and I about froze my hands and face. Three days later Hugh 'Whiskey' Newell was killed. He was a good pilot and well liked.'

The first leg of the flight south, from Yudam-ni to Hagaru, was completed by 4 December and the Division assembled there to evacuate its wounded. Between 1 and 6 December, Combat Cargo Command C-47s, together with Marine R4Ds from Marine Transport Squadron VMR-152, evacuated 4,312 wounded, including 3,150 Marines, 1,137 Army personnel and twenty-five Royal Marines. Marine Sergeant David Swann was on one of the last flights out. He had been stationed at Camp Pendleton in California when the Korean War began. The previous year he had returned from a tour of duty in Tsingtao, China, and was one of two sergeants assigned to the main gate at the camp as the 1st Marine Division started its build up and preparations for the 1st Marine Brigade to deploy to Pusan in the middle of July 1950. Around the country Marine Corps Reserve units were being mobilized to bring the Division up to war-time strength. By the middle of August the division was aboard ships en route to Korea via Japan, and Sergeant Swann was with them.

After the landings at Inchon and the liberation of Seoul, the Marines were relieved by Army units and transported around to the east coast, landing at Wonsan. They moved north from there and soon afterwards the Chinese troops started to appear. David Swann later told the author:

'I was in Hagaru when Lieutenant Colonel Drysdale, the C.O. of the British 41 Independent Commando unit and commander of Task Force Drysdale, was assigned the task of breaking through from Koto-ri to Hagaru. Of course, as you already know, that turned out to be a near wipe-out. I did meet some of the British troops that made it into Hagaru and in fact traded something for a nice warm British wool jacket that I was still wearing when I was wounded on 7 December 1950.

'On the breakout to the south, about five or six miles south of Hagaru on 7 December, we were ambushed in the same Hell Fire Valley area as the Commandos, and equipment and signs of the ambush were still visible. The going was very slow due to enemy along the hills, valleys and road. I was in the Division train and during an ambush at approximately 0700 hours while manning a light 0.30-caliber machine gun, I was wounded by a grenade that was tossed while I was reloading. We were alongside the road and the CCF were on the other side of a railroad track that ran alongside the road. I had wounds of the hands, arms, head, eyes and face. We arrived in the perimeter at Koto-ri at approximately 1200 hours. It was snowing and all air activity had ceased because of the heavy snowfall. I was put into a field hospital tent for the night. Next morning, also during a heavy snowfall, a C-47 landed and nineteen casualties were loaded aboard and took off and landed at Hamhung. The casualties were transferred to a C-54 aircraft and departed for Japan. This flight on 8 December was the only flight that made it in or out of Koto-ri that day. After spending time in the naval hospital in Japan I was then flown to the States, arriving in California on the morning of 25 December 1950. What a Christmas present that was for me.'

The second leg of the retreat, from Hagaru to Koto-ri, began as soon as the last of the wounded had been flown out. The Marines now had the air support procedure down to a fine art, with Forward Air Controllers circling the column and a four engine R5D (C-54) carrying a complete Tactical Air Direction Centre, controlling all support aircraft as they reported on station, and assigning them to the various FACs or the two airborne TACs who flew their Corsairs ahead and to each side of the advancing column.

By the evening of 7 December, the division rear guard was inside the perimeter of the 2nd Battalion, 1st Marines at Koto-ri. While the Marines were hard-pressed in the North Korean pocket, marine 'air delivery' pilots delivered many tons of supplies to them by plane and parachute. On one job near Majon-Ni, they parachuted 42,130 pounds of supplies in four hours, establishing a new record. Four hours after they received the urgent request the transports dropped 450 rounds of 105mm artillery shells, 100 rounds of 4.2-inch mortar, twenty-four rounds of 60mm mortar, six cases of hand grenades and 36,000 rounds of belted machine-gun bullets. They also dropped five gallons of antifreeze for tanks, 200 gallons of gasoline and 1,512 pounds of rations. The pilots who flew the record drop of 152 parachutes were Lieutenant Col Bruce Prosser, Captain H. D. Menzies, Lieutenants E. D. Storrs and Robert Carter, and Master Sergeant Larry Laugen.

James W. Laseter, a second Lieutenant of the 1st Marine Air Group, knocked out a North Korean self-propelled gun by firing a rocket directly into the operator's seat, while diving on the target at several hundred miles-an-hour. A low-flying reconnaissance plane checked out the area after the attack and reported a direct hit on the cockpit-like seat. Another candidate for a sharpshooter's medal was the Marine fighter pilot who was called in by Lieutenant John Theros, the ground control officer at the Chosin Reservoir, to knock out a single machine gun firing on ground troops from the hills. Using tracer bullets in the darkness, the plane came in from a flat angle, low over the streets of Hagaru, causing the Marines to duck for cover. In the morning a patrol went out and found the machine gun nest, thoroughly strafed the night before, with the gunner lying dead with a hole right between his eyes.

The third and final leg from Koto-ri to Chinhung-ni was going to be tough. The Marines had to negotiate the precipitous defile called Funchilin Pass, as well as a blown bridge just three miles from Koto-ri that had to be made passable. This was achieved by bridge sections being parachuted to the Marines who soon assembled them and continued their journey to Chinhung-ni on the plain below. The bridge was installed at the base of the penstocks of one of several hydroelectric plants fed by the reservoir. Eighteen months later, in June 1952, two of these plants were totally destroyed by MAG-12 and -33 in one attack; Chosin 3 by MAG-12 and Chosin 4 by MAG-33, the latter in one of the largest mass jet attacks of the war.

The Marines began their final movement by truck from Chinhung-ni to Hungnam early in the morning of 11 December and by the end of the day they were clear of the town. The 1st Marine Division along with a mixture of men from the 7th Division, the Royal Marines, and various ROK units, finally made it to Hamhung and were evacuated by ship to Pusan. The three shore-based fighter squadrons moved to Japan on 14 December and by 18 December the last of the 1st MAW equipment was flown out of Yonpo. From then on the air cover of the evacuation of Hungnam by sea became the responsibility of the light aircraft carriers.

Between 11 and 24 December, 105,000 troops and 98,000 North Korean civilians, along with 350,000 tons of supplies and more than seventeen thousand vehicles, were evacuated from Hungnam. Fortunately, the Chinese who were in serious straits themselves did not interfere with the evacuation.

Naval aviation and carriers played a large part in the successful evacuation of 193 shiploads of Marines, Army and Korean refugees from the Communist-surrounded seaport of Hungnam in December. Navy and Marine Corsairs and Skyraiders from Rear Admiral Edward C. Ewens's Task Force 77, and an escort-carrier group, dropped bombs, napalm and rockets on North Korean troop emplacements. Napalm tanks could be seen tumbling down from the planes and huge clouds of black smoke arose in the hills as they hit. In the final five days of the evacuation, with the beachhead growing smaller by day, strikes came faster and faster. More than 2,500 sorties by fighters and bombers were flown during the operation in close support of ground troops. The daily raids kept the Communists well dug in and prevented any big push at the beach area. All the time the ships were evacuating men and equipment from the beachhead, Marine and Navy transport planes flew heavy schedules, evacuating wounded men from Hungnam to Japan. Only a few short weeks earlier these same planes and ships were bringing in the supplies they later had to fly out. The evacuation of the port was completed on Christmas Day and the port, its warehouses, and tons of remaining supplies, were blown up in a spectacular series of explosions.

The battles around the reservoir and during the 'breakout' cost the UN troops – mainly Marines – some 6,000 casualties of the 25,000 men involved. Heavy as they were, these casualties would have been greater had it not been for the work of FEAF, Navy, and Marine aircraft. Planes from TF77 and the 1st Marine Air Wing handled most of the close support, while FEAF aircraft struck further afield. Joe Wosser reached the end of the year with seventy-five missions and finally rotated home on 12 February having completed eighty-seven missions.

The MiGs Arrive

A new phase of the air war began on 1 November when a Mosquito forward air controller was directing a flight of F-51s against targets near Sinuiju when they were bounced by six swept wing jets painted a 'burned green silver'. These new MiG-15s were being flown by Soviet pilots from the 72nd Guards Fighter Air Division and led by Hero of the Soviet Union, Major N. V. Stroykov, who had flown 245 combat sorties during WWII, and were based at airfields across the Yalu River in China. According to Soviet records, one Mustang was downed, but this is not confirmed by US records. The Soviet pilots were ordered to wear North Korean uniforms and only speak Korean when making radio transmissions. However, it was not long before the UN pilots discovered who they were flying against.

The MiG-15 was designed by Mikoyan-Gurevich to shoot down atomic-bomb armed Superfortress bombers with their two 23mm and one 37mm cannons. In production since 1948, the MiG was the Soviet Union's most effective fighter. With a service ceiling of 50,000 feet and a speed of 664 miles per hour at 40,000 feet it was a threat to all UN aircraft, not just the B-29s. Furthermore, although they wore Chinese Communist or North Korean markings, they were being flown by Russian pilots and some of them were very good at their job.

US Air Force records claim that an F-80C Shooting Star, flown by Lieutenant Russell Brown from the 51st Fighter Wing, shot down Senior Lieutenant Kharitonov on the 8th, but the Russians claim he escaped by diving. It is very difficult to assess the accuracy of the claims made by each side. Planes that appeared to be diving, trailing smoke, often made it home and sometimes more than one pilot would claim the same kill. The MiGs were far superior to the American jets, however, and they soon began to take a toll of the B-29s flying bombing and reconnaissance missions in the Yalu River area. In order to counter the new threat, the 4th Fighter Interceptor Wing, was ordered to Korea with its F-86A Sabres, along with the 27th Fighter Escort Wing with its F-84E Thunderjets.

On 9 November, an RB-29A from the 31st Strategic Reconnaissance Squadron, escorted by two flights of F-80s, was sent to the Sinuiju area to direct a strike by naval aircraft. Two MiGs made two passes at the bomber and it turned for home in flames, crashing at Johnson Air Base in Japan with the loss of five crewmembers. Task Force 77 made its initial effort against the International Bridges on the Yalu River that afternoon. It was the first time that the MiGs had met the Navy's F9Fs and they mistook them for F-80s. The Americans denied the Russian claim that Major Aleksandr Stulov and Senior Lieutenant Kaznacheev had each downed a Panther. The Navy admitted that it lost one Panther but not in combat; apparently it hit the landing barrier on the aircraft carrier USS *Valley Forge* and was wrecked.

On 10 November, Navy Skyraiders and Corsairs, escorted by Panthers, attacked the road and rail bridge near Sinuiju again and seven MiGs from the Soviet 139th Guards Fighter Air Regiment rose to meet them. A fierce battle ensued and the Russians later claimed three Americans shot down; a claim denied by the Navy. However, a Panther flown by Lieutenant Commander W. T. Amen, skipper of VF-111 from USS *Philippine Sea* (CV-47), scored the first MiG kill by a carrier plane. The fight raged from just above ground level to 18,000 feet in the air. Turning inside of a tight loop on the tail of MiG flown by Captain Grachyov, Amen closed the gap and opened fire, knocking down the enemy plane. The other MiGs fled across the Manchurian border. All the US planes returned from the successful assault on the bridges. 'I was coming head on at one of them and he didn't even try to get in a shot,' Amen reported after the fight. 'When I got on his tail he tried to evade but he wasn't very sharp.' Soviet records show this to be the first MiG to be lost during the war and it was the first jet kill to be confirmed by either side.

On 18 November, as the bridge campaign continued, F9Fs from USS *Leyte* (CV-32) and USS *Valley Forge* (CV-45) each got another MiG-15, bringing the navy's total to three. Navy F9F 'Panther' jets had also shot down two propeller-driven North Korean fighters in early July 1950, demonstrating the superiority of jets over the enemy's 'prop' planes. There the aircraft carrier navy's score remained for nearly two more years, since carrier planes soon returned to their usual eastern Korean 'beat', where MiGs were a happily rare commodity. In December an initial shipment of advanced Air Force F-86 'Sabre' jet fighters arrived on board the light carrier USS *Bataan* (CVL-29) and the escort carrier USS *Bairoko* (CVE-115).

The Sabres first encountered the MiGs on 17 December in the area of northwest Korea soon to become known as 'MiG Alley', and Lieutenant Colonel Bruce Hinton used up most of his supply of 0.50-caliber ammunition knocking one down. The MiGs were fitted with two 23mm and one 37mm cannons and had a much longer range than the Sabres. They could also operate at higher altitudes and had several other advantages over the Sabres. The Sabres were also at a disadvantage because they usually arrived in the area with dwindling fuel supplies, whereas the MiGs only had to cross the border to reach their airfields, declared out of bounds by President Truman. The first Sabre fell to the MiGs on 22 December and air combat between the MiGs and the Sabre would continue on virtually a daily basis until the end of the war.

Some American accounts claim that by the year's end, the Sabres and their experienced pilots would establish a mastery over the MiGs that would last to the end of the Korean War. This is far from the truth. The author recommends the book *Soviet MiG-15 Aces of the Korean War* by Osprey, written by respected authors Leonid Krylov and Yuriy Tepsurkaev. They have carried out extensive research in Soviet records and came to the conclusion that 307 MiGs were lost in combat, with 103 of their pilots. On the other side of the balance sheet they list UN losses at 1,025 – sixty-six B-29s, seven B-26s, two RB-45s, one RB-50, two F-47s, twenty-eight F-51s, 123 F-80s, 181 F-84s, 574 F-86s, eleven F-94s, one Corsair, 3 F6F Hellcats and 26 Australian Meteor F-8s.

Long Flight from Greece

Many countries sent ground troops or aircraft to Korea. South Africa sent a squadron of Mustangs, which were then replaced by Sabres. Australia sent an aircraft carrier HMAS *Sydney* to supplement the efforts of 77 Squadron which had been involved in the fighting since the start. The Greek government agreed to send a flight of C–47 transport aircraft to Korea as their contribution to the UN forces gathering to take on the Communists. One of the crew members Spyros Andreopoulos recalled:

'When Flight 13 was getting ready for departure from Elefsis Air Force Base in late November 1950, it was determined that a US Air Force C–47 would join us as an escort. The reason given was the lack of Greek consular help in many of the countries where Flight 13 would have to land for refuelling and maintenance during the transfer of the planes to Japan. Andrew Gorenko, Flight 13 Commanding Officer, chose me to fly in the American escort plane because I spoke English fluently and since it had been decided that the American escort plane would be the first to land at our various interim destinations, I would contact local officials concerning arrangements for refuelling and aircraft maintenance needs. I have no recollection of the plane's serial number but the names of the American crew were; Pilot Thomson, Co–pilot Irwin, Navigator Robinson, Wireless Operator Doran, Flt Engineer Pirnik.

'The Royal Hellenic Air Force observed strict weight limits on its C–47s. The maximum allowable weight was 7,000 lbs. As that maximum weight on our C–47s being loaded at Elefsis was reached, there was a tendency among the Greek pilots to put extra supplies on the US Air Force plane. As a result the escort plane was overloaded, and I can attest to that because we had to use every inch of runway to become airborne and at times barely succeeded. Keep in mind that we had auxiliary fuel tanks with gallons of gasoline, plus supplies, aircraft parts, maintenance tools and passengers – the ground crews.

'Greece only had a non-paid consul in Karachi who was nowhere to be found when we needed him. Greece did not have diplomatic relations with Pakistan at that time. It was still in the process of becoming a separate state from India. It was expected that the Americans would assist us, if needed, by contacting their established embassies and consulates in those countries. When we arrived in Karachi all of our Flight 13 crews were placed in a 10-day quarantine by the Pakistani government on the pretext that we may have landed in yellow fever areas on the way there.

Behind that pretext of course was the Pakistani government's political disapproval of the UN action in Korea. Since we could not locate the Greek consul in Karachi, it was the American crew with its contacts at the American embassy that led to negotiations for the lifting of the quarantine so that we could proceed to our next stop in New Delhi. I had a small part in that.

'One detail about the quarantine was that the Pakistanis housed the officers at some abandoned and decrepit Royal Air Force barracks, and the enlisted men at a plush and expensive hotel in the central district of Karachi. When the US Consul General and I paid them a visit at the hotel to let everyone know that we were working for their release, the Pakistani guards detained us both, and it took several hours before they let the American Consul General leave the hotel. I stayed with the rest. The hotel treated and fed us well during the week of our confinement. By the time the Pakistanis realized they had made a mistake and apologized, we thought they would also pay for the costs. How wrong we were! They sent a bill of several thousand dollars for all the hotel and food costs to my office at Tachikawa Air Force Base in Japan where we were then stationed. On orders from Squadron Leader Gorenko, I forwarded the bill to the Greek Air Ministry. I did not hear about it again.

'When we arrived in New Delhi, we were treated like heroes. The Indian Armed Forces organized tours for us to various temples and historical sites, as well as receptions and lavish dinner parties. During one of those occasions I asked our host, an Indian general, to explain the reason for the warm hospitality. He looked at me matter-of-factly and said, "We are celebrating an historic moment. You are the first Greek troops to land in India since Alexander the Great!"

'The mission of the American escort C-47 was terminated in Allahabad, India, where we had landed for routine maintenance and refuelling on about 15 November 1950. I recall Allahabad distinctly because after we took off from New Delhi, I had been asked by the American pilot to sit on his seat and admire the spectacular views of the Himalayas on our left in the distance while the crew sat on top of the auxiliary tanks in the back playing cards! (The plane was on auto pilot.) At Allahabad we had made a very rough landing that damaged the American plane's landing gear, among other things. (As I mentioned earlier the American plane was so overloaded that an accident was inevitable.) When it was determined that parts for repairs would not be available for weeks, I transferred to Captain Tzovlas's plane and continued with the rest of the Greek C-47s on to Rangoon, Saigon, Clark Field, Okinawa and our final destination, Itazuki Air Force Base at Fukuoka, Japan.'

The First Winter

By the middle of December 1950, the UN forces held a line running from the Imjin River on the West Coast generally along the 38th parallel to the East Coast. About this time UN members began efforts to arrange a cease-fire. These attempts floundered when the Chinese, flushed with their success, rejected the proposals. Nevertheless, the UN continued to work toward obtaining a cease-fire.

December also saw changes in the command structure in Korea. General Walker was killed in a jeep accident and was replaced by Lieutenant General Matthew B. Ridgeway. The new Eighth Army commander's initial encounter with the enemy was not auspicious. On New Year's Eve, CCF and North Korean troops attacked again. Although they suffered terrible losses, the enemy pushed the defenders back to roughly the 37th Parallel. This, however, was as far south as the Eighth Army would go.

The Communists soon began repairing the airfields in North Korea, in particular at P'yongyang and Sinuiji, the latter covered by AAA defenses on both sides of the Yalu River. On 23 January, forty F-80s suppressed the flak around the airfield at P'yongyang, while a B-29 force placed percent of its bombs on the target. The same day eight flights of F-84s strafed Sinuiji before the bombers arrived. Across the river MiGs were taking off from Antung and a thirty-minute dogfight ensued in which the 27th FEW claimed four MiGs destroyed and three 'probables', for no loss.

Because of their troop losses and because their supply and transportation system could not sustain it, the Communist offensive faltered, then stopped. The CCF's usual practice was to advance, attack, withdraw for supply, and then repeat the procedure. And this was what occurred now. But Ridgeway was perhaps more aggressive than Walker, and he decided to take advantage of the enemy withdrawal by launching a reconnaissance in force to Suwon followed by a two-divisional advance toward the Han River. By 16 February, the UN forces were back on the outskirts of Seoul and holding a line midway between the 37th and 38th Parallels. In these circumstances it was possible to return evacuated air units to Korea; in early February the Marines had moved three fighter squadrons in from Japan, and by the month's end 5th Air Force squadrons and supporting units were preparing to return.

Ridgeway's 'limited' offensive grew and by 9 April, Seoul was retaken and the front lines now ran generally southwest to northeast above the 38th

Parallel. Both Ridgeway and MacArthur had no illusions that the Chinese would retreat much farther, particularly from their main staging area bounded by the towns of Chorwon, Pyonggang, and Kumhwa, an area which became notorious as the 'Iron Triangle'. Ridgeway thus readied contingency plans to repel another Chinese offensive, plans that indeed became necessary to use.

As the UN troops moved north, the US government prepared further cease-fire overtures to the Communists, of which MacArthur was notified. The Supreme Commander suddenly undercut these plans on 24 March 1951, when he issued an ultimatum to the Chinese (without informing his superiors) that the war would be extended to the mainland unless they negotiated a peace settlement. This 'routine communiqué', as MacArthur later described it, resulted in several far-reaching consequences; by virtually taunting and challenging the Chinese, MacArthur undoubtedly ensured their continuing participation in the war; his ultimatum torpedoed Truman's cease-fire, for the President could hardly announce this when his commander in Korea was publicly intimating carrying the war to the Chinese mainland; he added fuel to a smouldering distrust by some UN allies about American policy in Korea; and it finally brought him down. Truman relieved MacArthur on 9 April and replaced him with Ridgeway.

Then, as Ridgeway had expected, a re-supplied and refreshed Chinese Army renewed its attacks on 22 April. They began their Spring Offensive with a thrust down the centre by the 20th Army and the ROK 6th Division collapsed under the weight of the attack. As the enemy poured through the gap between the 1st Marine Division and the 24th Infantry Division, the fighting was bitter and intense. Overall though, the offensive had little effect and the assault was checked within four days. With the enemy out in the open and moving, more than a thousand close support sorties by 5th Air Force and carrier-based aircraft inflicted very heavy casualties. The enemy lost almost half of their men and the Eighth Army recovered all its lost ground and even extended its gains in the eastern portion of the line. Eventually, the front settled down to a line winding from below Kaesong on the west to above Kansong on the shore of the Sea of Japan.

At sea, the navies sharpened the focus of their air and gunfire efforts. With three or four big carriers, a battleship, some cruisers and many destroyers on station, the US Navy undertook long campaigns to destroy North Korea's eastern railway system and other elements of its transportation and industrial infrastructure. British and smaller US carriers, plus gunfire ships, worked in the Yellow Sea. Minesweepers maintained firing channels for the gunnery ships, and small combatants of many nations enforced a rigorous blockade of the North Korean coast.

The Air Force concentrated on targets in the western side of Korea, using its B-29s for heavy bombing raids, whilst keeping the MiG-15 threat safely to the north and providing the great bulk of air transport services. The Air Force and planes from other UN nations joined US Marine aviation in directly supporting troops on the ground. USMC and USAF night fighters struggled to counter the only enemy airplanes that dared to approach the front lines, small propeller-driven 'night hecklers' that made very challenging targets.

By late June, the most recent Communist ground offensive had been decisively defeated. North Korea was being steadily punished from air and sea. Since the US and UN had decided not to advance further into the North, and with the enemy clearly unable to push south, there seemed little point in continued hostilities. Armistice feelers received favorable responses, and truce talks were in the offing. Most observers expected an early end to the fighting.

Escape through the Snow

By January 1951 the war situation had gone from bad to good to bad again. General Walton Walker and his successor, General Matthew Ridgway, had temporarily halted the retreat after the initial Chinese assault had driven the UN forces back below the 38th Parallel. But the Chinese were still pressing forward and had launched another attack which had forced the Eighth Army even further back into South Korea below the Han River, and were threatening to drive a wedge down through the centre of the UN line and capture Pusan.

Most of the ground forces had suffered heavy casualties and the men were exhausted, having been without adequate food or sleep for weeks. To try to stop the hordes of invading Chinese and North Koreans, airpower was in greater need than ever. The Mosquito aircraft were in great demand and the pilots of the 6147th flew two or sometimes three missions each day, remaining over enemy lines for as much as six or eight hours. Mechanics worked around the clock to keep the planes in the air.

On 15 January, Captain Clinton D. Summersill and Captain Wayne Sawyer were relaxing in their tent, enjoying their day off. They had flown eighteen missions in nine days and were tired. However, word arrived from Operations that they were needed to fill in for another crew and were to launch at 1230 hours.

They checked the six smoke rockets mounted under each of the wings and Summersill opened the baggage compartment and threw in his big fleece-lined boots. They were too large for him and he had to fly the plane in his paratrooper boots, so his feet were always numb when they returned from a mission. It was a situation that would have disastrous consequences for the young pilot. Sawyer crawled into the back cockpit and slid shut the 'greenhouse' canopy. He had already flown 150 missions as an observer and had crashed twice behind enemy lines. Both times he had escaped.

By 1400 hours they were over the front lines where a ROK division was facing a heavy concentration of enemy troops. The ground controller told them that a large enemy force was reportedly gathering for a break through, some eight miles behind the enemy lines. Could they try and pinpoint its location and then direct fighter bombers towards it? They were joined by sixteen Navy Corsairs and Skyraiders and Sawyer asked them to circle at a safe altitude while they looked for the enemy. Below them the terrain looked like the surface of the moon with deep ravines and canyons filled with snow. Suddenly, Sawyer spotted the Chinese below them and Summersill banked and dove towards the ground. It was not a good decision – the Chinese were now shooting at them and he was 200 feet above the ground, well within small arms range. Sawyer said, 'Clem they are shooting at us – we better get out of here!' Summersill pushed the throttles to full power but the manifold pressure was dropping and the engine was losing power. A Chinese bullet had found its mark and they were going down.

To compound his error Summersill had also flown into a blind, horseshoe-shaped canyon and was running out of options. He did not want to turn and glide back to the open end of the horse-shoe where the Chinese were massing; Mosquito pilots were usually shot on capture. He could not climb, so he was going to have to crash land on the canyon floor. The plane slid onto a large, upward sloping granite slab and skidded along for 100 feet. The belly fuel tank broke away and tumbled down the hillside in flames. Summersill's head smashed into the foam rubber crash pad over the instrument panel.

The plane ground to a halt and the men scrambled out of the cockpit as flames crackled around them. Sawyer's leg broke through some ice and became trapped in the rocks below and precious seconds passed before they could free him. Summersill turned to try to get his fleece lined boots from the baggage compartment, but one of the smoke rockets ignited with the heat and whooshed over their heads. The plane was well alight now and he had to abandon the attempt and start to climb up the hillside towards a cave in some rocks. The snow was up to their thighs and they were leaving a clear trail for the Chinese to follow.

In the cave they used the plane's first aid kit to tend to their wounds, while Sawyer put on a dry pair of socks. Both had lost their gloves in the crash and already Summersill could not feel his feet. They checked their maps and discussed their next move. There were 10,000 Chinese between them and the ROK troops, so they decided to go deeper into enemy territory and then turn south-east and infiltrate between the lines.

They heard Chinese voices in the distance and decided to move higher up the ridge and into a thicket where they would wait for darkness before moving on. By the time the Chinese neared the thicket it was dark and they were using torches to scour the undergrowth. The two men quietly moved away, heading for a 5,000-feet mountain to the northeast, figuring that it was the last place they would find any Chinese troops.

They started up the long, white slope of the mountain and were soon fighting their way through a blizzard, which thankfully covered their trail. At 2200 hours, eight hours after the crash, Summersill came to a halt. They had been struggling through waist deep snow which had caught in his trouser leg, melted and then run down into the inside of his boots, where it froze. His feet had been numb all along, but now he could barely bend his ankles. There was nowhere to shelter or to build a fire; they had to struggle onwards following their compass bearing to the northeast. Eventually they suspected something was wrong with the compass. It contained kerosene, which should not freeze until forty degrees below, but as they turned it, the needle remained pointing at northeast; it had frozen.

Two hours later they came to some trees and stopped to eat some food. They found some compressed beef in their emergency vests, as well as a few pieces of cheese, candy and bouillon cubes. Around four in the morning the ground started to level out as they reached the top of the mountain. But they were more exposed now and the wind blew with a vengeance. Eventually they could go no further and slumped to the ground. For an hour they crawled along, into the wind, heads down. Finally they collapsed onto the snow and fell asleep.

When they awoke it was almost daylight and the snow and wind had stopped. They struggled to regain their senses and walked around, beating the circulation back into their frozen limbs. Suddenly, they noticed a steep drop ahead of them, a mere fifteen feet from where they had collapsed. Someone had been watching over them that night.

They turned eastwards now to make their way along the enemies flank and began to make their way downhill. They had covered almost twenty miles in fourteen hours. Much of the day was spent sliding down the mountain on their backsides, avoiding the canyons and crevasses on the way. They were now so exhausted that they began to hallucinate or black out for brief periods. Finally they found themselves in a small snow-covered basin 300 yards wide, and decided to follow a creek as darkness descended again. Some time later they spotted two small Chinese one-man tents and gave them a wide berth as they pushed on through the snow. At midnight they halted and ate the last of their rations. Summersill unfortunately put a bouillon cube in his mouth and had swallowed it before he realised it was not candy. The cube was very bitter and salty and he would be sick many times as they continued their journey.

Around 0300 hours they came to a steep gorge, spanned by two eight-inch logs covered with ice and snow. As they crawled across Sawyer slipped and almost fell into the gorge. Summersill grabbed him and pulled him up to safety, but lost his 0.45 in the process. They continued to follow the path of the creek downhill until, as the first light of dawn broke the horizon, they saw a Korean home between the creek and the canyon wall. A light shone in the window and they crept cautiously towards it. Inside were six Chinese soldiers drinking tea and resting. They backed away and put as much distance between themselves and the hut as possible.

An hour or two later they came across a farmhouse. They could simply go no further and decided to see if they could find help and shelter. Sawyer covered Summersill with his 0.45 as he knocked on the door. An old Korean with a white beard appeared and Summersill dragged him around the side of the home and forced him to squat in the straw. He took out an Air Force 'pointee-talkie' containing fifteen or twenty sentences printed in Korean and English. The old man could not read, so Summersill tried his broken Japanese and sign language until the Korean went back into the house and returned with a younger man of about forty years. When Summersill showed him 'I am an American aviator' he became very excited and shook his hand violently. Quickly he ushered the two Americans inside.

Both men's boots were frozen solid and they had to use a heated flat iron to melt the ice around the laces. Sawyer's boots came off easily, but Summersill's were frozen to his socks. They inspected Summersill's feet and could see ice crystals under the skin. There was no doubt they were frozen solid.

The old Korean produced a bundle of loose cotton and a bottle of oil. He spread the oil over their feet, then wrapped them with the loose cotton, binding it in place with strips torn from a shirt. The old man's wife brought them two bowls of celery soup, followed by two bowls of steaming rice, and they ate while they communicated with the 'pointee-talkie'. When they pointed to 'Please find someone who can speak English and who can help us' the younger man nodded, put on his coat and left.

Within minutes both men had fallen into a deep sleep and the old woman covered them with blankets. When Summersill awoke he found a ROK lieutenant and sergeant standing in front of him. The young Korean had run twelve miles to the front and made contact with the ROKs. They immediately set out through enemy lines in a jeep and after eight miles parked and camouflaged it, and covered the rest of the distance on foot. The area had been heavily infiltrated by communist guerrillas and the lieutenant was anxious to set off before dark. The two ROKs and the old and young Koreans fashioned two stretchers from quilts and poles and set off carrying the two men.

Two hours later they were back at the jeep and on the way to the 5th ROK Division Headquarters. When they got there Summersill gave the Koreans all the money he had on him but they refused to take it. So he took their names and arranged for them to receive other remuneration. An ambulance arrived from the nearby 187th Regimental Combat Team and took them to a US aid station. That night they were put on board a hospital train for Pusan. Before they were shipped out to Japan they conferred and decided that they had walked forty miles in forty-three hours. An amazing feat under the circumstances.

Within days Sawyer was up and about. He only lost a tiny piece of his left big toe. He was later assigned to an Army unit that specialized in briefing men on how to survive behind enemy lines. Summersill's case was more serious and he was airlifted back to the States where his feet were amputated at the ankles. There were no double amputees serving in the United States Air Force and Summersill thought that his career was over.

While hobbling around on his new artificial feet at Walter Reed hospital in Washington, D.C., he came across a young Air Force Cadet who had been badly injured in an automobile accident. He was Hoyt S. (Sandy) Vandenberg, Jr., son of the Air Force Chief of Staff. They became firm friends and one evening Summersill walked into Hoyt's room to find his father sitting by his bed. He snapped to attention while Vandenberg Jr. made the introductions and explained Summersill's situation. General Vandenberg invited him to his office the following day and after listening to his story, called in three Generals and dictated an order decreeing that double amputees could remain in the Air Force. He told them, 'I want you to look around and see if we have a job for this man. As long as he can do his job efficiently and satisfactorily, he will wear an Air Force uniform.'

Night Hecklers

One unique Communist aircraft encountered in Korea was the Polikarpov Po-2 bi-plane which first flew in 1927. Designed as a two-seat primary trainer and made out of wood and fabric, it had a fixed landing gear and N-type struts holding the two thirty-seven feet wide wings together. With a top speed of ninety knots it had a combat radius of 184 miles. Four, or sometimes six, 55-pound bombs could be carried under the wings and occasionally missiles would be thrown from the cockpit. Armament consisting of two forward-firing 7.62mm guns and two rear-cockpit flexible 7.62mm machine guns may be fitted.

During the Second World War the Soviets used the Po-2 in a number of roles, including as a night nuisance bomber, sometimes dropping as much as 220 pounds of bombs on a single target. Rockets were attached to the wings of some Po-2s and these assault versions were used in the final battle for Berlin.

The role was taken up again in Korea and the Americans referred to the type as the 'Night Heckler'. Up against them were American Marine and Air Force night-fighters and they came across the type a number of times during the first half of 1951 in the Inchon-Kimpo-Seoul area. In June 1951, an Air Force B-26 was returning from a night interdiction mission when it came upon a Po-2 and followed it as it took evasive action flying between the hills. The B-26 lowered its landing gear and flaps to reduce its speed to that of the enemy aircraft and raked the Po-2 with 50-cal bullets before it blew up and crashed behind UN lines. A month later, one was downed by a F4U Corsair and another destroyed in the air by an F7F Tigercat.

Numerous night-combat and patrol flights had been vectored in pursuit of low, slow bogies, known to have been Po-2s. Vectoring was done by Tactical Air Control Centre (TACC) 'Dentist' located at Kimpo airfield. During the summer of 1951, the low number of night-fighter radar contacts was probably due to the combination of three factors; the wood-and-fabric construction of the Po-2, the extremely low altitude and speed of the aircraft, and the rugged terrain over which the Po-2s generally operated. This, combined with the low altitude, made airborne radar practically useless because of ground return.

On one flight, the attacking aircraft was within 100 yards and closing on a Po-2 but was still unable to contact the bogey on the scope of an efficiently operating radar set. On another flight, a pilot closed on a bogey through a cloud top at 1,800 feet and, upon breaking out of the cloud, found himself about to ram the Po-2's tail section. Later the pilot estimated the Po-2 to be within fifty feet of his fighter's nose section.

During February 1952 a similar incident occurred, but with tragic consequences. An F-94 Starfire was directed to the bogey by TACC, and the jet made three passes on the Po-2 before contact with both planes was lost by TACC. Later a UN pilot reported seeing a flash at 2,000 feet in the vicinity of the reported intercept. When the wreckage was located a few days later, it was deduced that the two aircraft exploded after collision.

Lockheed's F-94 Starfire was a temporary conversion from the company's T-33 two seat jet trainer, built as a stop-gap for the night-fighter role due to delays in the production of Northrop's F-89 Scorpion. The fuselage of the T-33 was widened to accommodate a more powerful engine with afterburning, and the airframe lengthened to make room for radar equipment. Only two squadrons equipped with the F-94 served in Korea, where they flew around 4,700 missions. Over two dozen were lost, mainly due to accidents.

One Marine night-fighter squadron observed that on every occasion but one, the Po-2 would begin violent evasive maneuvers as soon as the night-fighter was seen. During these manoeuvres the Po-2s would return fire from the rear cockpit while continuing its erratic flight. Furthermore, the communist pilots were not considered to be of a very high caliber. They flew mainly by the seat of their pants and did not seem to utilize to the limit the extreme maneuverability of their aircraft. They would also fly in and around cloud tops, but did not attempt true instrument flight.

A revealing example of the flight procedures used by the Po-2 pilots was found in the wreckage of a Po-2 downed by a F4U in July 1951. It was a chart which set forth standard navigation techniques and included the caution 'Don't believe in the compass'.

In runs made against Po-2s by Marine F7F-3N and F4U-5N aircraft, the bogey speed ranged from sixty to ninety knots. As a result, the night-fighters had to operate with full flaps, with landing gear lowered and at low power settings. In this flight attitude the attacking fighter is hindered by its lack of manoeuverability and continuous adjustment in power settings and attitudes made it impossible to not overrun the Po-2.

One of the more successful attacks was made by a Marine F7F with a relatively wide-angle deflection shot, resulting in the complete destruction of the Po-2. The pilot later remarked on the disintegration of the aircraft. Under 20mm fire, the Po-2s strutted, fabric-covered, wooden wings are the first portion to disintegrate. In another interception, a slight angle deflection shot from the rear accomplished the desired results. However, the Po-2 vanished from sight before its demise could be confirmed.

The ground troops often referred to the nocturnal visits of the Po-2 as 'Bedcheck Charlie' and they were more of an annoyance than a visitor to be feared. In the summer of 1953, just before the truce, the Communists used other night flying-propeller driven aircraft to drop bombs on Seoul at random intervals. Lieutenant Guy Bordelon became the Navy's only ace in Korea when he shot down four Yak-18s and a Lavochkin La-2 over a 16-day period whilst flying the F4U-5N Corsair with VC-3.

A Tail Gunner's Story

Escaping from a severely damaged bomber is a life-changing experience in itself, let along suffering ill-treatment and imprisonment in appalling conditions on the ground as well. Former B-29 tail gunner Dan Oldewage described his experience to the author:

'It was about 0430 hours; we were scoffing down breakfast so as to get to briefing about 0500 hours. The briefing would assign our aircraft, our position in the formation, our rendezvous point and, of course, the target for the mission. I'll not forget when they said our target for the day would be the railroad bridge connecting Sinuiju, North Korea to Antung, China – as deep into what was known as "MiG Alley" as you could get. The comment from the briefing officer, "if you should be captured, we have no clue as to what will happen to you", gave you a lot to think about. As for the MiG-15, it was a fine aircraft with lots of fire power, a 37mm cannon in the nose that could raise havoc, and very fast. Not a good match for the antiquated B-29s.

'Now about the 12 April mission. I'll give you my personal views based upon the sequence of events happening and from my position in the aircraft as tail gunner. A completed mission to North Korea from Kadena Air Base on Okinawa would normally be ten to eleven hours. I would have to go into the tail when the pilot started pressurizing the aircraft so I could be in my position for nine hours or more. Requirements to be a tail gunner mainly consisted of being able to like being alone and have better than average bladder control. Seriously, we did have contact with all the crew via the intercom and remembering to carry an empty bottle solved the other problem. The tail was an interesting position. It was very tight quarters; you were always riding backwards, you had an unobstructed over 180 degree lateral view and almost that much vertically. Also, because of the speed of the MiG, every attack initiated from the rear. Those pilots needed the slower closure time so they could be effective but, from our perspective, they were still too fast to give us accurate tracking time. My personal rule of thumb was to stay alert and spot them as early as possible, hold fire until fired on. My reasoning for this was the MiG's 37mm cannon had greater range than our 0.50-caliber machine guns, so if I didn't fire until I could see their cannon bursts, I would know then that they were within range. I defied all training principals of short bursts so you wouldn't burn the barrels; I fired continuously hoping they would run into my array of 0.50-caliber slugs. Everything took place so fast that you had to depend upon luck more than skill.

'To get on with my story; we were flying slot position in our particular formation. As we neared the target area our pilot called the lead aircraft with the fact that our aircraft was unable to pull enough power to stay with the formation. We were advised to drop back and fly lead aircraft on another formation several miles behind. We did so but had minimal fighter escort until we would join up with the following formation. In this process, we were jumped by MiGs – they would always pick off a plane that was obviously disabled. I spotted a reflection and called it out just before they turned in toward our aircraft. They were flying three abreast – a lead and two wing men. They were very good; we took several hits on their first pass. I felt the tail shudder as the left stabilizer took a hit leaving a hole seemingly large enough to crawl through. The area under my feet, including the floorboard, was hit, which gave me great concern since I would always lay my flak vest on the floor between my feet with my parachute, a chest pack, on top of it. The plane was out of control, the pilot announced on the intercom "prepare to bail out". Almost immediately the alarm bell went off. I tried my intercom, but I could not make contact with anyone, then I could see parachutes opening up, behind us – we were a lone aircraft at the time, so I figured it was the rest of our crew. Time to go. I reached for my parachute pack and snapped it on without looking for damage. I didn't want to know. I popped out my small escape window and jumped – how smart – I did everything correctly except tightening my leg straps. When my chute opened, I believe they could have heard me in the enlisted men's club back on Okinawa – I knew at that moment I could possibly never sire children.

'Being a slow learner, I tried, just once, to climb the shroud lines so I could tighten my leg straps. I could not do it and, in the process, I dumped my chute so when it reopened I got to enjoy the pain once more. I soon realized that the ground was getting much closer, and it appeared I was going to hit in an already harvested and dry rice paddy. As I neared my landing, I could see the plant stubbles sticking up like a bunch of needles – not good I thought – but it actually presented no problem. When I hit, almost instantly I was run down by my own dinghy. A seat pack suspended on the seat of my harness that contains a life raft and miscellaneous survival gear. That twenty-pound pack – with all the applied forces – hit my back with the force of a 300-pound line-backer. I was down, still alive but hurting badly. To this point I had no time for fear but, as I gathered my wits and realized the circumstances I was now in, I felt fear. Looking across to the edge of the rice paddy I spotted the peasant farmer. He was most likely more fearful of me than I was of him. Their propaganda had them convinced that Americans were murderers. So he was very cautious. I needed help so I placed my hands on my head to show I had no weapon and called out in my very best Korean "friendo", not realizing there was not a word "friendo" in the Korean language. He apparently forgave me of the fact that shortly before our meeting, he was an enemy who could very well have been a victim of the bombings. Go figure.

'Anyhow, this man helped me to his house, laid me out on the dirt floor, gave me boiled water and did his very best to give me some comfort as I thought I had a broken back and it hurt bad. His reward for doing this was a ballpoint pen and a small gold coin, plus a very rough time by the Korean police officers who were the first to arrive on the scene. They were looking for the 0.45-caliber semi-automatic pistol that all airmen were supposed to carry and were convinced that he now had it. My tail position was just too small for me to carry anything I didn't have to have. I don't know the end result of what happened to that fine man.

'Soon the Army folks arrived, and I was turned over to them. They were very young guys with all the authority in the world at that moment. They made me remove my shoelaces and tied my hands with them. We then proceeded to trek to the nearest village. Along the road we gathered a fairly large, angry and noisy crowd. At one point we stopped, and with a lot of shouting and pointing, they ordered me into a drainage ditch along side the roadway. The crowd cheered, the guards fired a couple of shots in the air, positioned me on the opposite side of the ditch, and I could hear them throw the bolts on their rifles. I was facing a firing squad but, surprisingly, I felt nothing – absolutely no feeling of fear. I guess the human brain functions way ahead of emotions sometimes. But the guards got to display their authority, the crowd was excited because they were in hopes of seeing an execution – me – I needed to do my laundry. Just kidding.'

The Dambusters at Hwachon

On 22 April, the Chinese and North Koreans launched their fifth offensive aimed at pushing the United Nations forces back from the 38th parallel. Fielding 700,000 men, the communists were determined to isolate South Korea's capital of Seoul with a double-flanking movement, and launched four Chinese communist army groups against the 75-mile front between the Hwachon Reservoir and Munsan.

When the 7th Marines dug in around Hwachon spotted movement on the nearby hills, they knew what was coming. Shortly after dark the stillness exploded as sirens, bugles, whistles, gongs and screams announced a huge Chinese attack. On their left the 6th ROK Division fell apart, exposing the Marines' flank and eventually they had to fall back.

With rising casualties, US planners desperately searched for a way to break the deadlock, and their attention was drawn to the Hwachon Dam. Located almost fifty miles northeast of Seoul, the 250-foot-high dam retained the waters of the Pukhan River, which were high due to the spring thaw. There were two scenarios to consider however. If the dam's sluice gates were destroyed, the released waters would flood the valley and possibly stop further UN advances. If the dam was left alone and the enemy held back the water by closing the gates, the river would be lowered to fordable depths and enable communist infiltration across the river against the exposed allied flanks.

The Air Force was the first to try to destroy the dam, using Boeing B-29 bombers, but they barely dented the twenty-feet-thick gates. Unfortunately, the bombing spooked the enemy, who promptly blew most of the vital Pukhan bridges and opened some of the gates, flooding the lower river.

On 11 April, the Army sent in Rangers and mechanized infantry, but they were heavily outnumbered and forced back by fierce resistance. A larger ground attack actually took the dam later in the month, only to be driven out by a ferocious counter-attack before they could destroy the sluice gates. Now it was time for the Navy to have a try.

At 1440 hours on 30 April 1951, Commander Task Force 77 Rear Admiral Ralph Ofstie received an urgent message from the Eighth Army. The Chinese had just resumed their 'spring offensive' and the hard-pressed troops on the ground desperately needed help. If two or more of the floodgates could be knocked out, it might prevent the enemy from releasing all of the impounded water simultaneously to the valley and bring operations to a standstill.

Carrier Air Group 19 on the *Princeton* was given the task. Since the twenty-feet-high and forty-feet-wide gates made a vulnerable target for aircraft, the enemy had strengthened the dam with rocks. The 4,000-feet ridges surrounding the reservoir meant that only two aircraft at a time could make their runs against the target, running the gauntlet of the enemy AA guns.

On the afternoon of the attack the *Princeton* turned into the wind and launched the first strike. Air Group Commander Richard C. Merrick commanded the strike force, comprising six VA-195 Skyraiders under squadron CO Lieutenant Commander Harold Gustav Carlson and escorted by Lieutenant-Commander E. A. Parker's flight of five Corsairs from VF-193. Each Skyraider carried two 2,000-pound bombs and multiple 11.75-inch Tiny Tim rockets intended for the sluice gates, while the Corsairs carried 100- and 500-pound bombs for flak suppression.

Carlson led the first pair in while the others orbited overhead and the valley erupted as the communist batteries opened up with everything they had. Swooping in low, the Corsairs blasted every anti-aircraft site they could identify, while the Skyraiders flew the gauntlet in rapid succession, dropping their bombs and firing their rockets.

Unfortunately, the strike was in vain. None of the bombs hit the vital gates and the one hit succeeded only in shaking loose a little of the dam's surface, while the rockets had no affect at all. The only bright spot in the day was that not a single plane was lost, although several sported numerous holes upon their return. At debriefing someone suggested using torpedoes. They would provide both the accuracy and the punch to tackle the dam, and by more luck than judgment some had been loaded onto the ship prior to sailing.

The flight crews worked through the night repairing the aircraft and arming them with eight MK 13s brought up from below decks, where they were buried behind the other ordnance. Ensign Robert E. Bennett, one of only three pilots who had practised anti-shipping tactics, said, 'We trained extensively at coordinated tactics against shipping on a previous cruise, before Korea, and we got good at it.' Still, most of them had never dropped a torpedo, much less tried anything this unorthodox. In fact, Bennett recalled that he had never even seen an aerial torpedo before Hwachon. They decided to include on the strike three VC-35 pilots who had already practised torpedo drops: Lieutenants Arthur F. Clapp, Frank Metzner and Addison R. English.

The high hills surrounding the reservoir continued to limit the approach to a two-plane section run-in, while the remainder of the group circled overhead. Making the run-in over the heights surrounding the reservoir required a letdown to drop altitude without exceeding torpedo drop speed.

In addition, the drop required limited water space to avoid grounding the torpedo, while still allowing sufficient time for the 'fish' to arm, and the departure from the target had to be made down a narrow valley lined with anti-aircraft guns. To top it all off, with just eight fish available, only a minimum error rate was acceptable.

Bennett explained, 'Too high and the torpedo would enter the water steeply and dive. Too low and the torpedo would skip off the water. There was difficulty also in slowing down to maximum drop speed, and if the ball wasn't centered, the torpedo wouldn't run true. The torpedoes were finicky little devils.'

Early on 1 May 1951, Merrick led his second strike, consisting of five Skyraiders from VA-195 and three from VC-35 Det 3, backed up by eight Corsairs from VF-192 and four from VF-193. Looking ungainly with their fish slung under their bellies, the Skyraiders had, nonetheless, been designed with just such a mission in mind, and they performed beautifully.

Arriving over the target at 1130, the pilots were amazed to find the valley ominously quiet. Expecting the guns to riddle them at any moment, they pushed themselves over and went in, only then being greeted by the first bursts of flak. Apparently, the enemy did not expect them to return so soon and was caught by surprise. While the Corsairs went after the guns or circled, each pair of Skyraiders flew in at wave-top level, struggling to hold their letdown to drop altitude so that they did not exceed torpedo speed.

Running the gauntlet took nerves of steel, each pilot dropping his torpedo and then climbing sharply up the great bulk of the dam as it suddenly loomed over him, waiting breathlessly during those agonizing seconds for his lightened aircraft to respond. During their run Clapp and English discovered the hard way that their torpedoes were faulty. Both men were stunned to watch their fish swerve at the last minute and avoid their targets completely!

Fortunately, the other six torpedoes ran true, slipping momentarily beneath the surface, but then regaining their calibration and racing on to slam into the gates. The explosions echoed off the hills and sent great waves roaring across the reservoir. The centre gate was ripped apart, the second gate was torn by a ten-feet gash and one of the abutments was damaged. Circling above, the pilots watched in awe as millions of gallons of water poured through the stricken gates in huge churning columns, flooding the valley for miles.

From this single raid, the enemy was denied control of the reservoir's waters for the rest of the war and VA-195 later adopted the nickname

'Dambusters'. Sadly, Merrick, the air group commander, was tragically killed in action on 18 May 1951 when his Skyraider took a large caliber hit on the wingroot. His relief, Commander Charles R. Stapler, was also shot down less than a month later on 10 June. Following their return to Naval Air Station Alameda, in California, the new CVG-19 commander, Commander William D. Denton, Jr., told a local newspaper, 'It's a damn bloody war. I think it's a more brutal war than WW II, frankly. In this war, you're going in every day. You know there'll be anti-aircraft artillery- lots of it – and you'll have to fly through it day after day.'

The war continued and Operation Strangle began on 31 May 1951, directed at the enemy's road system, and designed to accompany the UN counterattack toward the 38th Parallel. But when the Eighth Army reached its objectives in mid-June and slackened the pressure on the Communists, Strangle's effectiveness waned. In July, when it became apparent that the Communists were not worrying about the ground offensive and were using more men to keep the roads open, Strangle petered out. It was a fact of life that the Chinese soldier could exist on a lot less supplies than the American soldier. A 1951 joint Army-Air Force study estimated that a Communist division of about 10,000 men needed only forty-eight tons of supplies per day, compared to the 500 tons per day required to supply a 16,000-man US division. On a per-man basis, Americans needed about six times more supplies than the enemy did. The Chinese soldier was taught to use captured weapons and equipment as much as possible because this freed the Communist supply trains to bring more-needed items. Because his army still was not very mechanized, the Chinese and Korean soldier was used to carrying his own supplies. A single man could carry almost eighty pounds on his own back for long distances over rough terrain.

Measured against this requirement, the North Korean transportation net was more than adequate, and by early March the capacity of the west coast rail line was estimated at between 500 and 1,000 tons per day, and that of the east coast railroad at about 500, while highways in the west and east were capable of transporting 1,000 and 500 tons per day respectively. In these circumstances it appeared that the enemy could support half a million troops, with something over a third dependent on the east coast rail and road nets.

Interdiction of these routes depended, at least in the first instance, upon bridge demolition, and modern reinforced concrete bridges are hard to hit and hard to destroy, requiring the hitting power of battleship or heavy cruiser main battery fire, or of the Skyraider attack plane carrying three 2,000-pound bombs each. Experience gained as the campaign progressed showed force requirements of about sixty rounds of sixteen-inch gunfire or of twelve to sixteen Skyraider sorties per bridge destroyed. While the rail net could be thus fragmented the effect on highway travel was less decisive; a truck can be detoured more easily than a train and the supply of trucks from north of the border was a continuing one.

The enemy was also extremely energetic in their efforts to keep the lines of communication open. They built multiple parallel bridges to decrease the effectiveness of FEAF's bridge-busters. Usually they would build four such bypasses, but in one case, the Rail Bridge across the Yalu at Sinuiju, they built eight bypasses. They built bridges that were just a few inches under the water, and used removable bridge spans to prevent recon flights from detecting the repaired bridges. They were able generally to repair key bridges in about two days.

Their ability to repair road and rail cuts was no less impressive. Men were stationed at close intervals along roads and railways and they were able to make road repairs, without heavy equipment, almost overnight. A standard rail cut could be repaired in two to six hours and major cuts could be repaired in four to seven days. It was these Herculean efforts that helped to keep the interdiction campaign from being fully successful.

Despite MacArthur's attempt to develop national policy himself, the quest for a cease-fire had gone on, and on 10 July 1951, negotiators from both sides met at Kaesong to thrash out an agenda for an armistice. It would take two more years to accomplish this and during this time some of the bloodiest fighting of the war would take place.

Chapter 3

War of Attrition: July 1951–June 1952

Chapter Contents

July to December 1951

On 10 July 1951, negotiators from both sides met at Kaesong to work out an agenda for an armistice. However, it would take two more years to accomplish this and during that time some of the bloodiest fighting of the war would take place.

Far East Air Force was directed to maintain pressure on the Communists so that the United Nations could obtain the most favourable results during the armistice negotiations. Air Superiority remained the primary objective, but when Lieutenant General Otto P. Weyland took over command of FEAF in June 1951 he declared that they would cause, 'the maximum amount of selected destruction, thus making the Korean Conflict as costly as possible to the enemy in terms of equipment, supplies, and personnel.' Weyland hoped this new air strategy would also hurt the Soviets and Chinese through the loss of the equipment that they were supplying the North Koreans.

Three major interdiction campaigns were planned. One was named Saturate, and the other two had the same name, Strangle. Despite its name, Strangle was not intended to achieve the impossible and completely shut down the movement of supplies to the front lines. It was intended to disrupt the enemy's lines of communications to such an extent that he would be unable to mount a sustained major offensive. Both interdiction campaigns got off to a good start. The first Strangle, which began on 31 May 1951, was directed at the enemy's road system, and was designed to support the UN counterattack toward the 38th Parallel. But when the Eighth Army reached its objectives in mid-June and slackened the pressure on the Communists, Strangle's effectiveness began to reduce. In July, when it became apparent that the Communists were not worrying about the ground offensive and were using more men to keep the roads open, Strangle petered out.

On 30 July, in the largest single mass attack for the month on targets in the P'yongyang area, ninety-one F-80s suppressed enemy air defences while 354 USMC and USAF fighter-bombers attacked a number of military targets. To avoid adverse world public opinion during the on-going peace negotiations, the Joint Chiefs of Staff withheld information on the strike from the news media. However, on 4 August, Communist ground forces violated the Kaesong neutral zone, resulting in the suspension of truce talks for a week. On 22 July the Communist delegation fabricated evidence that a UN aircraft had bombed Kaesong, resulting in the suspension of the armistice negotiations once again. An attempt by the UN to reopen the peace talks at the end of September would fail.

In the summer of 1951 McDonnell's F2H Banshee arrived to join the combat, flying from USS *Essex* to escort B-29 bombers on a high altitude raid against North Korean rail yards. Faster than the Panther, but less robust, the Banshee was later switched to photo-reconnaissance with three cameras carried in its elongated nose. Some were flown from Pohang K-3, South Korea by VMJ-1 as part of the 67th Tactical Reconnaissance Wing based at Kimpo.

The second Operation Strangle began on 18 August 1951, and was directed at the North Korean railway system. On 25 August 35 B-29s, escorted by Navy fighters, dropped 300 tons of bombs on the marshalling yards at Rashin in far northeastern Korea. It was a major supply depot and had been previously excluded from target lists because of its proximity of

Jim Flemming of 77 Squadron Royal Australian Air Force was the first pilot to knock out a North Korean T-34 tank with his Mustang.

Australian Mustang pilot Lyall Klaffer inspects a 0.50-calibre bullet hole in his aircraft after landing at Taegu.

A Navy Panther ditches in the sea near one of the aircraft carriers. The ideal ditching procedure was wheels up and flaps down and if possible, with the canopy open to assist egress before the plane sank.

The Royal Navy aircraft carrier HMS *Ocean* with a Sea Fury on the catapult ready to launch.

An air rescue demonstration being carried out by an HO3S on the USS *Philippine Sea*, with the 'pilot' being winched up in a sling. Credit US Navy 80-G-420957.

A Marine Corsair attacking hilltop Chinese positions.

Lieutenant Joseph Wosser flew the Corsair with the Rattlesnakes of VMF–323 during the landings at Inchon and the retreat from the Chosin Reservoir. Credit Joe Wosser.

A North Korean IL-12 Stormovik fighter at Hamhung airfield in less than flyable condition. Credit Lyall Klaffer.

VMF-323 pilot Hugh 'Whiskey' Newell was killed while attacking Chinese positions during the Marines retreat from the Chosin Reservoir. Credit T.C. Crouson.

The flight deck of USS *Badoeng Strait* covered with snow and ice in November 1950 with VMF-323 Corsairs parked at the rear.

Identified by their yellow fuselage band and checker tails these 39th Fighter Interceptor Squadron Sabres on the flight line at Suwon are being readied for a sortie in 1952.

The Greek crew of the first C-47 to arrive with left to right W/Op Sgt Ion Chrysolaras, Major Andrew Gorengo, CO of the Hellenic Flight, 1st Lt Dimitrios Polymenakos, 2nd Lt Konstantinos Maglinis and kneeling, navigator 1st Lt V Pirasmakis. Credit Spyros Andreopoulos via Themis Vranas.

The Hwachon dam was breached by Navy Skyraiders from VA-195 using WWII torpedoes. This photo shows the impact of one torpedo at the centre of the dam wall.

Skyraiders from VA-195 flying from the USS *Princeton* breached the Hwachon Dam on 1st May 1951 with WWII torpedoes. On this mission B-518 is carrying twelve 250 pound bombs.

B-29 Superfortress 3992 'Flakshack' from the 91st SRS crash landed at Yokota air base in Japan when an engine failed on takeoff on 21st January 1952. One crewmember was injured jumping from the wing and the aircraft was wrecked.

A Tactical Air Control team jeep parked next to a knocked out T-34 tank. Credit Howard Tanner.

Brigadier Rockingham of the Canadian Brigade prepares for a flight in 'Rocky's Rickshaw' piloted by US Air Force air liaison officer Howard Tanner.

US Air Force Air Liaison Officer Howard Tanner points out the effect of cannon fire on the side of an armoured North Korean railway carriage. Credit Howard Tanner.

A Skyraider from VA-195 crashes along the deck of the aircraft carrier USS *Boxer*.

Joseph Holdens T-6 Mosquito with six smoke rockets mounted under each wing. Credit Joseph Holden.

Pilots from the 80th Fighter Bomber Squadron 'Headhunters' celebrate their 50,000 sortie in their F-80s with this artwork on 'The Spirit of Ho-Bo' in October 1952.

An 817 Squadron Firefly prepares to launch from the Royal Australian Navy carrier HMAS *Sydney* while a US Navy S-51 plane guard helicopter hovers nearby, ready to rescue anyone unlucky enough to ditch in the sea.

A Sea Fury from 804 Squadron taking off from HMS *Glory* in 1951. Alan Leahy's first RATOG takeoff failed and he ditched in the sea, struggling to the surface as the carrier sailed on past him.

Invader pilot Lt Robert C Mikesh (right) and his crew First Lieutenant John L Middleton navigator (left) and gunner A2C Kitchen (centre) pose for the camera in front of B–26 'Monie' named after Mikesh's wife Ramona. Credit Robert C Mikesh.

The devastating effect of napalm dropped by a B–26 on 23rd April 1951 can be seen on these two trains in a marshalling yard in North Korea.

This crash landed B–26 Invader wears the Grim Reaper badge of the 13th Bomb Squadron of the 3rd Bomb Group.

The crew of Superfortress 61872 from the 98th Bomb Wing line up with their parachutes before a mission at Yokota air base in 1952. They were on the same mission as 6392 when it was shot down with the loss of all but two of the crew. Credit John Baker.

This F-94B Starfire flown by Captain Ben Fithian and his RO Lieutenant Sam Lyons was the first Starfire to shoot down an enemy plane.

Australian Meteor pilot Ron Guthrie taking it easy on his veranda in 2007. He managed to escape his North Korean captors and was severely punished when he was recaptured. Credit Ron Guthrie.

Lieutenant Guy Bordelon was the only Corsair pilot to become an Ace during the Korean War flying his F4U-5N 'Annie-Mo' with VC-3 Det D, assigned to the USS *Princeton* but flying from Kimpo and Pyongtaek.

An RB–45C Tornado was shot down within days of beginning over flights of the border between North Korea and China. The type was then painted black in an effort to foil the enemy searchlights during night missions.

A posed Chinese propaganda photograph of Colonel Arnold (left) and his B–29 crew tucking into their first proper meal in two years during the visit of UN Secretary General Dag Hammarskjold to Peking. They were finally released two years after the war ended.

less than twenty miles to the Soviet border. The campaign continued regardless of the weather and on 23 September, in an excellent example of Shoran radar-directed bombing technique, eight B-29s from the 19th Bomb Group knocked out the centre span of the Sunchon rail bridge despite nine-tenths cloud cover. Initial results were encouraging, but the enemy quickly reacted with increased numbers of anti-aircraft guns along the tracks, increased activity by the MiGs against the bombers which drove them to less-effective night raids, and increased repair efforts. In addition, the attempts by the Communists to build airfields in North Korea resulted in many rail missions being diverted to attack the fields instead. Thus, by December, Strangle II also dwindled away.

While Bomber Command concentrated on the railways, it was business as usual for the night flying B-26s. On the night of 24/25 August they claimed over eight hundred trucks destroyed in the new campaign of night anti-truck operations. On 14 September, Captain John S. Walmsley Jr., of the 8th Bomb Squadron, on a night B-26 interdiction sortie, attacked an enemy train, expending his ordnance. He then used a US Navy searchlight experimentally mounted on his aircraft's wing to illuminate the target for another B-26. Shot down and killed by ground fire, Walmsley earned the Medal of Honour for his courageous act.

The men of the 3rd Air Rescue Service were also earning their pay. On 10 September, South of P'yongyang, an H-5 helicopter, with fighter escort, rescued F-80 pilot Captain Ward M. Millar, from the 7th Fighter Bomber Squadron. He had suffered two broken ankles during his ejection from the jet, but escaped after two months as a prisoner and then evaded recapture for three weeks. The helicopter also brought out an NKA sergeant who had assisted Millar, delivering both to Seoul. On 22 October two SA-16 Albatross flying boats rescued the twelve-man crew of a downed B-29, the highest number of aircrew rescued by SA-16s on any day in the war.

Towards the end of October, the enemy became more aggressive and flew sorties over North Korea daily for the first time in the war. Sometimes over one hundred MiGs would be in the air, consistently outnumbering their F-86 counterparts and downing three F-86s at a cost of five MiGs lost to Sabres. On 23 October, in one of the bloodiest air battles of the war, MiG-15s destroyed three B-29s and one F-84 and damaged five other bombers during a 307th Bomb Group raid on Namsi airfield. Within days the Pentagon ordered a halt to daylight bomber raids over North Korea.

On 25 October, in an unusually effective close air support strike, F-51 Mustangs inflicted approximately two hundred casualties on enemy troops in the I Corps sector. Enemy small-arms fire hit a rescue helicopter picking up a downed UN pilot and the H-5 made a forced landing in enemy territory. The next day, two other H-5s hoisted all four men to safety from the mountainside where they had hidden from Communist troops during the night.

The air war also spread to the islands off the peninsula on 6 November when eleven enemy twin-engine light bombers – probably Tu-2s – bombed Taehwa-do, a UN-controlled island. This raid was the first confirmed report of air-to-ground action by an enemy light bomber formation since the Korean War started. Three days later a C-47 landed on the beach of Paengnyong-do Island, off the southwest coast of North Korea, and rescued eleven crewmen of a downed B-29. The 19th Bomb Group had been attacking railway marshalling yards at Hwang-ju, Kowon, and Yangdok, Saamcham airfield and a barracks area. In other night attacks, 98th Bomb Wing B-29s bombed Taechon airfield, flew five close support sorties and a leaflet sortie, and struck Hungnam.

At the request of the Communists, peace negotiations resumed at Panmunjom, a village less than five miles east of Kaesong, in a newly established demilitarized zone on the 38th parallel. As progress was being made the UN Command ceased offensive ground operations.

Despite this, the air campaign against the railway system continued. On 16 November, 5th Air Force fighter-bombers made more than one hundred rail cuts between Sinanju and Sukchon and between Kunu-ri and Sunchon. They also damaged bridges, knocked out AAA gun positions, destroyed supply buildings, fired fuel dumps, and destroyed enemy railcars. However, two days later, MiG-15s forced three flights of F-84 fighter-bombers to jettison their bombs and abort their rail-cutting missions near Sinanju. On 24 November in night operations, 98th Bomb Wing bombed Taechon airfield and the marshalling yard at Tongchon and flew five close support sorties; 307th Bomb Wing bombed the marshalling yard at Hambusong-ji and the 19th Bomb Group bombed Namsi airfield, the Hoeyang highway bridge, and the marshalling yards at Munchon and Hambusong-ji. On the night of 14 December the 19th Bomb Group B-29s inflicted severe damage on marshalling yards at Maengjung-dong and on 19 December the 307th Bomb Wing sent ten B-29s to bomb marshalling yards at Chongju. On Christmas Eve, on a typical night time mission, B-29s from the 98th Bomb Wing cratered the runway at Taechon airfield and bombed the railroad bridge at Sinanju.

On 30 November, in one of the largest aerial battles of the war, F-86 pilots of the 4th FIG engaged forty-four enemy aircraft flying south to bomb a UN target. The Sabre pilots destroyed twelve and damaged three others. Major George A. Davis Jr., 334th FIS, achieved Korean War ace status by downing a Tu-2 and a MiG-15. He was the first to be an ace in two wars, since he had also been an ace in World War II. Major Winton W. Marshall, 335th FIS, also became an ace by destroying an La-9 and a Tu-2. Enemy ground forces attacked Taehwa-do Island, north of Cho-do Island, forcing the friendly forces to retreat to Cho-do. Eventually, 5th Air Force aircraft dislodged the enemy and friendly forces recaptured the island. On 3 December, enemy jets made their first air-ground attack of the war, bombing and strafing UN ground positions near Chorwon, almost sixty miles northeast of Seoul.

Meteor Bail Out at 39,000 Feet

77 Squadron Royal Australian Air Force exchanged their Mustangs for Meteor jets and began to fly combat patrols in MiG Alley. However, the Meteors were no match for the Soviet fighters. On 29 August 1951, eight Australian Meteors were well spaced-out and in combat formation as they cruised steadily at 39,000 feet. Five thousand feet below them another eight Meteors were flying a parallel path against the background of a deceptively peaceful Korean and Manchurian landscape. One of the pilots flying top cover was Warrant Officer Ron Guthrie:

'Suddenly I am startled by white-hot tracers streaming over and under my left wing like glowing ping-pong balls. Two MiGs have bounced us out of the sun and the air is filled with 23mm and 37mm cannon shells. I throw my Meteor into a hard left hand turn and press the "mike" button to call a "break" to the others in my flight. Too late! I have been hit behind the cockpit and my radio is useless. I am only talking to myself as I call "Anzac Item – break left – tracers!"

'The two MiGs shoot past my nose and I instinctively turn back sharply to the right hoping to get one of them in my sights. Through the illuminated graticule of the gunsight, I can see a red star on a silver fuselage and the pilot's head in the cockpit. I quickly adjust the gunsight control to correct for a retreating target as my finger curls over the trigger of my four 20mm cannons. The guns rattle. I am gratified and excited as pieces fly off the enemy aircraft which now rolls to the inverted position and dives out of sight.

'At this very instant I feel as though a load of bricks has fallen onto the rear end of my aircraft, which now shakes convulsively. Explosive shells from another MiG have destroyed my Meteor's tail. My aircraft – at this stage merely an uncontrollable mass of 'MiG meat' – begins to snap roll repeatedly. In shock, I prepare to make my first exit in a Martin Baker ejection seat – at this great height and over enemy territory? I realise my guns are still firing and release the trigger.

'The vibrating instrument panel catches my attention and two facts remain in my memory. The clock is reading six minutes past ten and the Mach meter – my gauge of speed-registers 0.84. As the speed of the dive increases beyond eighty-four per cent of the speed of sound the aircraft begins to shudder in compressibility. It continues to roll.'

Ron was about to become the first pilot to use an ejector seat in combat, at the fastest speed and at the greatest height. He urgently grasped and pulled the canopy jettison handle and found himself enveloped in a roaring swirling mass of frigid air into which he was about to eject. Taking a two-handed grip on the ejection seat loop handle above his head, he waited for the aircraft to finish its roll and on reaching the upright position pulled firmly on the control in order to fire himself out of the cockpit. At first nothing happened, until Ron realised that the downward motion of his arms was being obstructed by the pistol holster under his right elbow and a Red Cross pack on his left side. The third time he tried the altimeter needles were unwinding below 39,000 feet as a startling explosion produced an immense upward thrust out of the cockpit and he momentarily lost consciousness.

Ron came to a few seconds later, tumbling and swaying until the ejection seat's little drogue parachute deployed to steady the descent. He felt a little light headed and found that he could not breathe. This situation was quickly remedied by lifting his oxygen mask from where it had slipped to his throat. He was very relieved to feel the portable oxygen puffing onto his face. The sensation was odd as he just sat there strapped to the ejection seat, feeling quite stationary and quite detached, secured to his mechanical throne in space with no apparent means of support and no indications of motion.

The main thing now was to avoid capture by the North Koreans and Ron initially thought that from this great height he might be able to drift seaward and get into his survival dinghy and wait for Air-Sea Rescue to find him. With this plan in mind he unlocked the ejection seat harness and kicked. The seat and its small drogue chute fell away. Then a sharp pull on the ripcord handle produced a welcome jerk as the beautiful Irvin parachute, blossoming out above, stabilised Ron for his slow descent.

In an attempt to guide himself towards the ocean, Ron pulled down on one side of the canopy shrouds in the hope of producing some directional control. This had the unexpected and quite alarming effect of collapsing the chute and a sickening descent followed until the chute resumed its umbrella shape again. Vowing not to try that again, Ron resigned himself to landing on the ground and taking his chances with the enemy.

Ron recalled:

'Descending through the air seven miles above the countryside, my thoughts turned to home. How would my mother bear the shocking news? Have all my mates returned safetly to Kimpo? There had been a lot of MiGs spearing through our formation during that sudden attack. The Korean countryside below looked more hostile with every minute of the descent. What would be waiting for me down there? Am I too far north for a helicopter rescue?

The thought of falling into the hands of the North Koreans filled me with anxiety. Our intelligence briefings had been most discouraging in this regard. The Geneva Convention would mean nothing. Harsh treatment would be guaranteed. The possibility of being shot on sight by their military forces was a big worry.'

The emergency oxygen supply lasted to around twenty thousand feet, below which the ambient air was adequate for survival. The topography was becoming clearer and the mountains, rivers and towns were coming into focus. Unfortunately, this meant that if Ron could see the ground, the people on the ground could also see him. As the ground loomed below him, Ron began to experience something that every descending parachutist dreads:

'I could hear strange sounds like "fitttt-fitttt" and looked up at the canopy. Holes were appearing! Enemy troops were shooting and the bullets were zipping past very close! This was what we had been warned about at our briefings. In alarm, I attempted evasive action by pulling on the cords in order to swing myself from side to side. Again I spilt the chute and had to stop pulling. This was a frightening experience as I was so near the ground, but fortunately my parachute quickly re-erected.

'At very low levels the descent seemed to accelerate and the last couple of hundred feet slipped by rapidly. Descending towards a paddy field, for a moment it seemed I was going to land on two women bending over their work. In fact, my feet planted in the soft ground squarely between the two girls. I remained upright. The two ladies leapt into the air in fright and ran a short distance, then stopped as they saw there was no threat. I was still standing securely, with the spongy soil up to my ankles. As I unstrapped, the smiling girls each took one of my hands and one said "Russki Da?" Thinking quickly I repeated "Russki Da!" and they began to lead me away.'

Then bullets began to fly and Ron's guardians fled in fright. Seeking shelter behind a rice paddy wall, Ron drew his 0.38 revolver and could see three separate army patrols approaching his position. The nearest soldier began firing from the hip as he ran and Ron flinched at the chatter of the 'burp' gun and the impact of the bullets hitting the ground nearby. Taking careful aim Ron fired two shots at the soldier and was gratified to see him slump to the ground, bleeding profusely. Before he had time to fire again he was grabbed from behind and the pistol torn from his grasp. He was now surrounded by North Korean troops who crowded around and began to strip him of his Mae West and flying suit, followed quickly by his watch and signet ring. Ron was stripped down to his underpants and flying boots, and his hands were tied behind his back with a length of telephone cable. Accompanied by six guards he was marched away to a very uncertain future.

The following day saw Ron being questioned by two Russian pilots who claimed to have shot him down. They evaluated the Meteor very poorly, but felt that the Sabre was as good as the MiG, and one of the men claimed to have been shot down by a Sabre a few days previously. They also confirmed that Ron had in fact shot down one of the MiGs himself, before he had to bail out. This was quite a boost to his morale. Before they left they gave Ron some food – a small loaf of bread, some butter and a little packet of sugar. As he had just eaten he thanked them and said he would have it later. They firmly insisted it was now or never as they obviously understood the Koreans. How right they were – for soon after their departure the last morsels of the gift were snatched away by the guards who seemed to resent Ron's favoured treatment by the Russians.

When Ron was back in his holding cell, little more than a dank hole in the ground, he pondered with some apprehension the future interrogations that he would be facing. There were some sensitive facts which should never be revealed. There was 'Stovepipe', the code name for the high-flying Sabre spy plane the Americans positioned in MiG Alley to watch aircraft movements on the airfield at Antung. Even more secret was his knowledge of the spy with strong binoculars whom the Americans had concealed on an island in the Yalu estuary, very close to the MiG's airfield. The brave fellow reported in great detail and spoke directly to Stovepipe. He could identify the markings on the MiG fuselages and when the Russian fighter leader was seen, the excited spy would inform Stovepipe that 'Casey Jones' was leading a squadron of MiGs into the air. This information would be instantly relayed back to their controller 'Dentist' located in his radar van near their base at Kimpo. Verbally encoded, the VHF radio message was simple – 'Six trains leaving the station, Casey Jones at the throttle!' This vital warning was passed to friendly aircraft and the radar network.

The next day Ron was put in a truck and driven across the border into China, to a military training school in Antung, not far from the Chinese MiG base and just across the Yalu River from its sister city of Sinuiju. The interrogation programme commenced immediately and took two hours each morning and two more after lunch. The food was quite good and the interviewers were quite friendly at first. At the end of each session Ron was given a pack of Gold Wheel cigarettes, which he kept for use as currency and for making friends with the guards. They pronounced him as 'Ding Ho' – a good bloke, for his liberal distribution of the scarce cigarettes. He later recalled:

'The interviews were initially quite friendly sessions. Apparently innocent questionnaires about person history and personal likes and dislikes were frequently used. Obviously they were trying to get any bit of data which could suggest a way of influencing me. The story I built for myself was mainly false and I quite enjoyed stringing them along in this way. The female interrogators seemed pleased at my willingness to talk about my past and to give details. I kept telling them the truth; that I was a Warrant Officer and did not have any important military information. The questions, nevertheless, soon moved more frequently in that direction. I was asked "Where do you get the fuel for your Meteor jets?" The truthful answer came easily. "I have no idea – I am a pilot and only a Warrant Officer. I have never had anything to do with obtaining fuel!" Unfortunately this answer was not accepted and I was now in their bad books. I was having more success with lies than with the truth.

'However, I had pleasure in replying to the next demand for top-secret military information. "Where are the guns on your Meteor? Where do they fire from?" Naturally I could not pretend ignorance on such a technical matter. "Some of our guns fire backwards, so as to shoot at any aircraft behind us." I had little hope that this would keep the MiGs off our tails, but enjoyed explaining it to the young women nevertheless. The reaction was gratifying.'

Interminable, mind-numbing 'discussions' filled the hours. It was sometimes difficult for Ron to retain a respectful visage when confronted with such inanity. He was expected to sympathise with the downtrodden and starving workers in Australia and England whose flooded paddy-fields evoked no sympathy or help from callous capitalist bosses. His rebuttal of their fanciful stories generated angry reactions. The attempt to alter his values and loyalties was naive, and in many respects, quite juvenile. Lack of proper responses to their political pamphlets and Ron's unsatisfactory technical answers began to erode their friendship. Some of his military revelations were too bizarre even for those un-informed girls. He was warned about non co-operation and was obviously skating on thin ice.

Eventually, after three weeks of attempted brain-washing there was a final confrontation with the chief interrogator who informed him that he was a 'Super War Criminal' and that he was to be sent back to North Korea to be 'punished'. He was driven back across the bridge into Sinuiju and tied to a chair in the village square. For several hours in the midday heat, children were encouraged by the guards to spit on the 'foreign devil' and pull his nose – possibly in celebration of their cultural notion that foreigners have big noses. After this period of ritual humiliation, he was put back in the truck again and driven to the local police headquarters and jail. He was thrown into a stinking cell where about twenty Asian men and boys were sitting cross-legged on the floor in complete silence. With arms folded and heads bowed, they were to sit without moving or speaking for seventeen hours a day on pain of severe punishment. Ron was forced to sit in a space immediately adjacent to a stinking toilet and adopt the position of silent, motionless conformity.

His punishment had begun.

Black Tuesday
It was 23 October 1951 and the eight B-29s from the 307th Bomb Group were on the way to bomb the new North Korean airfield at Namsi, along the Yalu River. Around and above them flew fifty-four F-84 Thunderjets from the 49th and 136th Fighter Bomber Wings, and to the north, thirty-four F-86's from the 4th Fighter Interceptor Wing headed for the Yalu River to intercept any MiGs heading for the bombers.

Although ninety-eight American planes were in the air, the Soviets had done their homework and were more than ready for them. While North Korean and Chinese-piloted MiGs kept the F-86 screen occupied, forty-four MiGs from the Russian 303rd and 324th Fighter Air Divisions swept southwards to close in on the bomber formation.

The Russians entered the arena at 35,000 feet and dived down on the bombers lumbering along at 22,000 feet, their target hidden by a thick layer of undercast. They would be bombing blind using the Shoran guidance system and releasing under the guidance of the lead bomber.

The Thunderjets were no match for the MiGs which tore through their formation, cannons blazing. Even if the F-84s did get close enough to hit the speeding MiGs, their 0.50-caliber machine guns would often only damage the MiGs rather than destroy them. In that regard the Navy was far ahead of the Air Force, having already adopted the 20mm cannon as its standard aerial weapon. None of the Russian MiGs would be shot down that day.

For the B-29s it would be a different matter. The lead bomber was being flown by Captain Thomas Shields, and his bombardier, Captain Emil Goldbeck, would be the lead bombardier for the mission. Once he dropped his bombs, the entire formation would release theirs. If the target was covered with clouds, they had an extra crewman on board to operate the Shoran equipment.

As they passed the Initial Point Goldbeck peered through the Norden bombsight and waited for the Shoran operator to tell him when to drop his bombs. Suddenly, they were bounced by pairs of Russian MiGs firing their 23mm and 37mm cannons from close range. Shields's B-29 bore the brunt of the first attack and one of the engines caught fire. Thinking they would soon receive the order to bail out, Goldbeck released his bombs and, as required, the rest of the formation followed suit, the bombs falling to crater the North Korean countryside.

Shields turned for the coast, to try to make it to the Yellow Sea where they would stand a better chance of rescue. As he banked to the right, four other B-29s followed him. Three, however, continued on a heading of 250 degrees before swinging to the left. This split the force and divided the F-84 fighter cover, and the Thunderjets could only watch helplessly as the B-29s paid the price for the inability of their comrades to protect them. By the time they caught up it was too late. Within minutes the Superfortress piloted by Captain James Foulks Jr. was shot down.

Captain Robert Krumms B-29 was right behind Shields and suffered severe damage, and was last seen descending through the undercast. Both B-29s crashed into the sea and although his crew bailed out, Shields did not survive the crash.

During the next few minutes the MiGs severely damaged all but one of the remaining B-29s. Three heavily damaged B-29s landed at Kimpo and two of them never flew again. Two others landed at Kadena, one with six wounded men on board.

It was a humiliating defeat for the bomber force and its escorts, clearly demonstrating that the Soviet MiG pilots were the masters of the air – in daylight at least. Five days later USAF chief of staff Hoyt S Vandenberg ordered a halt to daylight bomber operations over North Korea. The wheels were also set in motion to send a second F-86 wing, the 51st FIW to join the 4th FIW in patrolling MiG Alley.

Air Liaison Officer

One of the better decisions made by higher command was the allocation of pilots to the ground units to direct close air support. The pilots were aware of the limitations as well as the abilities of the close air support aircraft and could ensure that they were used to best advantage. One of the Air Liaison Officers was Howard Tanner, who had begun his war flying the F-80:

'During May 1951 I was ordered to report to the Joint Operations Centre in Seoul, for immediate assignment to the Canadian "Princess Pat" (Princess Patricia) Brigade as the Air Force Liaison Officer with the end assignment as the first Air Force Liaison Officer for the 1st British Commonwealth Division.

'I was issued a radio control jeep and told to go to the headquarters 10th Corps for indoctrination on my way to join the Canadian Brigade. While at 10th Corps headquarters I was told to take the Corps aircraft and fly to the 5th Air Force Forward headquarters located at Taegu to take care of some administrative details. The flight back was no problem since I had flown over the area many times. Back at 10th Corps Headquarters I watched the Chinese Spring Offensive begin against the 10th Corps Divisions. The Divisions were well entrenched and the Chinese divisions took a terrible defeat.

'On my way to join the brigade I drove through Ouijonbu and had the opportunity to see the North Korean tanks Joe Rogers had destroyed. Joe was an outstanding fighter pilot – the best! He must have flown nearly two hundred combat missions in Korea. I joined the Canadian Brigade as it moved up to the front. Scouts were always sent forward to locate the area where the Brigade Headquarters would spend the night. At one area we had barely crawled into our cots when we were shaken by horrendous noises and bright flashes. It became obvious the scouts had chosen an area only a hundred yards in front of a camouflaged 155mm artillery unit. Needless to say we moved.

'When the Canadian Brigade was located in its combat area, I was loaned an L-5 liaison aircraft by the US Army to fly the Brigade

Commander Brigadier Rockingham on reconnaissance flights. The troops dubbed it "Rocky's Rickshaw" and painted it on the nose of the aircraft. When the 1st British Commonwealth Division was activated it was located at the point where the Main Line of Resistance (MLR) from the east coast met the MLR from Seoul just southeast of Kaesong. This was an important pivotal point because the defence of Seoul was manned only by two Republic of Korea (ROK) Divisions on the MLR.

'On 9 November Danny Kaye brought his USO troupe to the Division to perform the next day. However, at 2230 hours three Chinese Divisions attacked our Division. Danny Kaye sent his troupe back to Seoul, but he remained all night in our operations centre. General Cassels sent for me and when I arrived he told me he wanted Close Air Support immediately. I tried to explain that USAF policy prohibited Close Air Support after sundown. He then said; "I don't give a damn about USAF policy – I want Close Air Support NOW!"

'I then said I would need the assistance of the Division Intelligence Officer. The General turned to the IO and told him to give me anything I needed! He provided me with the coordinates of a straight line through each of the Chinese Divisions. Whilst flying with the 36th FBS I had dropped bombs under the control of the MPQ-2 radar during bad weather and I had seen the devastating effects of bombs armed with variable time fuses. Combining these two missions I called the JOC and requested three B-29 aircraft fully loaded with 500-pound bombs armed with VT fuses set at forty feet to be dropped 'in trail' under the control of the MPQ-2 radar – one B-29 for each set of coordinates.

'When I finished with the request, I was chewed out for violating USAF policy and the request was denied. I reported to General Cassels that the request was denied. He immediately called the Commanding General of the Eighth Army who in turn called the officer in charge of the JOC and told him to honour my request! The B-29s, loaded as requested, checked in with the MPQ-2 radar at 0230 hours and dropped their bombs.

'By 0330 hours all was quiet; no horns blaring, metal clanging or yelling and screaming. At dawn the battlefield was clean with no evidence of the attack the night before. Danny Kaye asked me for my wife's telephone number and spent Thanksgiving calling relatives of the men he had met in Korea. He told my wife I was looking very well and should be home soon. He was right. I arrived at Los Angeles airport at 0300 hours the morning after Thanksgiving.

'Several years after the conflict ended the Koreans sponsored visits for us who had been in combat. They provided us with hotel rooms, meals, guides and tour buses to revisit places where we had been during the war. One of the tours took us up to the DMZ – a very hostile environment! While there a crew chief/flight engineer who was shot down near the Yalu River early in the conflict said, "There's the Bridge of Freedom that I walked across during the prisoner exchange!" He had spent nearly the entire war in a prison camp just south of the Yalu River. During our talks I told him I had flown in his area many times; sometimes flying fighter cover over the B-29s. He asked me if I had released my auxiliary fuel tanks when the MiG-15s came in. When I told him I had, he told me the prisoners would pray that some would land in their compound because one tablespoon of the jet fuel would kill the worms in their digestive tracks! I was astounded!'

The Bridges at Toko-Ri
One of many films to be produced after the end of the Korean war was *The Bridges at Toko-Ri* based on a story written by James A. Michener. The author was aboard one of the navy carriers when the real raid took place and based his work on what he saw and heard during those eventful days. The actual raid was planned and led by Captain Paul N. Gray, the CO of VF-54 and his version of events was later submitted to the US Naval Academy and is reprinted here with their permission:

'On 12 December 1951 when the raid took place, Air Group 5 was attached to *Essex*, the flag ship for Task Force 77. We were flying daily strikes against the North Koreans and Chinese. God! It was cold.

'Our main job was to interdict the flow of supplies coming south from Russia and China. The rules of engagement imposed by political forces in Washington would not allow us to bomb the bridges across the Yalu River where the supplies could easily have been stopped. We had to wait until they were dispersed and hidden in North Korea and then try to stop them.

'The Air Group consisted of two jet fighter squadrons flying Banshees and Grumman Panthers plus two prop attack squadrons flying Corsairs and Skyraiders. To provide a base for the squadrons, *Essex* was stationed 100 miles off the East Coast of Korea during that bitter winter of 1951 and 1952.

'I was CO of VF-54, the Skyraider squadron. VF-54 started with twenty-four pilots. Seven were killed during the cruise. The reason thirty per cent of our pilots were shot down and lost was due to our mission. The targets were usually heavily-defended railroad bridges. In addition, we were frequently called in to make low-level runs with rockets and napalm to provide close support for the troops.

'Due to the nature of the targets assigned, the attack squadrons seldom flew above 2,000 or 3,000 feet; and it was a rare flight when a plane did not come back without some damage from AA or ground fire.

'The single-engine plane we flew could carry the same bomb load that a B-17 carried in WWII; and after flying the 100 miles from the carrier, we could stay on station for four hours and strafe, drop napalm, fire rockets or drop bombs. The Skyraider was the right plane for this war.

'On a grey December morning, I was called to the flag bridge. Admiral "Black Jack" Perry, the Carrier Division Commander, told me they had a classified request from UN headquarters to bomb some critical bridges in the central area of the North Korean peninsula. The bridges were a dispersion point for many of the supplies coming down from the north and were vital to the flow of most of the essential supplies. The Admiral asked me to take a look at the targets and see what we could do about taking them out. As I left, the staff intelligence officer handed me the pre-strike photos and the coordinates of the target, and said to get on with it. He didn't mention that the bridges were defended by fifty-six radar-controlled anti-aircraft guns.

'That same evening, the Admiral invited the four squadron commanders to his cabin for dinner. James Michener was there. After dinner, the Admiral asked each squadron commander to describe his experiences in flying over North Korea. By this time, all of us were hardened veterans of the war and had some hairy stories to tell about life in the fast lane over North Korea. When it came my time, I described how we bombed the railways and strafed anything else that moved. I described how we had planned for the next day's strike against some vital railway bridges near a village named Toko-ri (the actual village was named Majonne). That the preparations had been done with extra care because the pre-strike pictures showed the bridges were surrounded by fifty-six anti-aircraft guns and we knew this strike was not going to be a walk in the park.

'All of the pilots scheduled for the raid participated in the planning. A close study of the aerial photos confirmed the fifty-six guns. Eleven radar sites controlled the guns. They were mainly 37mm with some five inch heavies. All were positioned to concentrate on the path we would have to fly to hit the bridges. This was a World War II air defense system but still very dangerous.

'How were we going to silence those batteries long enough to destroy the bridges? The bridges supported railway tracks about three feet wide. To achieve the needed accuracy, we would have to use glide-bombing runs. A glide-bombing run is longer and slower than a dive-bombing run, and we would be sitting ducks for the AA batteries. We had to get the guns before we bombed the bridges.

'There were four strategies discussed to take out the radar sites.

'One was to fly in on the deck and strafe the guns and radars. This was discarded because the area was too mountainous.

'The second was to fly in on the deck and fire rockets into the gun sites. This was discarded too because the rockets didn't have enough killing power.

'The third was to come in at a high altitude and drop conventional bombs on the targets. This is what we would normally do, but it was also discarded in favor of an insidious modification.

'The one we thought would work the best was to come in high and drop bombs fused to explode over the gun and radar sites. To do this, we decided to take twelve planes; eight Skyraiders and four Corsairs. Each plane would carry a 2000-pound bomb with a proximity fuse set to detonate about 50 to 100 feet in the air. We hoped the shrapnel from these huge, ugly bombs going off in mid air would be devastating to the exposed gunners and radar operators.

'The flight plan was to fly in at 15,000 feet until over the target area and make a vertical dive bombing run dropping the proximity-fused bombs on the guns and radars. Each pilot had a specific complex to hit.

'As we approached the target we started to pick up some flak, but it was high and behind us. At the initial point, we separated and rolled into the dive. Now the flak really became heavy. I rolled in first, and after I released my bomb, I pulled out south of the target area and waited for the rest to join up. One of the Corsairs reported that he had been hit on the way down and had to pull out before dropping his bomb. Three other planes suffered minor flak damage but nothing serious.

'After the join up, I detached from the group and flew over the area to see if there was anything still firing. Sure enough there was heavy 37 mm fire from one site, I got out of there in a hurry and called in the reserve Skyraider still circling at 15,000 feet to hit the remaining gun site. His 2,000 pound bomb exploded right over the target and suddenly things became very quiet. The shrapnel from those 2,000 pound bombs must have been deadly for the crews serving the guns and radars. We never saw another 37mm burst from any of the fifty-six guns.

'From that moment on, it was just another day at the office. Only sporadic machine gun and small arms fire was encountered. We made repeated glide-bombing runs and completely destroyed all the bridges. We even brought gun-camera pictures back to prove the bridges were destroyed.

'After a final check of the target area, we joined up, inspected our wingmen for damage and headed home. Mr. Michener, plus most of the ship's crew, watched from Vulture's Row as Dog Fannin the landing signal officer, brought us back aboard. With all the pilots returning to the ship safe and on time, the Admiral was seen to be dancing with joy on the flag bridge.

'From that moment on, the Admiral had a soft spot in his heart for the attack pilots. I think his fatherly regard for us had a bearing on what happened in port after the raid on Toko-ri.

'The raid on Toko-ri was exciting, but in our minds, it was dwarfed by the incident that occurred at the end of this tour on the line. The operation was officially named OPERATION PINWHEEL. The pilots called it OPERATION PINHEAD.

'The third tour had been particularly savage for VF-54. Five of our pilots had been shot down. Three not recovered. I had been shot down for the third time. The mechanics and ordnance men had worked back-breaking hours under medieval conditions to keep the planes flying, and finally we were headed for Yokosuka for ten days of desperately needed R and R.

'As we steamed up the coast of Japan, the Air Group Commander, Commander Marsh Beebe, called Commander Trum, the CO of the Corsair squadron, and me to his office. He told us that the prop squadrons would participate in an exercise dreamed up by the commanding officer of the ship. It had been named OPERATION PINWHEEL.

'The Corsairs and Skyraiders were to be tied down on the port side of the flight deck and upon signal from the bridge, all engines were to be turned up to full power to assist the tugs in pulling the ship along side the dock.

'Commander Trum and I both said to Beebe, "You realize that those engines are vital to the survival of all the attack pilots. We fly those single engine planes 300 to 400 miles from the ship over freezing water and over very hostile land. Overstressing these engines is not going to make any of us very happy." Marsh knew the danger, but he said, "The captain of the ship, Captain Wheelock, wants this done, so do it!"

'As soon as the news of this brilliant scheme hit the ready rooms, the operation was quickly named OPERATION PINHEAD, and Captain Wheelock became known as Captain Wheelchock.

'On the evening before arriving in port, I talked with Commander Trum and told him, "I don't know what you are going to do, but I am telling my pilots that our lives depend on those engines and do not give them more than half power, and if that engine temperature even begins to rise, cut back to idle." That is what they did.

'About an hour after the ship had been secured to the dock, the Air Group Commander screamed over the ships intercom for Gray and Trum to report to his office. When we walked in and saw the pale look on Beebe's face, it was apparent that Captain Wheelock, in conjunction with the ship's proctologist, had cut a new aperture in poor old Marsh.

'The ship's CO had gone ballistic when he didn't get the full power from the lashed down Corsairs and Skyraiders, and he informed Commander Beebe that his fitness report would reflect this miserable performance of duty. The Air Group Commander had flown his share of strikes, and it was a shame that he became the focus of the wrath of Captain Wheelock for something he had not done.

'However, tensions were high and in the heat of the moment, he informed Commander Trum and me that he was placing both of us and all our pilots in hack until further notice. This was a very severe sentence after thirty days on the line.

'The Carrier Division Commander, Rear Admiral "Black Jack" Perry, was a personally soft and considerate man, but his official character would strike terror into the heart of the most hardened criminal. He loved to talk to the pilots and in deference to his drinking days, would reserve a table in the bar of the Fujia Hotel and sit there drinking Coca Cola while buying drinks for any pilot enjoying R and R in the hotel.

'Even though we were not comfortable with this gruff older man, he was a good listener and everyone enjoyed telling the Admiral about his latest escape from death. I realize now he was keeping his finger on the morale of the pilots and how they were standing up to the terror of daily flights over a very hostile land.

'The Admiral had been in the hotel about three days and one night he asked some of the fighter pilots sitting at his table, "Where are the attack pilots? I have not seen any of them since we arrived." One of them said, "Admiral, I thought you knew. They were all put in hack by the Air

Group Commander and restricted to the ship."

'In a voice that could be heard all over the hotel, the Admiral bellowed to his aide, "Get that idiot Beebe on the phone in five minutes; and I don't care if you have to use the Shore Patrol, the Army Military Police or the Japanese Police to find him. I want him on the telephone NOW!"

'The next morning, after three days in hack, the attack pilots had just finished marching lockstep into the wardroom for breakfast, singing the prisoners song when the word came over the loud speaker for Gray and Trum to report to the Air Group Commander's stateroom immediately.

'When we walked in, there sat Marsh looking like he had had a near-death experience. He was obviously in far worse condition than when the ship's CO got through with him. It was apparent that he had been worked over by a real pro.

'In a trembling voice, his only words were, "The hack is lifted. All of you are free to go ashore. There will not be any note of this in your fitness reports. Now get out of here and leave me alone."

'Posters saying, "Thank you Black Jack" went up in the ready rooms. The long delayed liberty was at hand.

'When writing about this cruise, I must pay homage to the talent we had in the squadrons. LTJG Tom Hayward was a fighter pilot who went on to become the Chief of Naval Operations. LTJG Neil Armstrong, another fighter pilot, became the astronaut who took the first step on the moon. My wingman, Ken Shugart, was an all-American basketball player and later an admiral. Al Masson, another wingman, became the owner of one of New Orleans' most famous French restaurants. All of the squadrons were manned with the best and brightest young men the US could produce. The mechanics and ordnance crews who kept the planes armed and flying deserve as much praise as the pilots for without the effort they expended, working day and night under cold and brutal conditions, no flight would have been flown.

'It was a dangerous cruise. I will always consider it an honor to have associated with those young men who served with such bravery and dignity. The officers and men of this air group once again demonstrated what makes America the most outstanding country in the world today. To those whose spirits were taken from them during those grim days and didn't come back, I will always remember you.'

January to June 1952

As the war ground on into 1952 the bombing offensive against the railway system achieved occasional successes. On 12 January F-84s caught three supply trains at Sunchon, racing for the shelter of a tunnel. They blasted the tunnel mouth shut, trapping the trains in the open, and then destroyed the boxcars and at least two locomotives. That night, ten Okinawa-based Superfortresses dropped 396 high-explosive 500-pound bombs on the railroad bridge east of Sinanju across the Chongchong River, rendering the bridge unusable.

On 10 February while leading a flight of three F-86s on a patrol near the Manchurian border, Major George A. Davis Jr. engaged twelve MiG-15s in aerial combat. Davis shot down two enemy aircraft and completely disrupted the enemy formation, but the MiGs destroyed his aircraft as well. Because he executed his attack against superior numbers and successfully protected the fighter-bombers his flight had been escorting, Davis posthumously received the Medal of Honour for his valour.

The third interdiction campaign, Saturate, was planned to be a more continuous campaign, with missions flown both day and night, and with the attacks concentrated into smaller target areas. Saturate ran from 3 March to mid-May, 1952.

On 11 March, fighter-bombers dropped 150 tons of bombs and approximately 33,000 gallons of napalm on a four-square-mile supply storage and troop training area near Sinmak. 5th Air Force operations officers reported this to be the most intensive napalm attack on a single area in the war. That night ten B-29s struck the Sinchang-ni choke point, ten miles east of Sunchon, with ninety-one tons of high explosives, rendering the point impassable. On 25 March, 5th Air Force flew 959 sorties, concentrating on interdiction of the rail line from Sinanju to Chongju and making approximately one-hundred-and-forty-two cuts in the track. On 8 May, in the first of four major interdiction strikes, 5th Air Force fighter-bombers flew approximately four-hundred-and-sixty-five sorties against the enemy supply depot at Suan which was located about forty miles southeast of P'yongyang, in the largest one-day attack since the war began. Over a thirteen-hour period, the UN pilots damaged or destroyed more than 200 supply buildings, personnel shelters, revetments, vehicles, and gun positions. Enemy anti-aircraft fire downed an F-86 on a dive-bombing strike against the Kunu-ri marshalling yards, the first loss of a Sabre on a fighter-bomber sortie. On 13 May, twelve F-86s attacked targets in Sinuiju and Uiju airfields. In the early afternoon, Sabres struck the marshalling yards at Kunu-ri and, in the late afternoon, bombed Sinuiju with 1,000-pound bombs. Unfortunately, Colonel Walker M. Mahurin, commander, 4th FIG, who had led all three missions, was shot down and captured.

On 13 May, in the last of four major interdiction strikes, 5th Air Force flew

275 fighter-bomber sorties against a steel factory complex in the Kijang-ni area, destroying eighty percent of the target. Because of poor weather, an H-19 helicopter from 3rd ARS flew most of a sortie on instruments and picked up a downed Marine Corps Skyraider pilot – one of the first instances of a primarily instruments helicopter rescue.

Unfortunately, heavy enemy defences, coupled with a lack of fighter-bombers (instead of seventy-five assigned aircraft each, the two main fighter-bomber units in Saturate had only eighty total aircraft), caused the operation to swiftly lose effectiveness just as the two Strangle's had.

Air interdiction in Korea was succeeding up to a point, but it was not as successful as was hoped. Several factors were responsible for this. One was that night interdiction was generally unsuccessful because of the lack of proper aircraft, instrumentation, and bomb weight and bomb types, particularly delayed action bombs. Another was the enemy's capability for rapid repairs, along with the anti-aircraft defences they deployed along the roads and rail lines. A third reason was that at this point the war was stalemated. Although brief periods of fighting occurred, too often the enemy was able to choose when he wanted to fight and when he wanted to rest and resupply.

On 12 May 1952, General Mark Clark replaced Ridgway and became the UN/Far East Command Commander. Like Weyland, Clark favoured a more aggressive approach toward the Communists, although restrictions still affected how they could operate. Air power really was the only way to maintain effective pressure without incurring unacceptable loss of life. The first targets of this air pressure strategy were the North Korean hydroelectric plants. All of the major plants, except for the Suiho facility on the Yalu, were targeted initially, but Suiho quickly joined the list. FEAF planned that the first attacks would take place over a two-day period, reducing the time the enemy could react.

They began on 23 June 1952, with 5th Air Force and Navy planes hitting the Suiho plant and when they were over, more than ninety per cent of North Korea's electric power complex was inoperable. However, these attacks caused worldwide repercussions. A number of countries publicly denounced the bombings, thus mitigating the effects of the bombings and causing the Communists to take heart that the war in Korea would remain limited.

The war would continue for another twelve months.

Flying Blind

On more than a few occasions pilots found themselves lost in the skies over Korea. Some would lose their lives while others were lucky enough to find help at hand.

On 2 November 1950, Captain John K. Bassett was flying his B-29 home from a mission over North Korea when his aircraft was struck by lightning in a heavy thunderstorm over the Sea of Japan. The lightning bolt entered the aircraft through the radio antenna, passed through the body of a waist gunner and exited through the side of the plane, causing considerable damage. Apart from blinding and burning the gunner, who collapsed in a state of shock, the lighting destroyed all of the electrically operated radio and navigation equipment, except for the magnetic compass, which seemed to be working correctly.

However, after following the compass course for a while, the navigator informed the pilot that the lightning had magnetized the compass to a point where it was giving a false reading of more than sixty degrees. Bassett later recalled; 'We were still flying on instruments, with a wounded man aboard who needed prompt medical attention and had no idea what our position was. I called over the radio "blind" to any aircraft monitoring that frequency and, in a few minutes, I received a very welcome reply from an RB-29 who was also returning from Korea. I explained my predicament to him and by "homing in" on my radio transmissions, he located us, and in a few minutes was flying on our wing. He shepherded us back to our base without further incident.'

Ken Schechter was just twenty-two years-old when he took off from the USS *Valley Forge* on 22 March 1952. This would be his 27th mission flying the Skyraider with VF-194 the 'Yellow Devils' against enemy marshalling yards and railway tracks. It would also be his last. On the ninth of his planned fifteen bomb runs at 1,200 feet, an anti-aircraft shell exploded in the cockpit.

Instinctively, he pulled back on the stick to gain altitude. Then he passed out. When he came to, he could not see a thing. He was flying blind. There was a severe throbbing in his head and he was in agony from numerous cuts, including his upper lip which was almost severed from the rest of his face.

He called out desperately over the radio, 'I'm blind! For God's sake, help me! I'm blind!' as he continued to climb. Fortunately his room mate on the *Valley Forge*, Lieutenant Howard Thayer, heard the call and saw Schechter's plane about to disappear into a heavy overcast at 10,000 feet. Once he entered the overcast he would be doomed and Thayer called out, 'Put your nose down! Put your nose down! I'm coming up.'

Once the two Skyraiders had levelled off, Thayer looked across at Schechter's plane and saw that the canopy had been blown away and his friend's face was a bloody mess. The area around the cockpit was splattered with his blood and Schechter's face was being buffeted by the 200 mph slipstream. He was also being deafened by the noise from the engine, and sending and receiving radio transmissions was very difficult.

Schechter poured some water from his canteen over his face and for an instant he caught sight of his instrument panel. However, it disappeared immediately and he was blind again. He then jettisoned the rest of his bombs and turned south towards Wonsan, a port on the coast. Thayer told him to prepare to bail out, but Schechter was adamant that to do so would be suicide. On his second mission over Korea, his wingman was forced to ditch in the freezing ocean off Wonsan. He was wearing a rubber immersion-suit, but it was an early version and did not keep the water out. Only one of the two carbon dioxide cartridges that inflated his life vest worked and he was unable to inflate and get into his life raft. Help would be slow in coming to the downed pilot. A rescue helicopter based at Yo-Do Island, a mere five miles away, was unserviceable and the two destroyers that usually lay offshore Wonsan had moved fifty miles northwards. By the time he was pulled from the water ninety minutes' later he had frozen to death. It was not a fate that Schechter wanted to share.

The two planes turned south again and headed towards K-18, a Marine airfield thirty miles behind the front lines. By now Schechter was drifting in and out of consciousness and the blood running down his throat made him want to vomit. He could not reach the morphine in his first-aid kit and it was a race to get him on the ground before he fell unconscious for ever.

Thayer decided to try to guide his friend down to a 2,000 foot dirt airstrip named 'Jersey Bounce' immediately behind the front line that the Army used from time to time for its light planes used for artillery spotting. As he turned his aircraft towards the airstrip, Schechter decided to make a wheels-up landing, rather than risking a collapsed undercarriage as he landed blind.

Thirty feet away, Thayer flew alongside his friend, duplicating his manoeuvres as he talked him down. 'We're heading straight. Flaps down. A hundred yards to the runway. You are fifty feet off the ground. Pull back a little. Easy, easy. That's good. You're level. You're OK. Thirty feet off the ground. You're over the runway. Twenty feet. Kill it a little. You're setting down. OK. OK. OK. Cut!'

Forty-five minutes after the artillery shell exploded in his cockpit, Schechter bumped his plane down on the dirt runway and skidded to a halt in one piece. The plane did not catch fire. It was a good landing all things considered.

Almost immediately an Army jeep with two men pulled up and helped the pilot out of the cockpit and drove him to a shack on the edge of the airfield.

Soon a helicopter arrived and flew him to K-18 where the doctors at the field hospital gave him pain killers and started to tend his wounds. A transport plane flew him on to Pusan where he was taken aboard a Navy hospital ship for immediate surgery. The doctors restored the sight to his left eye, but not the right, and he was retired from the Navy in August 1952.

Sadly, Howard Thayer perished in 1961 in a landing accident in the Mediterranean Sea when both he and his squadron commander flew their A-4s into the water while on a night approach to their aircraft carrier.

Alone on an Island
USAF records show that of the 1,690 Air Force pilots and crewmembers shot down over enemy lines, around one hundred of them made their way back to friendly lines. Colonel Albert W. Schinz was one of them. At the time, he was thirty-three years-old and had flown 174 combat missions in the South Pacific during WWII, downing four Japanese Zeros. When the Korean War broke out he was in the Pentagon and joined the 51st Fighter Interceptor Wing as its second in command. The wing commander was Colonel Francis Gabreski who had 33 and a half kills under his belt from WWII. 'Gabby' was a 'Tiger' whose sole purpose in life was to shoot down MiGs and ensure that the 51st downed more than their rivals the 4th Fighter Interceptor Wing. This meant that all of the other jobs that had to be done; administration, supply, personnel etc, fell to Schinz to take care of.

The extra work meant that Schinz could not fly as often as he wanted to, and in four months he had logged only thirty-eight missions and claimed one-and-a-half MiGs. He decided that 1 May 1952 would be a good time to go up again and see if he could improve on the Wings total of MiG kills. It would be May Day, when the Reds traditionally brought their MiGs out in force so there would be plenty to choose from.

The plan was simple, Schinz would lead the four Sabres of Maple Flight towards the Yalu River where they would turn sharply and look across the border towards the enemy airfield at Antung to see if the MiGs were active. Colonel Albert Kelly, the 51st Group Commander, would fly as his wingman. Kelly was an experienced Second World War pilot on his first Korean combat mission.

Ten minutes before take-off time the pilots eased themselves into their cockpits and checked out their equipment; the jet pilots acceleration suit known as a G-suit, crash helmet with radio and oxygen mask attached, a back parachute, rubber dinghy and an escape and evasion kit containing Korean money and watches and fountain pens to be used as bribes for any friendly

North Koreans they may come across if they were shot down. Unlike most of the pilots however, Schinz did not take a gun or knife with him; a decision he would certainly regret.

The jet engines were started and the yellow generator carts and wheel chocks pulled out of the way as the Sabres taxied towards the end of the runway. At 1230 hours they took off for the half-hour flight from Suwon to MiG Alley. Even though they carried two wingtip tanks, the Sabre burnt so much fuel that the pilots had to stretch it out if they wanted to dogfight with the MiGs and still make it safely back home. Time after time they would flame out on the way back and make a dead-stick landing back at Suwon.

The area looked quiet as they reached the Yalu River, cruising along at 30,000 feet, searching for MiGs below. Suddenly, over the radio came 'sunglints at two o'clock high!' This was bad as it meant the MiGs were above them, at 38,000 feet or more. In fact, there were more than two dozen MiGs dropping their bomb-shaped silver wing tanks and test-firing their cannons before they began their dive on the hapless Sabres below.

Maple Flight toggled their own fuel tanks and pushed their throttles to full power. It was too late though, and the MiGs were soon upon them, cannons flashing. One of Kelly's tanks refused to drop away and this reduced his speed considerably. They could not outrun or outdive the MiGs, so they tried to out turn them instead. Kelly flew in three complete circles to shake the MiGs, but Schinz found them on his tail and the 37mm shells began to rip into his fuselage and wings. Schinz threw his plane into a severe Split-S manoeuvre. He was upside down and pulling through the manoeuvre when a light on the dashboard told him that he had lost his hydraulic system. A flashing red light came on to signify a fire in the tail pipe.

Schinz was at 8,000 feet when the rudder pedals became useless and the joy stick could not be moved forward or aft. Fortunately, he was heading south towards the sea and one of the prescribed safety routes, and by varying the throttle settings he could fly along like a roller coaster, dipping up and down. He discovered to his consternation that his radio equipment was out of order and the other members of the flight had lost him.

It was clear that he would not make it to the Air Rescue outpost at Cho-do Island and, as he descended over the Yellow Sea, he searched the area below for another island to aim for. He was now at 1,500 feet and it was time to leave his dying aircraft. At that moment he flew over a large island with a village at the northern end and two reefs on the southern end that appeared to be unoccupied. He put his feet in the stirrups of the ejection seat, pulled the left arm-rest knob and then the right knob. The canopy blew off and as the plane descended through 1,000 feet he fired his ejection seat and hurtled up and out of the plane.

Schinz should then have released his heavy ejection seat (to which he was still strapped) before popping his parachute, as the parachute is not strong enough to withstand the initial opening shock with both still attached. Usually such an error was fatal, but this time the chute held together long enough for him to release the seat and watch it follow his plane into the water below.

Schinz landed in the water 100 feet south of the island, between the two reefs, and inflated his yellow Mae West life preserver. He had watched a training film in which it was suggested that you could use your parachute as a sail to drag you towards an island, but his feet became tangled in the bottom risers and he began to sink. Without his survival knife he could not cut himself free and for five minutes he fought the chute as it tried to pull him under. Finally he managed to inflate his rubber dinghy and, on the verge of losing consciousness, he dragged himself into it.

When he regained some of his strength he tied his orange and white parachute to the dinghy so he could use it as a distress signal later. Inside the dinghy he found a URC-4 two-way radio, two night-signal flares, dye-markers and shark repellent. He had neglected to fix his escape and evasion kit to his parachute harness and it had been lost when he bailed out. He pulled out the radio, plugged in the battery and extended the antennae. Confident that the other members of the flight would be looking for him, he called into the miniature speaker. The radio was dead. He then discovered that the paddles that should have been with the dinghy were missing and the tide was slowly carrying him out to sea. No matter how hard he flailed his arms the tide carried him away from the island and by now exhausted, he fell asleep.

Seven hours later he awoke in darkness to the sound of breakers. The tide was now flooding and he was drifting slowly up to a rocky beach. The dragging chute was slowing down the dinghy and he released it, discovering in the process that a second survivor's kit was hanging down underneath it. He pulled it aboard and started flailing his arms again, taking five more hours before his raft bumped up onto the beach. He dragged the raft up to some rocks, climbed aboard and fell asleep again.

During the coming weeks Schinz would find himself coming closer to God. When he awoke in his sodden clothes he tried to light a fire with his Zippo lighter, but sea water poured out of the cap and it would not light. He fell to his knees and sobbed. He collected a small pile of twigs and paper and prayed to the Lord to make his lighter work. It did.

When his clothes were dry he decided to explore the island. It was deserted, but had been occupied by civilians and soldiers at one time. He found four huts which he began to dismantle to feed his fire. He also came across three G.I. ration packs which would last him a week. He selected a small lean-to which became 'headquarters', and then found a stream and an old tin can in which to boil water for drinking. In a nearby field he found a few ears of corn, spring onions and a patch of dandelion greens. At least he had food of a sorts and water to keep him going until he was rescued.

One night he heard a B-26 flying overhead and fired one of his flares into the sky. The three bright-red balls soared into the sky, but the plane droned on into the distance. Over the next week he constructed a number of SOS signs from grass and cotton balls found in one of the huts and eventually built one twenty-five feet wide and fifteen feet high.

When his food and firewood supplies began to dwindle, he trudged overland to the village a couple of hours away and lay down on a hill to observe and make sure it was deserted. There were about fifteen large huts and one large building which may have been a church or school house. When he ventured into the place he found it deserted, with filth and the remains of dead animals everywhere. Finding nothing of use, the stench drove him back whence he came.

During his wanderings he found various items of usable junk and equipment such as a rusty shovel, a knife, a G.I. can which was unpunctured, some dishes and a large bag of dried beans that proved edible after a day of soaking and boiling. By now, he had been on the island for fourteen days and his 36-inch waist was now down to 20-inches. He had lost fifty pounds in weight! He decided to move to the deserted village and carried all his meagre belongings in two exhausting journeys. In the morning he awoke and was so weak he could hardly move. He prayed to God for food, and when finished, walked into the nearest hut and discovered twenty-five bags of rice that had not been eaten by the village rats. It was another miracle and it was followed by the discovery of a deep-water well. Soon the rice was cooking and Schinz ate like a pig. He slept soundly for the first time in two weeks.

Schinz found a cave nearby which was full of cotton and he decided to make a giant SOS forty-five-feet long and fifteen-feet wide. Then, while exploring the beach he came across three oil drums, one containing aviation gasoline and the others, diesel oil. He soaked a pile of cotton and rags with the oil and when he saw a plane in the distance, he set it alight and dense black smoke billowed into the air. The plane turned towards the island and circled overhead. Schinz waved his arms furiously at the F-51 then gazed with amazement as it dropped its two wing tanks in the middle of the village and flew away.

Days passed and on 23 May he heard the sound of aircraft again. He lit his fire. All day long, aircraft flew over the island, but there was no sign of a rescue helicopter. For the next week Schinz laboured to make a large MAYDAY sign out of cotton and tried to supplement his rations by catching birds which he ate, bones and all.

On the morning of 6 June, his thirty-seventh day on the island, two F-51s flew over again and Schinz lit his signal fire, dragged his dinghy and Mae West out into the open and stood pointing at them. Again the planes flew away. That evening disaster struck as he heard the sound of a B-26 in the distance and tried to ignite a trip flare that he had found in a slit trench. The flare exploded in his face, temporarily blinding and deafening him and peppering his hands with pieces of shrapnel.

After his hearing and eyesight had returned he set to work with boiling water and a needle to dig the pieces of shrapnel out before they became septic. That night he half buried another flare near the fire, with a trip wire stretched to his bed in his hut and fell into a restless sleep. At 0230 hours he awoke suddenly to find a bright light shining in his eyes and rifle barrels pointing at him. A hand grabbed his shirt collar and then moved to his silver eagles. A voice said in English; 'American! American Colonel!' On hearing the English Schinz shouted, 'I surrender! I surrender!' But the Korean put his arm round him and pounded him on the back shouting; 'OK, OK, OK, we are friends. We help!'

The men were South Korean soldiers who had been on a routine sea patrol around the islands and had spotted the fire as they sailed by. Believing Schinz to be part of a communist unit that had recently occupied the island, they had come ashore to kill him.

In the morning Schinz was taken by boat to Cho-do Island. He had lost forty pounds in weight. It turned out that the Air Rescue people had been watching his activity on the island for some weeks, but they thought it was a communist trap to capture a rescue helicopter as there were no downed aircrew believed to be in the vicinity. However, after the distress signals persisted and the May Day sign was clearly discerned in aerial photographs, a commando party was put together to investigate the island. The South Korean soldiers had reached him first.

Rescuing the Rescuers
On 27 May 1952, Ensign Harlo E. Sterrett from VF-653 was flying a Corsair from the *Valley Forge* on a rail-cut mission near Hapsu, North Korea, when

he was hit by small-arms fire and bailed out of his stricken airplane. He landed near his burning plane on the western side of a hill and waved to his mates as they circled overhead, urgently requesting a rescue helicopter. An HO3S was despatched by the fleet, but low on fuel and operating in marginal weather, the helicopter turned back before reaching the crash site. The following day tragedy struck when the downed pilots close friend, Ensign Roland G. Busch crashed as the tried to locate Sterrett's position. He was thought to have perished in the crash.

The Commanding Officer of Task Force 77, Rear Admiral John Perry, requested the assistance of Marine Helicopter Squadron 161. Their HRS-1 helicopters were superior in performance to the HO3S and would have a better chance of making the rescue.

Within hours, two Marine helicopters were aboard the *Valley Forge* where Admiral Perry briefed them on the situation. The senior Marine, Major Dwaine E. Lengel, informed the Admiral that he considered a rescue attempt to be feasible, but that they would need to go early in the morning in order to maximise the performance of the helicopter. He also informed the Admiral that it was USMC policy that the helicopter is not sent in until the downed pilot was in sight. They were too valuable to risk loitering in the pick-up area and would prefer to make one run in, pick up the pilot and immediately head for friendly lines.

The first ResCap of four F4U-4s was launched at 0730 hours on 29 May and headed for the crash site. Major Lengel, his co-pilot Captain Eugene V. Pointer, and crew chief T/Sgt C.E. Gricks, sat in their helicopter 'HR-1' waiting for news from the ResCap. Four more ResCap planes would be launched with the helicopter and two of them would remain 200–300 feet above the helicopter where they were to do the navigating. An AD-3N Skyraider was to be stationed high above the rescue area to act as a radio relay in case communications were poor.

Whether or not Sterrett was still in the area was open to debate. If the North Koreans had found his crashed plane they would probably be searching for him, and if two days had passed without a rescue helicopter showing up, it was very likely he would have left the area to try to make his own way to friendly lines. He could also have been killed or captured.

However, at 1000 hours, 'Birdcap One', the flight leader of the ResCap, radioed that the downed pilot was in sight and that he had withdrawn into the edge of the woods near the clearing where he had been spotted two days before. At 1030 hours HR-1 was in the air heading on a bearing of 342 degrees for the seventy-two mile journey to the crash site. They were carrying 850 pounds of fuel making a total gross weight of 6,390 pounds, and climbed slowly to 5,000 feet where they would wait for the second ResCap flight. The helicopter crossed the beach at 7,000 feet and an airspeed of seventy knots indicated, with 'Birdcap 7' navigating. Major Lengel later recalled:

'I was flying the helicopter at this time. We were circling the object at about thirty feet and forty knots indicated airspeed. Captain Pointer saw a red object on the ground up the slope from the yellow disc. We were proceeding down the slope when I felt the helicopter begin to lose turns. I immediately started to milk the collective to try to regain my turns. The RPM indicator needle was showing about 2,150. I tried to nose the plane down the slope to pick up some additional airspeed and RPM. The RPM was now down to about 1,900. We were moving down the slope at about forty to fifty knots indicated. There was a tree stump about six to eight-feet high and a foot in diameter directly in our flight path. There was insufficient control to avoid this stump and we hit it with the bottom forward portion of the cabin.

'The helicopter nosed over, and as the rotor blades dug into the ground, the helicopter rolled over on the right side. Captain Pointer and I both began to call for Gricks. We were concerned over his condition as he was not secure in the cabin. Both of us in the pilot's compartment released our seat belts and shoulder harnesses and proceeded to leave the helicopter through the left hand pilot's compartment window. Fortunately T/Sgt Gricks had crawled out of the cabin through the main cabin entrance and was waiting to help us from the helicopter.

'The helicopter was lying over on the right side with the forward part of the main cabin resting on a large rock. This left the main cabin access door about a foot from the ground. The tail cone had been sheared off and had been thrown over the main cabin and was down the slope approximately ten yards. At this point our status changed from the 'Rescuer' to 'Awaiting Rescue'.

'In our pre-flight briefing, we had covered our course of action in the event we were forced down in enemy territory. I immediately secured the URC-4 radio from the cabin and proceeded up the slope to establish contact with Birdcap Leader. I advised him that we were proceeding up the slope and that if he wanted to contact us by radio to fly over and wobble his aircrafts wings.'

The three men were well equipped to spend a couple of hours on the ground. They were wearing Marine Corps issue dungarees and the pilots were wearing field shoes and T/Sgt Gricks a pair of Army combat boots. They were armed with two 0.30-caliber carbines and 100 rounds of ammunition, one 0.45-caliber Thompson sub-machine gun with 200 rounds of ammunition and two 0.38-caliber pistols with twenty-four rounds of ammunition. Two full canteens of water, three survival vests, two first-aid pouches, one first-aid kit, one pair of field glasses, one map case with pencils and three unmarked maps of the area completed the ensemble.

They proceeded to walk up the hill in an easterly direction. The slope was fairly steep and at 7,000 feet altitude they tired easily. They would walk for five minutes and then have to lie down and rest. After about 100 yards they entered the trees where the undergrowth was very thick and continued up the hill to the top of the ridge. They found a clearing about ten yards in diameter and decided to call Birdcap Leader to see if he could locate their present location. With the use of the radio and waving the two yellow life vests that they had brought with them from the wreck, they vectored to aircraft to their position. After being spotted, they asked Birdcap Leader to fly over them in the direction of the nearest large clearing. They were told that it was 100 yards away and one of the planes flew over them to show them the way.

In the meantime, the ResCap planes were making diversionary runs on various surrounding hills, so as not to attract attention to the area of the wrecked helicopter. A North Korean officer was spotted about a mile away on the railroad track, but they did not strafe him because they did not want to stir up the local population any more than necessary. Back at the large clearing the crew spread their two life vests on some bushes where only the planes could see them and settled down for a long wait. Before Birdcap Leader and his flight left the area, Major Lengel asked them to advise the other rescue helicopter on the *Valley Forge* to leave its crew chief behind, in order to lighten the helicopter as much as possible. The Major considered that the reason he had crashed was because he had got into such a position that he was out of the wind and had too little forward airspeed. He also suggested that a second rope ladder be carried and that the helicopter make a low pass, maintaining forward speed at all times.

About two hours later a Corsair flew over and wobbled his wings. Radio contact was established and he advised he was being relieved on station in 15 minutes by Cherry Tree Nine. In due course Lieutenant Wessel, the pilot of Cherry Tree Nine, appeared and gave them the bad news that they would not be picked up that day. The weather was closing in on the ship, but a rescue attempt would be made as soon after sunrise on the morning of

30 May as weather would permit. A method of authentication was agreed upon so the ResCap that found them could positively identify them, in case they had been captured and were being used to lure the rescue helicopter into a trap. The authentication would consist of the ResCap leader asking, 'Dwain, what is your daughter's name?' The reply would be 'Judy'. If radio communication was not established, they were to make a 'J' out of panels on the ground.

Lieutenant Wessel then asked if they needed any more equipment. They replied that they could do with some more water and rations. The ship had already anticipated their needs, and two ADs were inbound with five survival bombs and a water one. The first AD made his run and released his load a little too high and the parachute was carried over the hill and away from them. The next drop was made from lower, but the parachute did not open and the bomb fell into the woods 100 yards away. The other four survival bombs landed 200 yards away. They collected as much of the survival gear as they could carry and moved to a new spot in a densely wooded area.

They then made their first big survival mistake. They had all heard the survival lectures and the two officers had been through the Pickel Meadows survival school and they should have constructed a shelter. However, they were very tired and merely placed their new sleeping bags close together and covered them with ponchos to keep them dry. But underneath them was six inches of dead pine needles and leaves, and when it rained that night the rain ran down hill and seeped under their sleeping bags. By morning they were soaked.

After a sleepless night they constructed a lean-to shelter and collected rain water in a poncho. The weather was wet and overcast and there would be no rescue attempt that day. That evening they heard voices in the distance and heard blows being struck on a metal object. Presumably someone had found one of the survival bombs and was trying to force the lid off.

At 0800 hours the next morning they heard aircraft above them and a flight circled down to break through the overcast. They established radio contact and advised them that a rescue helicopter, HR–13, was on its way. They moved to the edge of the woods and waited until they had the helicopter in sight. They moved down the slope to a clear area and Sergeant Gricks laid out one of the fluorescent panels. Captain Pointer stood by with a yellow smoke flare to give the wind direction and Major Lengel maintained contact with the pilot.

Captain Lesak made one pass to see how the helicopter would react and to judge what speed he would need to make the pickup and went round a second time. They were trailing a ladder and it was moving at about ten or twelve miles an hour across the ground. Sergeant Gricks leapt for the ladder and began to slowly pull himself up the rungs, discarding his carbine and heavy boots on the way. When they came back round to pick up Captain Pointer he caught the ladder, but fell off again. The next time he made a good catch but his weight caused the helicopter to sink and he was dragged for twenty yards before the helicopter gained height.

By now the helicopter was running low on fuel and Captain Lesak radioed that Major Lengel would only have one chance to catch the ladder before they had to depart the area. As the helicopter came in again, Lengel managed to grab the bottom rung but was unable to get a leg onto the ladder and dropped off after 100 yards. He ran back up the slope and asked Lesak to give it one more try.

This time the ladder was a bit lower and Lengel managed to get his leg through the bottom rung and climbed up a few rungs, put both legs through and sat down. Captain Lesak and Lieutenant Wessel climbed to about 6,000 feet and increased their airspeed to sixty knots. Very slowly Captain Pointer and Major Lengel made their way up the ladder. By now their hands were very cold and numb and it was hard maintaining a grip on the ladder. Finally Pointer reached the cabin and Gricks pulled him inside.

As Lengel neared the cabin the heat from the exhaust warmed his hands which made climbing easier, but upon reaching the cabin door he had insufficient strength left in his arms to pull himself in. Both Gricks and Pointer grabbed his jacket but they were weak as well and could not pull him the last couple of feet. He finally managed to get his right leg onto the last rung below the door, gave a big kick and rolled into the cabin. The two officers had been on the ladder for about twelve minutes.

A few minutes later they landed on the cruiser USS *St. Paul* where they refuelled and proceeded back to the USS *Valley Forge*. They landed at midday on 31 May, fifty hours after they took off.

While the rescuers were being rescued, Ensign Sterrett had been discovered by the North Koreans and shot in the leg. He spent three months recuperating before being moved north to the notorious Pak's Palace prison camp, and then on to the Yalu River where he was handed over to the Chinese. In Camp 2 Annex he was reunited with Ensign Busch and they remained in captivity until they were released on 31 August 1953.

B-29 Search and Rescue Mission

The orderly banged on the door at 0700 hours, 12 June 1952, and informed the six enlisted crewmen that they had to get dressed in flight clothing and hurry to the chow hall. They were required to be in the briefing room in forty-five minutes. An RB-29 from the 91st Strategic Reconnaissance Squadron had been shot down the previous evening just off the coast of Vladivostok. Their aircraft commander Captain Eugene T. Hassing was a good friend of Sam Busch, commander of the downed plane and he had volunteered them for a search mission. The briefing officer told them that it was a very serious situation and that a message had been sent to Moscow not to interfere with the search aircraft.

In order to hasten their departure other crews were pre-flighting their plane while they were being briefed. They would not be carrying bombs this time, but they were loaded with extra ammunition for the guns, just in case. At 0830 hours B-29 9727 'Hot to Trot' left the runway at Yokota for the start of a mission which would see them in the air for almost fifteen hours.

It was a very clear day over the Sea of Japan as the plane headed for Vladivostok. In the tail gunner's position Airman First Class Roland Robitaille remembers the aircraft making a wide turn and when it was completed he was looking at the airfield north of Vladivostok. The plane descended and the crew began searching the sea below them for signs of the downed bomber. Robitaille later recalled:

> 'I happened to look at one o'clock low and saw a B-29. I called in "aircraft commander from tail gunner". "Go ahead tail gunner". "B-29 at one o'clock low." Almost instantly, the aircraft went into a left bank. I got to look at it for about fifteen seconds, until the left bank put me in a position that I could no longer see it. In that short time I noticed it sitting high in the water. The aircraft looked fully intact. The aircraft commander must have made a perfect ditching. All men aboard should have escaped injury unless some were hit by gun fire. Shortly after we went into a left bank, our left gunner called in on the intercom that he sees the B-29 directly beneath us. Someone answered for him to get off the intercom and not clutter the intercom. What he saw were the two open doors to the life raft compartments and they were empty. They are situated above the wings in the fuselage.'

Time passed and the plane was still in a left bank, but nothing was being said on the intercom. Robitaille decided to take his chances on a butt chewing and called the aircraft commander again to ask if he had the B-29 in sight yet. 'What B-29?' came back from the commander. Robitaille indignantly reminded the commander that he had called it in and the Radar Operator confirmed that he had heard both the tail gunner and left gunner report the B-29 in the water. By now fifteen minutes or more had passed since they flew over the downed plane and it took time to return to the area. However, the plane was nowhere to be found, but there was a wake in the water that started below them and went directly to Vladivostok. They continued searching as darkness fell, but with fuel running low they had to return to base.

Back at Yotoka the officers were interrogated, but nobody asked any of the six enlisted men any questions. And that was the end of that. It was pretty clear that the crew had ditched successfully and got into their life rafts. Thereafter the Soviets probably captured them and either towed the floating plane to Vladivostok while the search plane was still in the area, or perhaps helped it on its way to the bottom. Perhaps if the aircraft commander had paid more attention to the reports from his gunners, or if there had not been a ten-hour delay between the loss of contact with the plane and the launching of the rescue mission, there may have been more answers.

On 3 July 1952, another B-29 was shot down near the Yalu River and two of the crew were taken to Mukden in China for interrogation. Whilst undergoing questioning their Chinese interrogators suddenly started asking about Major Samuel Busch, the commander of the B-29 lost on 12 June. The questions were repeated a number of times, which is surprising considering that the Major was thought to be lying with his crew at the bottom of the Sea of Japan. Both crew members returned home at the end of the war convinced that the Soviets had Busch and were looking for information to assist with their interrogation. Neither Major Busch nor any of his crew members came home again.

Tales from the Mosquito
The Mosquito Squadrons had one of the highest battle damage rates and one of the lowest loss rates of any airplane operating in Korea. Joe Holden told the author:

'I ended up flying twenty-three combat missions in January 1952 and I received three minor instances of battle damage in that first month. I once figured out that we received battle damage on every seven to eight missions; normally it was a lone bullet hole somewhere on the airplane and since unlike Jet airplanes prop airplanes they have a lot of hollow places, the battle damage was usually insignificant and easily repaired.

'Often you get some battle damage and don't even know it; other times you know for sure. The best close support airplane was the AD Skyraider and the second best was the F4U Corsair usually flown by Marine pilots. The AD (also called Able Dog) carried more ordinances then a whole flight of other aircraft except the Corsair which only carried about the same amount of ordinance as a flight of three other aircraft. We had been requested to strike a series of bunkers in enemy territory. We made a low reconnaissance and there were around a dozen bunkers in the target area. Fortunately, we received a flight of Corsairs. I was informed of the ordinance load and can't recall the exact numbers anymore but it was considerable. The strike went nicely and all the ordinance was on target.

'At the end of the mission the flight commander requested I give a comprehensive "Bomb Damage Assessment". I usually made an estimate which was reasonably accurate and I didn't like to go back into the area so soon since the guys we just bombed were still pissed off. But if they requested a really good one I would go back in and do my best to give exact numbers. I requested that I be given strafing cover when I made my low level pass. I was right behind the lead fighter and was able to keep up with him. The T-6 was red lined at 205 mph. However, I had discovered that it would go much faster than that without breaking up. I suspect that the Corsair was going close to 270–280 mph and I could keep up with him OK. They had done a really good job and wreaked havoc on the target. Just before I pulled off there was a loud bang and the whole airplane shook. I pulled up sharply and the airplane seemed to be handling well, and a quick scan of the parts of the airplane I could see did not reveal any damage. I gave the bomb damage assessment to the fighters and headed for home. After I landed I told the crew chief that I knew we had been hit, but when we looked the plane over we could not detect any damage. A couple of days later when I was getting ready to fly the crew chief came running over and told me they had found where we had been hit. Most airplanes have what are called "Jack Points" which have been beefed up so that the airframe can be jacked up without causing damage to it. There is one for each landing gear. It is a flat place with a nipple on it and there is a dimple on the jack which the nipple fits in to. This is to prevent the area from slipping off the jack. There is a jack point on the T-6 about three feet in front of the tail wheel and the nipple had been neatly severed from the hard point. This explained the loud noise and the impact on the whole airframe.

'All Forward Air Control missions had a two-man crew. The guy in the back was usually an Army member from one of the UN participants. On 1 May I had a good mission. My observer was an Army Captain whose last name I can no longer recall, but his first name was Pat. Our area was on the East Coast and about an hour into the mission we were flying along a road searching for targets. I knew several of the tricks the enemy used to avoid detection and one of their favourites was to space soldiers about the distance you would expect fence posts to be placed apart. If they saw us, they would merely stand in place and we would not usually see them.

'Suddenly Pat told me to look out the right side of the airplane. He said there were a number of vehicles on the west side of the road partially camouflaged. We went down to a few hundred feet and since I was flying I couldn't concentrate on the target. Pat told me there were over thirty trucks and at least two tanks.

'We reported this to our control airplane "Mosquito Shirley", a C-47 with extensive communication capability that had direct contact with Headquarters. We reported what we had found and were informed that we would be receiving fighters shortly. When I heard the call sign "Jell" I knew they were F-84s and we ended up getting three flights for a total of twelve aircraft and directed them on to the target. One pilot told us we were getting anti-aircraft fire, and we saw an explosion on top of a ridge just west of us. He told us the AA had been destroyed and we thanked him. It took about ten minutes to work each flight because we had to mark different areas as the target was spread out over about a half-mile. After the last fighter pulled off we could see several fires and we made a low pass to assess the damage that was inflicted. Pat said he felt most of the vehicles were at least damaged, and confirmed that one tank had suffered a direct hit and was on its side. We were relieved on station and I think the next FAC got a few more fighters. When we got back to the Base we were debriefed and told we were both being submitted for a Distinguished Flying Cross.

'One of my observers was a French Canadian with a heavy accent, named Pierre Lamintain. He was a fairly large person and always carried a Thompson sub machine gun when he flew. There is a funnel-shaped device under each seat which is connected to a hose in case nature calls while you are flying. Hopefully, if you used it, all would drain through the tube and be siphoned out under the fuselage. Apparently Pierre was not familiar with this device. The first time I flew with him I was manoeuvring over enemy territory when a blast of wind came into the cockpit. It took me a few seconds to recover enough to check it out. It seemed Pierre had to go, so he had undone his parachute, opened the canopy in the back, partially stood up in the seat and was urinating on the enemy. I was careful because I didn't want to accidentally bounce him out of the airplane. When we finished the mission and landed, I explained to Pierre in detail what to do the next time he had to pee.

'I had one more mission with my friend Pierre. He was really quite jovial and seemed to be happy to be flying with me. He also had his trusty Thompson sub machine gun with him. We took off and proceeded to the target area, where it was requested that we make a low recce on an area on the back side of a mountain. I did as requested and as I was flying along a trench line I again got a blast of air. This time I realized that Pierre had opened his canopy and decided to shoot at the troops in the trenches with his Thompson. I said a silent "oh shit" and pulled up sharply. Fortunately, Pierre was at the end of his tour and wouldn't get to scare me again.

'I can recall being almost immobilized by fear only once. Most of the danger to our operations was from small arms and it was rare to encounter a serious anti-aircraft capability close to the front where we spent most of our time. There were a few 37mm anti-aircraft weapons, but we usually were low enough that even if we were hit, it merely punched a fairly large hole in the airplane – unless it penetrated a vital part – because it had to travel a greater distance to arm.

'One day I was flying along when I noticed tracers coming up on my left, ahead of me and to the right. All I could do was duck my head and take violent evasive action. Both my adrenalin and heartbeat were elevated. I don't know how, but I exited the area unscathed. I am sure that the weapon was either a captured American quad-mounted fifty-caliber machine gun or a Russian ZPU4. Our airplanes had no armour plate. Some of the guys carried a tent stove-top which was fairly sturdy to sit on, but I always felt since we wore a seat pack parachute, most small caliber bullets would be deflected or absorbed by the parachute.

'Probably the best mission I had during my tour took a long time to come about. While we were still at K-6 one of my friends showed me some pictures he had taken on a mission on the east coast. He told me that he had been randomly looking for targets when he spotted something that looked at first like a normal village. He noticed there were a lot of tracks going into the village and then stopping. When he finally got right on the deck he realized they were not actually houses, but were open underneath and a vehicle was hidden under each roof. At least one was a tank. He called the control ship explaining the target but was told there were no assets available.

'Every time I flew that area I checked what I still think was a planned truck park. Several months passed and I never found any vehicles under the structures. Then one day I flew over the area and there was something under each structure. I estimated that there were at least thirty vehicles in that village. When I was sure I had a good target, I called the control airplane, described the target and asked for fighter resources. I too was told that no resources were available.

'A short time later I got a call giving me a call sign and asking if they could be of help. After a brief exchange I realized I was talking to a Navy Battleship sitting about six or seven miles off shore. I knew that the Navy had several Battleships in the area and there were usually at least two on duty all the time. I believe the one I was working with was the *Iowa*.

'I knew that it would not be prudent to orbit between the ship and the target, so I moved out of the way, gave them a set of co-ordinates and described the target in detail. They fired one round which was very close, so I gave them a correction and they fired a salvo of three rounds which landed in "the village". I was shocked at the power of the rounds. I had fired Navy ships before, usually Destroyers, and I think they used five-inch guns, but this was amazing. To all intent and purposes the target had been obliterated. I don't know whether it was because the structures were so flimsy or because the shells were so powerful, but it was probably a combination of both. In any event the target no longer existed.

'I had detected a couple of times that I was getting ground fire, but had not felt or seen any evidence that I had been hit. I thanked the Navy for their exceptional job, gave them an assessment of the destruction done, and my time on target was about over. I heard my relief check in and about that time noticed a puff of smoke come from the cowling. I asked him to check me over and he joined on my wing and indicated he did not see anything. I got a call from the Battleship asking if they could be of any assistance and I told them I was recovering at K–18, which was only about five minutes' away, and thanked them for their concern. Somewhere along the mission they started to refer to me as "little buddy" and I kind of liked that. I actually started my Military service in the Navy during WWII. I saw several more puffs of smoke before I landed safely at the Marine Base.

'As I taxied to my parking area I noticed the crew chief staring at my airplane. After I shut the motor down he shouted at me, "Where have you been?" As I climbed off the wing I noticed a couple of holes in the airplane and was looking at them when he said, "You haven't seen anything yet". He led me to the front of the airplane which was covered with oil. I noticed several holes in the engine, one through a push-rod housing and another through a cylinder. When we got done counting I had over thirty hits on the airplane and I was told there was no more oil in the oil tank. Some days you are just lucky. If the mission in May was worth a DFC, this should have been worth two!

'I flew my 100th and last mission on 5 August 1952. As I flew my last few missions I got higher and higher and avoided any danger as much as possible. K-47 was almost in a bowl, surrounded by mountains. The runway, if I recall correctly, was about five-thousand feet long. One day two F-84s landed on it, and both pilots did a commendable job by getting their airplanes stopped on the very end of the runway. I had flown the F-84 and knew how difficult it was to stop in that distance. After they stopped, one of them ejected from his aircraft. I can't imagine that it was done deliberately, but perhaps he inadvertently pulled up the ejection handles trying to get out. In any event it occurred. I can't recall how he faired.

'Another time we had been weathered in for over a week and nobody had received any mail. One day we heard an airplane droning around in the soup. Eventually we saw him break out of the clouds and everyone cheered. We all rushed to the parking ramp in anticipation. It was a C-46 and he unloaded four boxes and departed. It turned out it was four cases of cabbage. I sure wouldn't have risked my life to deliver cabbage.'

Attack on the Sui-Ho Dam

When the war began, North Korea had six hydroelectric systems and six small thermoelectric plants supplying electricity to North Korea and to some areas of China. All were on the list of strategically-important targets compiled by the Joint Chiefs of Staff (JCS). On 21 September 1950, FEAF bombers had attacked a plant of the Fusen system near Hungnam, completely destroying its transformers, and thereafter recommended that all of the plants should be destroyed. General MacArthur directed the attacks to proceed, but before that could happen the JCS authorized MacArthur to enter North Korea and advised that targets of 'long-term importance' including the hydroelectric plants, should not be destroyed. In addition, the State Department wanted to avoid provoking the Chinese into entering the war so a ban on bombing the Sui-ho Dam was put in place on 6 November 1950. Even after China's massive intervention at the end of November, the ban was not rescinded, and in fact it was confirmed by the UN Command when the truce talks resumed in July 1951.

A year later things had changed and in order to apply political pressure on the communists at the stalled truce negotiations, the decision was taken to attack the Sui-ho Dam. The dam's generating facilities provided power for much of western North Korea and for the Port Arthur and Dairen regions of northeast China. Located on the Yalu River, the concrete dam was the fourth largest in the world and had been constructed by the Japanese in 1941. It was 2,800 feet (853 m) in length, 300 feet (97 m) thick at the base, sixty feet (18 m) wide at the crest, and 525 feet (160 m) in height. Its reservoir storage capacity was more than twenty billion cubic meters, and it powered six turbine generators each with a capacity of 100,000 kilowatts.

The attack on the Sui-ho Dam was, in fact, a campaign of several large air attacks by Navy, Air Force, Marine and South African Air Force units on thirteen hydroelectric generating facilities that took place on 23 and 24 June 1952. It was followed seventeen days later by another series of air attacks on the capital city of P'yongyang.

Task Force 77 had four aircraft carriers available for the attacks; the USS *Philippine Sea*, the USS *Princeton,* the USS *Boxer* and the USS *Bon Homme Richard*. The first mission was to be launched at 0800 hours on 23 June, with strikes beginning at 0930 on all targets. However, weather reconnaissance aircraft reported unbroken clouds over the Yalu River and FEAF Commander General Otto Weyland postponed the attack twenty minutes before it was due to begin. As the morning passed, however, the weather system moved south, and Weyland ordered the attacks to proceed. This time the attackers could use the heavy clouds as concealment enroute to their targets, with the strikes beginning at 1600 hours.

The carriers launched their propeller aircraft at 1400 hours and their jets at 1500 hours in order to coordinate their arrival at the same time. The Air Force fighter-bombers, having the longest distance to fly, took off at 1430. Because the Sui-ho Dam was located less than forty miles (65 km) from the MiG-15 fighter base complex at Antung/Tai Ton Chao/Phen Chen in China, where 150 MiGs were stationed, a coordinated simultaneous arrival over the targets was crucial in order to limit the effectiveness of the defenders.

The carrier aircraft crossed the Korean coast at Mayang-do, northeast of Hungnam, and flew low over the mountains at 5,000 feet (1,500 m) to mask their radar signature. The propeller and jet divisions rendezvoused approximately fifty miles (80 km) east of Suiho shortly before 1600 and climbed to the attack altitude of 10,000 feet (3,000 m) for a high-speed run-in.

Eighty-four Sabres from the 4th and 51st Fighter-Interceptor Wings were the first to arrive in the Sui-ho target area to provide cover against MiG attack. In a breach from the protocol which forbade flying over Chinese territory unless in hot pursuit of a MiG, a part of the force was tasked with preventing the MiGs from taking off by flying low over their bases. One of the Sabre pilots was Frederick 'Boots' Blesse who would later become a Major General. He later recalled:

'On 23 June 1952 the commanders called in half-a-dozen dependable leaders and said, "There's gonna be a huge air strike today on the Sui-ho reservoir; over 100 air-to-ground airplanes to completely knock out that dam's electrical generating capability. We expect a massive attack from the MiGs when that happens. We'd like to give you twenty-four aircraft apiece, but you only get one flight, and your objective is to keep those MiGs on the ground. Don't let them get airborne for about twenty minutes, while these guys make their strikes and get out."

'Phen Chen was my target. I knew the base like the back of my hand. I had watched it being built, reported it to the intelligence officers, swore them to secrecy and said, "Put an 'X' right here because they're building an airfield there." About once a week I'd whip over to see what they had done. Next, I observed a whole bunch of boxes on the south end and figured they were moving in airplanes. Soon two or three MiGs appeared on the runway. Before I left, they could have flown 200 airplanes from that air base.

'On the day of the raid I got two kills over Phen Chen without firing a shot. Two MiGs were taxiing out when I brought my flight over the field. When they started take-off I kept my wingman high and told the element leader to protect the two of us. I kept the wingman up above me because I didn't know what I was going to run into down there. I came down right over the approach end of the runway and these airplanes were about halfway down. The tower apparently told them, "An F-86 is coming down the runway right behind you." Big, blue, smoky streaks came off the tyres as they tried to stop. But it was too late. They had passed the point of no return. They both ran off the end of the runway. Two airplanes were sticking like that, their engines pumping out jet fuel. They didn't shoot at me, and I didn't shoot at them. I had two airplanes that were totally destroyed at the end of the runway. I climbed back up and we continued to circle. All the other airplanes turned around and taxied back. Not a single MiG took off from Phen Chen that day. And that's exactly what they wanted us to do. Other guys were doing the same thing. I never reported those two kills. And four or five other flights had assigned airfields, keeping those planes on the ground during the air strike.'

Incursions into Manchuria by pilots of the 51st FIW under an unofficial policy nicknamed 'Maple Special' to surprise MiGs over their own airfields, had resulted in heavy losses for the Soviet 64th IAK during the previous months, with at least half of the MiGs destroyed in April and May 1952 shot down during take-offs or landings. The Soviets developed a counter-tactic to cover takeoffs from Antung with combat air patrols launched from Mukden and Anshan, but on 23 June, despite good weather over Antung, inclement conditions prevented covering MiGs from taking off. According to US sources, 160 MiGs took off before the arrival of the covering force and flew deeper into China, possibly fearing that the airfields were the targets, and none attempted to intercept the strike force.

At 1600 hours, thirty-five Navy Panthers began to suppress the anti-aircraft fire from fourty-four heavy caliber guns and thirty-seven automatic weapons emplacements around the dam. Twelve Skyraiders of VA-65 from USS *Boxer* then began their dive-bombing runs on the Sui-ho generating stations, followed by 23 Skyraiders from USS *Princeton* and *Philippine Sea*, releasing eighty-one tons of bombs in little more than two minutes.

Between 1610 and 1700 hours, Air Force jets added 145 tons of bombs on the Sui-ho generating plant with seventy-nine sorties by F-84 Thunderjets of the 49th and 136th Fighter-Bomber Groups and forty-five by F-80 Shooting Stars of the 8th Fighter-Bomber Group.

At almost the same time, fifty-two Mustangs of the 18th Fighter-Bomber Group and the South African number 2 Squadron struck Fusen plants 3 and 4, west of Hungnam, while forty Marine Skyraiders and Corsairs of MAG-12 bombed Choshin No. 4, and thirty-eight Panthers of MAG-33 hit Choshin No. 3. The lower Fusen plants and the Kyosen complex were bombed by 102 Corsairs, eighteen Skyraiders, and eighteen Panthers from the carriers. In all, on 23 June Task Force 77 flew 208 strike sorties and FEAF 202. At 1900 hours, two RF-80 photo-reconnaissance aircraft of the 67th Reconnaissance Wing, escorted by six flights of F-86s, returned to Sui-ho, while Marine F2H-2P Banshee photo-recon planes of VMJ-1 and Navy F9F-2P Panthers of VC-61 overflew the eastern systems to assess damage.

Two F-80Cs of the 8th FBW were battle-damaged by flak over Sui-ho, and written off after crash-landings in Taegu. The only Naval plane lost was a Corsair flown by the squadron commander of VF-63 which was heavily damaged over Kyosen No. 4 and made a water-landing in which the pilot was rescued. A VA-115 Skyraider from *Philippine Sea* had its hydraulic system damaged by flak over Sui-ho and diverted to K-14 airfield at Kimpo, South Korea, for a wheels-up landing, and another from VA-75 was severely damaged when it was struck by debris from a bomb explosion but recovered aboard *Bon Homme Richard*. The only other battle damage reported by the attacking units was by Carrier Air Group 11 off the *Philippine Sea*, a Corsair hit in an accessory compartment over Kyosen No. 3, and a Skyraider at Sui-ho struck by small arms fire.

Most of the targets were re-struck the next day, in both morning and afternoon missions. In the morning missions, Air Force F–84s and Navy Skyraiders attacked Sui–ho, judging it totally destroyed. *Princeton* aircraft bombed Fusen, Mustangs of the 18th FBG hit the unscathed Choshin plants 1 and 2, and planes off *Boxer* and *Philippine Sea* struck the remainder of the Kyosen plants. In the afternoon *Princeton* completed the destruction of Kyosen No. 3, but incurred the loss of a Corsair of VF-192 in the process, although the pilot was rescued at sea.

Approximately ninety per cent of North Korea's power-production capacity was destroyed in the attacks, with eleven of the thirteeen generating plants put totally out of operation and the remaining two doubtful of operating. China suffered an estimated loss of twenty-three per cent of its electric requirements for northeast China, and other intelligence estimates stated that industrial output in sixty per cent of its key industries in the Dairen region failed to meet production quotas. For two weeks North Korea endured a total power blackout.

Both China and the Soviet Union immediately sent technicians into North Korea to repair or rebuild damaged generators, but for much of the summer of 1952 only ten per cent of the energy production was restored, primarily by its thermoelectric plants.

Unfortunately, any effect that the attacks had on the communist hierarchy and its representatives at the truce talks was immediately negated by the reaction of the left wing politicians in London. In Parliament, Labour Party leaders Clement Attlee and Anuerin Bevan attacked the operation as risking World War III. The Labour Party saw an opportunity to cripple the ruling Conservatives and immediately called for a vote in the House of Commons to censure the Churchill government. The government barely survived the vote after US Secretary of State Dean Acheson publicly took the blame, stating the US was at fault for not consulting the British as a 'courtesy'.

The other factor crippling the political effect of the strikes occurred in the United States and was just the opposite of that in Britain. Critics of the Truman administration in Congress quickly seized on the military success of the strikes to question why the attacks had taken almost two years to be approved.

Chapter 4

Slow Crawl to a Truce: July 1952–Sept 1953

Chapter Contents

July to November 1952

ON 11 July, in the first raid of Operation Pressure Pump, nearly every operational air unit in the Far East attacked thirty targets in P'yongyang, in the largest single strike so far of the war. They destroyed three targets, including the North Korean Ministry of Industry, and most other targets sustained heavy damage. Four days later 5th Air Force fighter-bombers flew approximately 175 sorties against the Sungho-ri cement plant and a nearby locomotive repair facility. On the last day of July in one of the largest medium bomber raids against a single target, sixty B-29s destroyed ninety per cent of the Oriental Light Metals Company facility, only four miles from the Yalu River in spite of encountering the largest night-time interception effort to date by the enemy. The attacking bombers suffered no losses.

Psychological warfare efforts continued when FEAF initiated a new general-warning leaflet-drop program over enemy territory. The new leaflet identified specific towns and targets to be destroyed by air attacks. Whether this was done to strike fear into the troops and civilians reading the leaflets or not, it certainly gave the enemy plenty of time to prepare their anti-aircraft defenses. On 30 June in thirteen sorties over enemy territory, C-47s dropped more than twenty-two million leaflets, over one-sixth of all dropped during the month. On 8 August, B-26s flew three night voice-broadcast sorties totaling almost four hours over enemy-held positions near the east coast. On 22 and 23 June, on successive nights, three C-47s flew sixty-minute voice-broadcast sorties near the front lines, indicating a greater emphasis by UN Command on psychological warfare.

On 6 August, FEAF organized Detachment 3, 6004th Air Intelligence Service Squadron, to increase the effectiveness of the evasion and escape techniques taught to pilots. The detachment continued ongoing experiments, such as 'snatching' downed personnel by especially-equipped C-47s. It also emphasized aircrew training in emergency procedures, the use of radios and survival equipment, and the rapidly evolving helicopter rescue procedures.

On the night of 19 August, FEAF aircraft dropped general-warning leaflets over P'yongyang concerning the next night's attacks when thirty-eight B-29s bombed supply areas around the enemy's capital. On 29 August, at the request of the US Department of State, FEAF conducted the largest air attack to date against P'yongyang during a visit by China's foreign minister, Chou En-lai, to the Soviet Union. The State Department hoped that the attack might lead the Soviets to urge the Chinese to accept an armistice rather than expend further Communist resources in the war. FEAF aircraft, protected by USAF Sabres and RAAF Meteors, flew approximately 1,400 air-to-ground sorties. The thirty-one targets sustained moderate to severe damage, but 5th Air Force lost three aircraft to ground fire.

In September, twenty-five B-29s attacked the generator building at the giant Sui-ho power plant which supplied electricity to Manchuria. Prior to and during the attack, USAF B-26s and USN aircraft dropped low-level fragmentation bombs to suppress enemy searchlights, rendering eight of approximately thirty unserviceable. At the same time, four B-29s orbiting to the east jammed enemy radar. Enemy fighters shot down one medium bomber and flak damaged several others, but the B-29s dropped their bombs on target, again rendering the plant unserviceable. FEAF concluded that searchlight suppression and electronic countermeasures probably had saved the B-29s from greater losses.

On 18 November, when the Navy attacked the North Korean border town of Hoeryong in the far northeast, unmarked, but obviously, Russian MiG-15s flying from Vladivostok attempted to attack the fleet. Carrier-based Panthers engaged several MiGs and downed one of them. That night six B-29s from the 98th BW attacked the Sonchon supply centre, thirty-five miles from the Manchurian border. The weather in the target area was clear, and enemy interceptors used new tactics to shoot down a B-29. The enemy dropped flares so that searchlights could lock on to the bomber, and four fighter passes riddled it, forcing its crew to abandon ship over Cho-do.

On 22 November, the 8th FBW lost two F-80s to ground fire during close support missions for IX Corps. One of the pilots, Major Charles J. Loring Jr., leading a flight of four F-80s, was hit near Sniper Ridge by enemy ground fire. He deliberately crashed his aircraft into the midst of enemy gun emplacements, destroying them completely. Loring was posthumously awarded the Medal of Honor.

Fireflies from the Ocean

On 17 June at 0710 hours, Peter Arbuthnot sat in the cockpit of his Firefly preparing for his sixth catapult takeoff. The flight deck crew attached a tension cable to his tail wheel and one to the hook on the fuselage below the cockpit. With the tail wheel locked and the rudder bar held in the central position, Peter selected 'Flaps down' into the take-off position. He advanced the throttle to full power and raised his left hand. On the deck the operations officer raised his green flag and looked expectantly at the young pilot. Gripping the stick with his right hand, he dropped his left arm down towards the throttle. Seeing the pilot was ready to go, the deck officer dropped his flag, signalling to the Bosun to pull the lever to activate the compressed air catapult. The strop holding the tail wheel snapped and with a loud hiss the air-powered catapult sped along the deck, dragging the Firefly with it. With a thirty-knot wind blowing towards him from the front of the ship, Peter needed a speed of ninety-five knots to take off. As he cleared the end of the deck he felt that the aircraft was not going to fly and automatically lowered the nose to pick up speed. He dropped towards the water while the Westland Dragonfly rescue helicopter turned towards him. Slowly but surely the Firefly clawed at the air and began to climb.

Peter retracted his undercarriage and began to climb at 125 knots, raising his flaps in stages and retrimming as required. Underneath his wings he was carrying sixteen sixty-pound rockets and a full load of shells for his 20mm cannons. As his comrades followed him off the catapult he circled the carrier and prepared to go to war.

Peter Arbuthnot always wanted to join the Royal Navy. He did not pass the interview for Dartmouth in January 1944 and joined HMS *Worcester*, the Merchant Navy training college. He left in 1947 and joined Port Line as a deck apprentice. After serving his time, in April 1950 he joined the Navy as an Aviation Cadet. In January 1951, he started his pilots training at RAF Syerston, flying initially Percival Prentices and then Harvard 2Bs. He was awarded his wings in October and went to RNAS Lossiemouth for OFS 1 where he converted to Firefly Mk 1s. In January he transferred to RNAS Eglinton for OFS 2, where he flew the clipped wing Fireflies Mk 4, 5 and 6. During the course he qualified on deck landings after making fourteen in HMS *Triumph*. The course ended on 12 May and all the pilots began a three-week ground-attack course. After a week Peter was given a pier head jump to 825 Squadron, commanded by Chico Roberts, in HMS *Ocean*.

Peter arrived at Iwakuni on 8 June after a five-day flight with BOAC, including three night stops and two engine changes. The CO told him that a batsman would arrive to give him some ADDLs, as on Number 2 Patrol two new pilots from Culdrose were flying their new Sea Furies on board from Iwakuni on Replenishment Day. One went into the barrier, and in the next four days, they each put another into the barrier so they were sent home and Peter was looked on with great suspicion. However, the batsman, Tiny Bowen, arrived and after five sessions said he would take Peter on board.

Peter joined HMS *Ocean* on 12 June at the start of her third patrol. On the first flying day he flew twice in the morning doing deck-landing practice, taking wave-offs whilst aircraft were being shot off the catapult. In the afternoon he went on a coast familiarization with the CAP. Both landings were successful and the following morning he joined Harry Hawkesworth's 32 Flight, flying as Number 4. The flight took off on the second sortie on 16 June. Peter's aircraft carried sixteen sixty-pound rockets, two full nacelle tanks and two sixty-pound heads in the back seat. It was his sixth catapult launch and he thought it was not going to fly, but he scraped it off the sea and joined up with the flight. The target was troop positions in the Hanch'on area. No results were seen.

A patrol lasted ten days, one day steaming to the operational area - usually some twenty minutes flying from the South West point of North Korea - four more days flying, followed by a day's replenishment from a RFA tanker, then four more days flying and a day's return to either Sasebo or Kure. The carrier remained in port for six or seven days, then off again to replace the American carrier. On a normal flying day HMS *Ocean* made six sorties, usually comprising ten Sea Furies, of which two were acting as CAP, and four Fireflies. 825 Squadron had twelve aircraft while 802 had twenty-four Sea Furies, and there was a Dragonfly helicopter for search and rescue. The Sea Furies carried either 500 or 1,000lb bombs. If the latter, then they used RATOG for takeoff. The Fireflies carried sixty-pound rockets; a maximum of sixteen, but usually twelve. This was reduced to eight from August due to a shortage of rockets. All these has been manufactured in 1944-45 and usually failed to explode because the detonator pins must have seized up. At the beginning of August 825 Squadron was dropping 500lb bombs. Peter's log book shows that he dropped a total of eight bombs, of which six were dummies and two had delayed-action fuses. The bombers' targets were mainly bridges, as the North Koreans were very good at repairing them during the night.

On 11 July, some 1,250 sorties were flown by the UN forces against P'yongyang, the North Korean capital. HMS *Ocean* flew two sorties of eight Fireflies and sixteen Sea Furies each. Chico Roberts led both strikes and Peter flew as his Number 4 on both strikes. The Fireflies target was a number of large crates in a railway yard in the southeast of the capital. The CO approached the city from the east at 14,000 feet. As he got near he began a gentle dive towards the target. There was very heavy radar-controlled 88mm flak. Peter could smell the cordite and was hit by shrapnel; luckily on the nose fairing of his starboard nacelle tank. As the flight reached 8,000 feet, Chico rolled into his attack. Peter became 'attached to the target' and did not fire at 1,500 feet, but at 900 feet – much to the fury of Dave Williams, leading the second Flight. However, all rockets landed in the target area. On the afternoon strike there was much less flak and the rockets again landed in the target area. No *Ocean* aircraft were lost and Peter's shrapnel was the only damage.

On 27 July Peter was on a sortie with 32 Flight. When they reached the coast the cloud base was 1,700 feet so Harry took the Flight through cloud, steering northeast. They reached the top at 5,000 feet, and as they passed north of Chinnampo the cloud broke up to 4/8ths. Harry found a large warehouse, which was rocketed. The Number 3, Pete Watkinson, was hit and his radiator began to leak. While making for the coast, the Flight was bounced by three MiG-15s. Bob Brand was hit in the port wing tip and Pete was hit in the starboard tail plane, causing a hole some three feet wide at the root. This damage made the tail plane flap about, making smooth flying difficult. The Number 3 ditched safely off Cho-do Island, while Peter made a wheels-up landing on the emergency strip known as 'Tinfoil'. Harry and Bob returned to the carrier after watching over Number 3's ditching.

The tenth, and last, patrol ended on 31 October with the discovery of petrol contamination. Peter had started his engine for his 120th sortie when a flight deck man signalled 'cut' and that was the end of his operations. Later in the afternoon the CO and his Flight made the final sortie. The ship returned to Sasebo and then sailed to Hong Kong, where her aircraft were handed over to HMS *Glory*.

Sea Furies from Glory

Alan Leahy joined the Royal Navy in 1943 and was awarded his wings in 1944. When he arrived in Korea in 1952 he joined 801 Squadron on HMS *Glory* for its third and last tour of the war. Lieutenant Leahy was the third senior man in the squadron, as the Weapons Officer and a Division (Flight) leader. At the top of the tree was the Squadron Commander, followed by the Senior Pilot, Alan and two other Division leaders. Of the eighteen pilots on the squadron, seven of them would die in combat and one would become a prisoner of war. He told the author:

'As far as weapons were concerned, there was not a lot of choice at that time. We had 20mm cannon and three-inch rockets plus 500-pound and 1,000-pound bombs, but we only used the cannons and 500-pound bombs. You could not use rockets and bombs at the same time. If you wanted to use rockets you had to take the bomb racks off first. It was very time consuming and not the thing to do on the flight deck in the middle of winter. The Fireflies used 20mm cannons and rockets. We never got to use napalm, as the Americans did.

'We flew missions from our carriers off the west side of Korea and the Americans flew from the east side. We performed ten-day patrols, then returned to Japan to Sasebo or Kure to resupply, then back again. While we were away, the Americans filled in with two small carriers, the USS *Badoeng Strait* and USS *Bon Homme Richard*.

'The missions flown by the Sea Fury pilots fell into five categories. One was Interdiction, which meant the disruption of both road and rail traffic on our side of the country to help stem the flow of supplies to the enemy front line. This included the destruction of bridges and tunnels. Combat Air Patrol was usually flown in pairs, waiting for enemy aircraft to appear.

We always had two aircraft in the air on CAP, not necessarily to intercept enemy aircraft, but if anyone was shot down the CAP would be sent right away to try to keep the enemy troops away from them while a rescue was organised. TARCAP was short for Tactical Air Reconnaissance Combat Air Patrol and was mainly applied to the task of making life better for the Americans occupying Cho-do Island where powerful air defence radar was based to warn of aircraft approaching from China. Enemy artillery was hidden in caves in cliffs on the coast line opposite Cho-do Island, and when they emerged to open fire we would try to bomb them. Infiltration missions included targets such as troops hiding in villages or schools. The locations would be passed to us by Partisans operating in the North. The pilots often worried that the huts they were bombing were occupied by innocent civilians, but when one of the pilots, "Pug" Mather, was shot down and taken prisoner, he passed through a number of these villages and noted that troops and guns were indeed concealed in the villages. Bombardment Spotting where the pilots would correct gunfire from UN ships could be interesting to say the least. One such event occurred when the Senior Pilot worked with the battleship USS *Missouri*. You went through a routine where they would say "Ready" and "Firing" and you would look for the splash. The Senior Pilot looked for the splash, but he could not see a thing. So he looked around and saw that their first salvo was splashing down seven or eight miles south of the target. When he told the "Mighty Mo", they switched off and would not talk to him again. I was the next pilot out and I positioned my aircraft where I could see the target quite clearly. Not long after hearing the command "Fire" my Sea Fury jumped about twenty to thirty feet up in the air, and when I looked I could see a big shell slowly rotating as it hurtled away to the east. When I told them they switched off on me as well. The next guy out was called MacAndless and he managed to convince them that they were miles off target. Eventually they got the coordinates right and their salvo of 16-inch shells knocked hell out of the caves opposite Cho-do Island.

'Close air support of the Commonwealth front was another role for us. We would be directed to the target by a "Mosquito" forward air controller flying a North American Harvard who would fire a smoke rocket and then describe the target in relation to where the rocket hit. After the attack the "Mosquito" would give us a bomb damage assessment of what we had achieved. Hitting traffic on the roads was very difficult as the Chinese moved most of their supplies by night. So they started launching us about an hour before dawn in the hope of catching a convoy with its lights on. You would roll into your dive at about 4,500 feet and release your bombs at 1,500 feet, but then the convoy lights would go out and the other three members of your division would not have a target. It was impossible to join up again in the dark, so they would go off and look for their own targets.'

Alan was a victim of the faulty ammunition problem that occurred at various times during the war:

'I was carrying out a strafing run and firing at the target when there was a hell of an explosion in my port wing. Some of the 1940 ammunition had exploded in the barrel. It was a problem that caused the loss of at least one Firefly as the ammunition exploded nearer to the fuselage, resulting in the loss of a wing. When I looked out of the cockpit I could see right through the wing and when I got back on the ground I could stand up through the hole. The explosion had also shredded my tail plane, which caused it to flutter – I thought I had been hit by flak. I got it back to Paengnyong-do, the island off the south coast and landed on the beach.

'There were three ways to take off from an aircraft carrier. The first was a free take-off when one had the full-length of the runway to use; the second was a catapult take-off, to be used when the carrier had a full suite of aircraft. However, the light carriers only had one steam catapult which could become unserviceable. If this happened the only alternative was RATO – Rocket Assisted Take Off.

'Although the system was efficient, it could be damned dangerous. One of the problems was the location of the RATO Gear firing button. The decision was originally made to fit the button at the end of the throttle twist grip, replacing the radio press-to-transmit (PTT) button. However, after one pilot pressed the button by mistake, thinking he was activating his radio and launched his aircraft at the carriers island and causing the death of one man who was blown over the side, it was moved. However, the pilot could no longer see the button once it had been moved to its new position above the contacting altimeter. He had to duck his head to see it tucked under the coaming over the instruments.'

Lieutenant Leahy came a cropper one day in 1952 when he attempted his first RATOG launch from HMS *Glory*:

'When it became my turn to be launched, I went up to full power with the RATOG master switch ON and the tail wheel control locked. When cleared to go I took off down the deck towards the man who marked the spot where the rockets were to be fired. When I reached the firing point I depressed the firing button. The rockets should fire simultaneously within half-a-second of pressing the button. If they do not do so, the take off should be abandoned. In my case, the rockets did not fire.

'The briefing had been very clear. "If your rockets do not fire, close the throttle and apply the brakes and you will stop before you reach the end of the deck." However, I did not do as briefed and looked under the coaming to see if I had put my finger in the punkah louvre next to the RATOG firing button by mistake. By the time I looked up again, it was too late. My Sea Fury taxied over the bow with my brakes still hard on.

'When my Sea Fury struck the water, I could see from the disc of the propeller hitting the sea, that we were vertical. When I opened my eyes the cockpit was full of water and bubbles, and I started to get out. I released the seat harness and then the parachute harness and stood up in the cockpit. The speed of the aircraft sinking and turning upside down forced me back against the cockpit hood, which had been open for take off. On the front of the cockpit hood were two spigots, designed to stop the hood from fluttering at high speed by slotting into the top of the windscreen. However, I was trapped by these spigots sticking into the back of my Mae West and thus I had to get back down into the cockpit and turn around facing the tail so that I could cover the spigots with my hands and then lever myself out using the canopy. Clear of the aircraft, I saw it sinking upside down beside me. All this time I had been waiting for the ship to hit one or the other or both of us.

'Now that I was clear of the aircraft I thought that it might be better to stay where I was until the ship passed me, although that thought did not last more than a fraction of a second as I was running out of breath. Inflating my Mae West, I swam up and at an angle away from where I thought the ship was. I surfaced about twenty to thirty feet away from the ship's side, abeam the starboard propeller, and took a huge breath only to end up choking badly. My oxygen mask was still strapped to my face and the tube attached to the mask was still under the surface. After taking the mask off and getting my breath, I climbed into the dinghy and waited for the lifeboat from the attendant destroyer *Chieftain* to rescue me and then return me to *Glory*.

'On reflection, I think that most occasions of RATOG failures on board ships were brought about by the pilot failing to make the master switch. I cannot remember if I made the master switch or not, but I believed that I had. Nevertheless, it was certainly my fault that I went over the bows instead of stopping on the flight deck. Next time I tried, the whole system (including the pilot) worked perfectly.'

Night Invader

When Lieutenant Robert C. Mikesh arrived at airfield K-9 at Pusan, South Korea, in August 1952, B-26 Invader tactics were about to change. The Communists moved their men and supplies by road and rail under cover of darkness, rather than during daylight hours and new tactics were being drawn up to try to counter this. Up to this time, the procedure was to carry out a low-level dive at moving truck lights for a strafing or bombing run. However, at the sound of the aircraft, the drivers would turn their lights out, leaving only the pilot's memory as to where the trucks might be. In addition, anti-aircraft positions now covered most of the frequently used routes and the cost of B-26s shot down compared to trucks destroyed made a change of tactics inevitable.

In the future, level-bombing runs from an altitude of not below 4,000 feet above sea level in mountainous terrain were the order of the day. The squadron that Mikesh had joined – the 37th Bombardment Squadron – had just been stood down from flying combat missions in order to train in the synchronous level bombing techniques that would be used on future night missions. The other two squadrons of the 17th Bombardment Group would continue to fly daytime missions and then transition into the new night-interdiction tactics. Their sister organization, the 3rd Bombardment Group at Kusan, covered the western half of the North Korean supply routes, and their 13th Bombardment Squadron was also stood down for training in the new tactics. Morale in the two training squadrons was not very high as it meant that the crews would now take longer to achieve the fifty combat missions necessary before they could return home to the United States.

It was 10 December 1952. First Lieutenant John L. Middleton, the Bombardier of RB-26C 44-34517, peered into the darkness through the glass windscreen in the nose of the bomber and keyed his mike, 'Skipper I can see the lights of K-3 down below.' This was the airfield where the Marine units flying the F7F-2N Tigercat and F4U-5N Corsair night fighters were based, and at times flew night-interdiction missions along the coast of North Korea, while the B-26s flew further inland. They worked under flares fired from ships lying off the coast and their light could easily be seen if they were working their area.

'Hello. HOT HOUSE – PACIFY EIGHT ONE. Estimating King Four six at three four – prebriefed inbound. Over.' The pilot, twenty-three-year old First Lieutenant Robert Mikesh, turned the plane north-westward for the thirty-four-minute journey to airfield K46, and thence on to K47 which he was to fly over eleven minutes later. On reaching K47 he switched over to the White Channel and reported to BROMIDE – the call sign for the Tactical Air Control Centre that they would be working with that night, and who would monitor their mission over enemy territory.

As they approached the stationary front line, the invisible line between the opposing forces, they saw the hundreds of searchlights shining on strategic points or on the faces of the opposite hills to reflect light throughout the front-line area. They formed an irregular pattern of lights from one coastline to the other. Between the front-line and the Bomb-Line, the bombers had to be under radar surveillance and with ground approval to drop any bombs, to ensure protection for any UN patrols that may have penetrated enemy territory. This time, however, their targets were way beyond the Bomb-Line, further north where the enemy was trying to bring supplies south to the Chinese and North Koreans dug in opposite the UN lines.

'Turn right. Zero-one-one. This should line us up on the roadblock', came the next comment from the Bombardier. Earlier that evening, and indeed every evening, a 'last light' fighter bomber would have made one or more road cuts at strategically-selected locations along the enemy supply lines. This was a major aspect of the new night-interdiction strategy. Road cuts were usually made at a fork in two roads, a ford, or better still, at a road along the side of a hill that was susceptible to hill slides. Four well-placed 500-pound general purpose bombs carried under the wings of the B-26 could cut the road and on successive passes, the six internally carried M-29 canister bombs would open on the way down and scatter small 'Butterfly' bombs over the roadblock area. These would go off at timed intervals – sometimes lasting up to thirty-six hours – to discourage those making roadside repairs. Once the roadblock was in place, subsequent bombing missions would be laid on with the intention of catching traffic backed up, making an easy and lucrative target.

As they approached the area where the road cut should have been, there was nothing but darkness. 'Bob, I don't see one light down there', said the Bombardier. 'Let's swing around for two passes and drop the wing bombs, two at a time, just to see if we can hit something that might be there.'

The 260-pound bombs exploded with a flash as they hit the ground, but there were no secondary explosions from trucks carrying fuel or ammunition. 'Let's try the Recce route Bob and see if we can do better there', said the Bombardier, and they turned northeast towards RED 11, a well-travelled highway where they had achieved success before.

RED 11 ran generally north for 25 miles towards Wonsan, and like most supply roads on the eastern half of North Korea, it followed a valley flanked on both sides by a ridge of steep-sided mountains. They were in luck tonight. As they approached from the southwest they could see several clusters of headlights from truck convoys moving south.

The Bombardier was already bent over the Norden bomb sight, synchronizing on something moving on the ground below. His instruction 'Follow the PDI now, Pilot' was followed by a half-standard turn to the left as Mikesh centered the Pilot Direction Indicator needle. This was an instrument that took its reading from the bomb sight itself, giving the pilot the direction and amount of left or right correction to make.

'Open bomb bay doors', came the next instruction from up front. 'Steady, steady. Bombs away!' came the cheerful cry from the nose section. Mikesh closed the doors and counted up to seven, before pulling hard left and looking downwards. He could see the flashes as the bombs exploded around the lights of the trucks in the convoy. Then two large yellow bursts indicated secondary explosions from fuel or ammunition cargoes on the trucks.

Suddenly, 'BREAK LEFT! BREAK LEFT!' came urgently from the gunner A2C. Kitchen and Mikesh twisted the wheel hard left to avoid the line of bright 'ping-pong balls' floating up towards them. Then more anti-aircraft shells were off to the left of them and they turned hard right and dived to change altitude, in case the AAA was radar-guided. Each bright ping-pong ball was a tracer round, so the gunners could see its path in the darkness. But for every one tracer there were five others that could not be seen.

As they continued north they could see more truck headlights in the distance, but they suddenly switched off as the B-26 approached. The Communists had an alarm system of sentries on the hills, who would fire flares as the bombers approached, warning them to turn their lights out. Another convoy was visible in the distance, but before they turned their lights off the Bombardier had obtained a synchronization on the middle truck and the Norden bombing system was about to earn its keep.

A flick of a switch and two more bomb shackles released four clusters of six twenty-eight-pound fragmentation bombs. If any one of them exploded within 100 feet of a truck, its destruction was virtually ensured. As they banked hard left, they saw a big ball of well-sustained orange flame – possibly a fuel-supply point of forty-five-gallon drums rather than a supply truck.

'Wow! Did you see that?' asked Mikesh as he turned hard right so that Kitchen in the right seat could see the results of their efforts.

The next three drops had negative results as the trucks turned their lights out before they could get lined up on them, but they dropped anyway and hoped for the best. By now there was only thirty minutes of their two-hour sortie remaining, and they were down to two clusters of bombs. At the northern end of the route they came across another convoy and all of the lights went out except one. The Bombardier kept it in the centre of the cross-hairs, and adjusting for the speed of the truck, released the last few bombs.

They sparkled as they exploded, but there were no secondary explosions. The seconds passed, and then suddenly a blue flame appeared, followed by another as something exploded – gasoline, alcohol, perhaps. It was important to record the colour of the explosions at the post-mission debriefing. It had been successful after all.

Even though they had no bombs left, they decided to remain in the area anyway to harass the supply trucks crawling southwards. Over to the east along the coast they could see several streams of anti-aircraft fire. Someone was catching a packet and it was not until the morning that they would discover that one of their B-26 crews on their forty-eighth mission was lost that night in the area. They may have witnessed the lethal stream of anti-aircraft fire that shot them down. Few crew members survived from downed B-26s.

As they headed north, there was a sudden flash from behind them, followed by another, then another as they crept closer. 'BREAK! BREAK! BREAK!' came from the other two crew members, and Mikesh turned sharp left to try to shake the exploding flak. One last shell exploded in the area that they had just vacated. It was a narrow escape. This was flak like they had never experienced before. Russian-made radar-tracking guns, probably operated by Soviet gunners, rather than Chinese or North Korean.

Mikesh turned the Automatic Direction Finder needle from the stationary position to the homing mode. It swung to the nose position to lead them to the friendly Mike-Roger homing beacon on the south side of the front line. As they crossed the bomb line, they called BROMIDE to tell them they were on the way home to K-9.

When they came in to land with snow falling and a strong cross wind, the visibility was so bad that they had to land under GCA (Ground Controlled Approach) radar guidance. This was essential with minimum visibility as there were hills to the north and both sides of the airfield, which made a go-around a risky prospect. They were the last aircraft home that night and before the storm had finished, it had dumped ten inches of snow on Pusan, the heaviest snow fall in fifteen years.

In the days immediately following the snow fall, two B-26s crashed on take-off two nights apart. They struck the banked snow at the sides of the runway, resulting in nose-gear failures which then broke off the navigator's nose sections. Both navigators were killed in the accidents, and it subsequently became policy that no one would occupy the nose compartments on take-offs and landings.

The war of attrition would continue into 1953, while peace negotiations slowly progressed at Panmunjon. Finally, 'Operation Little Switch', the first exchange of sick and injured prisoners, took place in April.

At last there was light at the end of the tunnel.

B-29 Bail Out – The Chances of Survival

Dozens of B-29s were lost during the Korean War. Sometimes all of the crew survived; sometimes none of them did. There were many variables that could influence the chances of survival. In theory, if you bailed out at height, your chances of survival were better than bailing out at low level. However, sometimes the theory did not work out in practice.

It was 6 August 1952 and 98th Bomb Group B-29 44-2237A 'Tondemoni' (which means 'Never Happen' in Japanese) was first in the queue for take-off. As they carried out their take-off checks they realised that they had a bad mag drop on Number 4 engine. After discussion with the flight engineer, it was decided that it would burn off after warm-up and they began their take-off roll. However, the engine began to smoke badly and burst into flames as they cleared the runway. To try to gain some altitude they salvoed the bombs and were at approximately six-hundred feet when the Number 2 engine blew.

The bail-out alarm sounded. They had a passenger in the rear and he was the first to go out the right rear door. Tail Gunner Kerrin H. Coyne was right behind him, but because the flames were now trailing back past the door, he had to wait until he had fallen through the fire before pulling his D-ring, to prevent his parachute from catching fire. He went out head first and received some rope burns to his neck due to the risers jerking him into an upright position. He swung once in his parachute then hit the ground almost immediately, narrowly missing some high-voltage lines nearby.

He spent some time trying to find the rest of his crew. The plane landed very close and was burning furiously with the full load of fuel on board, and the ammunition started to explode. The CFC Gunner, Left Gunner and Right Gunner had followed Kerrin out of the rear door and they landed close together. The aircraft commander was the first out of the front, followed by the Navigator, Bombardier and then the Pilot. The Pilot had to go back and regain control to straighten up the aircraft. He also tried to get the Flight Engineer to exit, but he froze at his station. The radar operator never got out. The survivors were taken to Yokota Hospital where they were given sedatives and whiskey.

On 7 October 1952, an RB-29 from the 91st SRS was on a reconnaissance mission over the southern Kurile Islands north of Hokkaido, Japan, when it was intercepted by Soviet fighters from the 368th Air Defence Fighter Aviation Regiment, scrambled from South Sakhalin airfield. They intercepted the plane south of Demin Island and alleged that the RB-29 opened fire on them first. Two La-11 fighters attacked the aircraft and it went down into the sea. They claimed that the plane had violated their airspace on three occasions and they shot it down. The pilots reported that no parachutes were seen and the eight man crew were never located.

Night was falling on 19 November 1952 when B-29 44-86392 took off from Yokota Air Force Base in Japan and set course for North Korea. Their target for that night was the Sonchon Supply Area. 6392 and one other from the 345th Bomb Squadron, 98th Bomb Group, were to approach the target from the east at 23,000 feet while another flight of three B-29s were to approach from the west side, with both flights arriving over the Initial Point at 0029 hours. If all bombers arrive over the target at the same time, the anti-aircraft defences cannot concentrate on one bomber and the chances of survival are greater. Tonight, however, all was not going to plan. Unexpectedly heavy head winds had delayed the two ships and when they arrived over the target, the other flight had dropped their bombs and begun their flight home, without receiving any flak or being intercepted by fighters.

The two bombers began their approach to the target at 23,250 feet and dropped their bombs sixteen minutes later at 0045 hours. As the last bombs cleared the bomb bay they took photographs for the air intelligence guys and broke away to the left for the return trip. Just as they reached a heading of 212 degrees, a flare exploded approximately five-thousand feet above the aircraft, and at the one o'clock position. As they made a sharp left banking turn to avoid the flare's light, a second flare exploded between the ten and eleven o'clock position again at about five-thousand feet above.

Major Sawyer, the aircraft commander, made a sharp right turn and immediately a third flare exploded at the same altitude as the two previous flares and at the two o'clock position. Within seconds, a score of searchlights began turning towards the aircraft. The second bomber in the flight later reported that a total of seventeen searchlights were locked onto them. Technical Sergeant Morton, the ECM Operator, frantically tried to jam the radar-operated searchlights and called the pilot in frustration that, 'There are too many frequencies and I haven't enough equipment to jam them all!'

Just after the searchlights lit up the plane, the Bombardier First Lieutenant Peck called out, 'Two fighters at twelve o'clock high!' The tail gunner A/2C McToughlin then called out, 'Two fighters sitting out at six o'clock high.' About thirty seconds later an unidentified fighter made a firing pass at the aircraft from six o'clock level, but no hits were observed. The four bursts of what looked like red tennis balls floated away into the darkness. Thirty seconds later a second fighter came in from the same direction, but this time the number 2 engine was hit and started smoking heavily.

All the time the gunners in the Superfortress were blazing away at their attackers. Despite this, as Major Sawyer was feathering the number 2 engine, they received a third pass from the same direction and number 3 engine caught fire. As the aircraft commander feathered that engine, a fourth fighter opened fire on the plane, scoring hits on the leading edge of the right wing between the leading edge and the number 3 engine. The wing started to burn at this point. Then the searchlights went out and the fighter attacks stopped.

At the time the last pass was made, the radar equipment was momentarily useless because they had been performing violent evasive action which blanks out the equipment. After they levelled out, however, they were able to observe that they were over and coming down the west coast of Korea. The very first definite fix that they got that could be given to the directing forces was 110 miles northwest of Chinnampo. The reason that that was necessary was that their IFF (Identification Friend or Foe) was inoperative and had been for the whole flight, so they could not show May Day.

Major Sawyer tried to gain height as they limped away from the target area, and the Flight Engineer Technical Sergeant Tiller, and the right gunner A/1C Whitman, anxiously gave a running report on the fire and how close it was getting to the fuel tank. Time was now running out and Sawyer notified everyone to prepare to bail out as the pilot First Lieutenant Swingle, started his distress calls on Dog Channel.

Sawyer told the crew to make sure that they had their dinghies on, because they would probably be in, or close to, the water when they landed. 'Dutchboy' was contacted on Dog Channel right after the searchlights went out and as they were passing a point approximately ten miles north of the Chongchon River they were given a heading of 200 degrees as an initial steer. As they passed abeam of P'yongyang, the North Korean capital and five miles offshore, a corrected heading of 220 degrees was received from 'Dutchboy'. At that time the aircraft was descending at a rate of 500 feet per minute, at an indicated airspeed of 280 miles an hour. At a point ten miles northwest of Chinnampo a third corrected heading of 236 was received as the crew prepared to abandon their aircraft. The route southwards generally paralleled the coast, keeping about five miles from the shore at all times.

The situation was so critical that the crew could be given the bail-out order at any time and thus they did not take the time to remove their parachutes in order to put on anti-exposure suits and then refit and readjust their parachutes. It was to have terrible consequences.

On board, the aircraft was kept trim and flown manually until two minutes prior to actual bail-out. The radar equipment continued to function and the VO (Video Operator) First Lieutenant Winchester was able to make radar fixes up to the time he left his station to bail-out. Finally, the systems began to fail; the vacuum system and the majority of the generators were out; the fluxgate compass was out, and shortly after receiving the last steer, the VHF radio faded out. The last message received by 'Dutchboy' was that they were sending up flares. Major Sawyer called them a short time later and asked them if they had shot off the flares, but by that time the radio was already dead and he got no answer. Not seeing any flares he thought he was too far from Cho-do to make it.

By this time the fire was burning in the wing very close to the gas tanks and streaming back as far as the right scanners blister, and the final decision to bail out was made. The boys in the waist were ready to go out; they were lined up and requested the bomb bay doors be opened. The radio operator requested that the forward bomb bay be opened so he could bail out. The tail gunner came forward to get rid of his heavy winter flying equipment. The ECM operator and the assistant radar operator were lined up at the after escape hatch ready to go.

Approximately two minutes later, although Sawyer had not seen any flares, he gave the order to bail out, both verbally, and on the alarm bell. The actual location of the island of Cho-do was unknown, but he felt that they could wait no longer. Shortly before he gave the order to bail out, the Navigator First Lieutenant Bird called and asked that he hold it off as long as possible as he had popped his chest chute, necessitating his changing it to a spare back-type chute. There was no spare chest chutes so he had to change harness too.

About ten seconds prior to the time Major Sawyer called for bail out, the ECM operator, who was to be the first one out of the rear, misinterpreted something that was said and went out. The bail-out was very fast in the back.

Three men went out ahead of the VO through the after escape hatch. Just before he followed them, he called the Aircraft Commander and told him that he was leaving and was the last one left in the rear of the aircraft.

As the VO made to leave he found he was too close to the aft end of the escape hatch and the dinghy caught. He had to pull himself back in and move towards the front of the ship to go out of the front side of the hatch. He did not know it at the time, but the delay may have taken him nearer to the island below and thus saved his life. When he hit the rough slip stream he pulled the rip cord and felt the shock as the parachute opened above him.

As the plane descended below 4,000 feet the crew bailed out, as follows:

After escape hatch; ECM Operator, Spare VO (passenger), Tail Gunner, VO.
After bomb bay; Central Fire Controller, Left Gunner, Right Gunner.
Forward bomb bay; Radio Operator, Navigator.
Nose wheel hatch; Spare Aircraft Commander (passenger), Bombardier, Engineer, Pilot, Aircraft Commander.

The estimated time to clear the aft section was forty seconds, and the front section, one minute. At the time Sawyer bailed out, the aircraft was at approximately 2,800 feet and he observed it making a slow 270 degrees turn to the left and it hit the water approximately half-a-mile north of the northern tip of the island of Cho-do.

Major Sawyer later described his exit from the aircraft:

'After observing the crew members bail-out and getting interphone calls from the rear saying the last man was leaving, I got out of the seat and stepped over the crash bar which was in position, climbed down the rungs on the side of the nose wheel well and let go. As soon as I was clear of the aircraft I pulled the rip cord and the chute opened normally with no perceptible shock, although I lost my helmet.

'I started to slide back into the seat when I observed the first flare approximately one-and-a-half-miles north, and I could see that I was over the island and close to the ground. I slipped the chute to prevent severe oscillation and to be sure of hitting the island. However, because of the closeness to the ground, I soon stopped this measure and hit the ground backwards at the start of a new oscillation. I struck on the side of a hill and was rather gently lowered to a prone position on my back. I then rolled over, collapsed my chute, and got out of my harness. I could see a glow from lights to the north, so I started to walk in that direction. Shortly after starting off I encountered a ROK Marine. I asked him if there were Americans to the North and the ROK nodded, "Yes", and then I left him. I then walked the balance of approximately one-and-a-half miles to the Americans.'

The VO later recalled:

'I hit the water a little bit sooner than I expected to and just sort of sat down in it. I had unfastened my chest strap prior to hitting the water, so I got rid of the top part of my harness, but I could not unfasten the leg straps. I inflated the Mae West and then got one leg strap unfastened. I found that my canopy was still billowing, ducking me under the water periodically so I had to stop and spill it. Then I got rid of the rest of the chute and had a little trouble opening up the dinghy. I could not find the zipper on it, but I finally succeeded in getting my hand inside and pulling the CO2 release cord. This popped the dinghy out, fully inflated, and after hanging on to it for a short time to get my breath back, I succeeded into getting into it.

'After getting into the dinghy I realized for the first time that I was very cold. But the minute I put the hood up over me and the flap over my legs, I was considerably more comfortable. To the south of me I could see the search plane looking for us. It was dropping flares and flying a search pattern. Due to my coldness, and I guess just plain excitement or nervousness, I took out only one of the paddles and foolishly didn't search the dinghy thoroughly enough for useful equipment. I did find a whistle which I blew several times in an effort to contact some of the others who might be in the area. I then attempted to paddle towards what I think was Cho-do.

'I wasn't making any headway and soon realized that this was due to the fact that my chute harness was still attached to the dinghy and acting as a sea anchor. After that, there is a period that is completely blanked out. I came to the next morning and could again see planes flying a search pattern to the south of me. It was just about dawn. I dumped my sea marker-dye out of the Mae West, used a smoke flare to attract their attention and opened the flap of the dinghy to the yellow side to make it more obvious. At the time that the smoke flare went off I realized that the search plane had altered course to come directly over me. It came over and circled my position. There was a B-26 and a chopper. That is the last

I remember as I passed out again, and, except for the faint recollection of being in the hold of a boat, I don't remember anything until I was in the aid station on Cho-do.'

The men of the 3rd Air Rescue Detachment on Cho-do took good care of Sawyer until the next morning when he was reunited with Lieutenant Winchester and flown in a C-47 to K-16.

They were the only members of the crew to make it. The rest perished in the water and were never recovered.

The Starfire Arrives

The 319th Fighter Interceptor Squadron became operational at Suwon on 23 March 1952. Their job was to fly missions at night or in all weathers in the Lockheed F-94B Starfire. However, due to the sensitive radar systems in the plane, it was not permitted to fly missions north of the Main Line of Resistance until 1 November 1952.

On 2 November 1952, the first night air-battle between jet aircraft of the opposing sides took place when a Marine Skyknight shot down a MiG-15. On 7 November the Russians took their revenge and brought down the first F-94B Starfire. Lieutenant I.P. Kovalev was guided to the Starfire by a ground-based radar station and at 10,000 feet the two aircraft collided. The Starfire crashed in flames, and Kovalev bailed out. He landed in a rice paddy where Chinese troops found him and returned him to Antung. The American pilot, call sign 'Volleyball 95,' was not found in the wreckage on the beach and it is assumed that he bailed out and was rescued. Kovalev was awarded the Order of the Red Banner.

The first Starfire kill occurred on 30 January 1953 when Captain Ben Fithian and his Radar Observer Lieutenant Samuel Lyons caught a propeller driven aircraft west of P'yongyang and sent it down in flames. On the night of 3 May, Second Lieutenants Stanton Wilcox and Irwin Goldberg radioed 'Splash' to indicate that they had downed an enemy aircraft and then suddenly disappeared forever. They had either flown into the water or had a mid-air collision with the wreckage of the enemy aircraft. A week later Captain John Phillips and his RO Lieutenant Billy Atto bagged the first MiG-15 to be destroyed at night by an F-94. They climbed to 40,000 feet in MiG Alley and started a gentle let-down to 30,000. They found themselves on the tail of two MiGs and opened fire on the one on the left, while the other swung around to get on the tail of the F-94. Phillips fired again and his target exploded while the other MiG broke away for Manchuria.

On 7 June 1953 Lieutenant Colonel McHale and the squadron's lead radar observer, Captain Sam Hoster, encountered a MiG-15 while they were escorting a B-29 mission near the Yalu River. They became the first jet night fighters in history to shoot down an enemy fighter while defending a bombing mission. Unfortunately, the team was lost on the night of 12 June when they disappeared while attempting an intercept against a bogie southwest of Cho-do.

Robert Arndt was a radar observer in an F-94 of the 319th Fighter Interceptor Squadron and he described the job of an RO:

'I was never in a combat situation in Korea because I arrived there in September 1953 after the armistice was signed. However, we did fly combat air patrols along the Demarcation Zone and the tactics we used would probably have been the same if we did encounter a combat situation. There were two basic scenarios used for combat in F-94 All Weather Fighters.

'The first would have been used when encountering a target aircraft under visual and probably daylight conditions. The second procedure would have been used in weather or at night. Under each scenario, the fighter would be controlled by a Ground Controlled Intercept (GCI) site which would detect an enemy aircraft on its radar and then direct the fighter towards the target for interception. An approach to a target could be from any direction or altitude, including head-on, side, or tail chase attack. It was the radar observer's job to find the target and to direct the fighter into an attack position. Normally, the fighter's radar could pick up the target at a longer range than the pilot's visual ability and thereby assist the pilot in acquiring the target. If the target was at a low altitude, it was almost impossible to find it on radar because the radar echo would be buried in radar return from the ground until the fighter was very close to the target. Modern fighter radars are capable of separating ground return from a target.

'It was interesting to see the difference in range in finding a radar target, depending on the target type and configuration. For instance, the pick-up range on an F-86 was several miles greater than the pick-up range on another F-94. And the return on an aircraft with propellers was much greater still. A B-36 bomber made wonderful radar return with its six propellers. As I recall, the maximum range of the F-94's Hughes E-1 Fire Control System was 30,000 yards or about seventeen miles. Pick-up range on an F-86 would often be about 25,000 yards, whereas it was usually limited to about 15,000 yards on another F-94. Pickup range on a B-36 would be a strong target at 30,000 yards.

'The E-1 system had an automatic search mode. The radar antenna would sweep from side-to-side in a box pattern, displaying all radar return from targets, clouds and the ground. The RO controlled the elevation of the antenna to look level, up or down. Once a target was seen, the RO used a hand control to manually position the antenna. He placed a cursor on the target and "locked" onto the target. Thereafter, the radar would automatically track the target and provide appropriate information to the E-1 computer. Elevation of the target, relative to the attitude of the fighter, was monitored by frequently pressing a small button on the radar indicator which provided a separate blip on the radar screen.

'The E-1 system was somewhat temperamental because it used radio tubes instead of solid state electronics. It took a brief while for the system to reach its normal operating temperature for which it was calibrated. Even then, the system would easily drift out of alignment, which severely affected its range. The system was designed to provide target position, range, weapons' ballistics and lead-firing information to the pilot.

'The pilot was provided with two sights. The first was a "pipper" projected onto a glass plate behind the windshield. The second was a scope on his instrument panel where he would manoeuvre the aircraft to centre a dot inside a small circle. When in a firing position, the RO would also provide target range to the pilot. Experienced pilots could normally sense the appropriate range, particularly in a visual attack mode. When properly calibrated, the total weapons system was very accurate.

'If the attack was visual, the RO assisted the pilot in acquiring the target, while managing the radar to lock onto the blip. The RO continued to provide primarily target information to the pilot who could visually manoeuvre the aircraft into a firing position.

'In an all-weather or night attack, it was the RO's responsibility to position the aircraft into a firing position. This required a fair amount of skill and experience to interpret range, altitude, closing speed and position of the target, particularly if the initial position was from a head-on or front quartering initial acquisition. The RO had to displace the fighter off to one side at an appropriate distance so the fighter could roll into an attack position. A weather or night attack normally ended up in a tail chase situation, hoping that the target would not be aware of a fighter on its tail. North Korea had its own equivalent of GCI control and was often able to tell its aircraft if another fighter was in the vicinity and behind him. Once the F-94 was in an attack position, it was the pilot's job to centre the dot on his scope and pull the trigger.

'It was impossible for an RO to determine the attitude of the target. If the target became aware of being pursued, he could dive, zoom up, bank and turn to the side, or do a split-S and dive away. A split-S was by far the most difficult evasive manoeuvre for an RO to follow. He had no way of knowing that the target had rolled over and was about to dive away. At very close range, the target usually moved a little to one side or the other and started to drop down from a straight ahead position. At very close range the target could easily escape the limits of the radar antenna.

'Intercept situations in Korea after the war usually involved North Korean aircraft flying south towards the DMZ and turning at the last minute to avoid flying into South Korean airspace. An aircraft threatening the DMZ usually got the attention of GCI controllers, which often resulted in a scramble or diversion of a fighter on combat air patrol. A frequent annoyance was so-called Bed-Check Charlies, which were usually slow moving light aircraft. The aircraft had relatively little material to reflect radar and usually flew at a very low altitude. Bed-Check Charlies frequently flew through the DMZ and into South Korea. After a short incursion into South Korea they would quickly return to North Korea. Although my pilot and I were frequently diverted to chase them, we never found them by the time we reached the area. Their low altitude made it difficult for the GCI sites to find and track them.'

Clarence Fry completed sixty-seven sorties over North Korea with the 319th Fighter Interceptor Squadron. Here he describes a mission for which he was later awarded a Distinguished Flying Cross:

'It was not the first of our combat air patrols along the Yalu River. My attention was first aroused when the GCI (Ground Controlled Intercept) controller on Cho-do Island gave me a call and indicated that he was vectoring me towards a "bandit" aircraft. That was our term for positive enemy aircraft. We had heard the term "bogie" many times on previous missions, since there were always bombers and fighter bombers operating in the area. My first reaction was to confirm with my RO (Radar Observer) Arthur Watson, that the vector we were being given was towards a bandit. We both agreed that such was the term we heard and at that point the pucker factor increased many fold.

'When we got within the range of our airborne radar, Art picked up the target. I had been descending and slowing down during the GCI vector.

Once within radar range, Art picked up the target and got a lock on. With the lock on, I got a target symbol on my repeater pilot scope and began to control the aircraft to get the target within the parameters needed to engage. My scope had a range circle which shrank in size the closer to the target I got. There was an inscribed circle on the pilot scope indicating that range to the target was 800 yards. This was the range that I was trained to commence firing. There was also an inscribed circle at 200 yards range which was to indicate that the attack should be broken off to avoid collision. We lost some of our crews in this type of engagement when the attacking plane collided with the target. One of those lost in such a mission was Lieutenant Colonel Robert McHale our commanding officer and his radar observer.

'My pilot guidance on the scope was a small dot indicating the target. I was to control the dot such as to bring it within a small circle in the centre of the scope. Throughout all of this I was aware that my altitude was very low and my airspeed close to stalling. I had to carefully fly to an engagement point without stalling out and crashing into the sea off the west coast of North Korea. I began firing on the first pass at the maximum range. I saw no sign of strikes. We were firing armour-piercing incendiary bullets from our four 0.50-caliber machine guns, which in night engagements provide small winks of light when striking the target. I made two more passes without any positive results.

'On the third pass, Cho-do GCI advised me to break off the attack since I was approaching the range of their anti-aircraft guns and those guns were instructed to fire at anything moving. Being a young fearless fighter jock, I ignored the order and pretty soon I had more flak surrounding me than I cared for. I got out of there pronto.

'I never made any claims for damage or destruction of the enemy aircraft. In the world of night fighters, it is difficult to make a claim unless you get the enemy aircraft burning. In later years I realized that the aircraft I was attacking might have been cloth covered and therefore strikes by the API ammunition would not have been noticed. We got back to K-13 Suwon, our home field, and provided our intelligence officer with a post-mission brief describing our encounter.'

Skyknights and Bed-Check Charlies
Intercepting and destroying the Po-2 Bedcheck Charlies was far from easy. It was 26 November 1952 and the F3D was acting as Strip Alert at K-8. At 1905 hours they received instructions to scramble. When they reached

20,000 feet they were directed to report to 'Dutchboy'. They were vectored to 360 degrees to intercept bandits at twenty-five miles. 'Dutchboy' said that bandits were at 3,500 feet and immediately the Skyknight began to descend from 20,000 feet. At 2005 hours 'Dutchboy' began giving vectors and distances. They were now closing on the bandit. They were about four miles over the water, directly west of prisoner of war camps 10 and 12. At this point they received another vector at 015 degrees, and, still over land, they received word that the bandit was in an orbit. The pilot later recorded:

'We began orbiting to the right until 'Dutchboy' gave a vector of 090 degrees. Turning to this heading, we started overland at 3,000 feet. Then we were told to vector 360 degrees. Upon turning to this heading, we awaited further instructions but all 'Dutchboy' gave was that they had the bandit approximately one mile ahead but no altitude information. Upon hearing this, we opened speed brakes and let down to 600 feet. While in descent at 190 knots for ten seconds, I made a visual on a biplane of the Po-2 type as it passed over a small lake or swampy area. The plane was at 10 o'clock and slightly below.

'I immediately turned into the aircraft which was at 200 feet altitude flying at about 100 knots, and fired at it at the same time, with no results observed. We passed just over him in a left-hand turn. I then went into a port-orbit search, but with no success. The time was then 2015 hours. On returning from this area, we attacked eight trucks. One truck was destroyed. 'Dutchboy' advised return to base, which we did.'

It was a busy night for the Po-2s. In another sector, six enemy aircraft, probably Po-2s, dropped five bombs on Cho-do Island, in the fourth attack to date. No damage was reported, but two F-94s and one F3D were vectored into the area. The F3D established contact with the Po-2, but the Red pilot's luck held and the F3D was unable to manoeuvre into a firing position due to the slow speed of the enemy aircraft.

There were better results the following month. An F3D Skyknight from VMF(N)-513 cornered a Po-2 over the sea off the mouth of the Chongchon River and, after one firing pass, the enemy aircraft was observed to be out of control. As a result of the night fighters' automatic radar-controlled gunfire, one of the Po-2's wings was shot off and the aircraft was last seen spinning into the water. However, around the middle of the month F3D Skyknights and F-94 Starfires patrolling the northwest coast of Korea made contact with enemy aircraft on at least ten occasions, but only one of them was shot down.

From the radar point of view, ground return is a major obstacle in the tracking and shooting down of enemy aircraft, especially the slow, small ones.

Another role for the Po-2 was the dropping of propaganda leaflets over the battle lines, and near Seoul and Inchon on the western coast of Korea. The leaflets were published in newspaper format and dealt with 'Peace' and the troop-rotation policy of US frontline troops.

One day a US L-4 plane flying at 1,000 feet approached elements of the US 3rd Division. The aircraft was displaying unusual white circles under each wing and banked sharply to send showers of leaflets fluttering down to the bemused troops below. The aircraft carried out this manoeuvre twice and then flew away. It later transpired that a second lieutenant from the South Korean Air Force had defected to North Korea in an L-19 aircraft on 3 December, landing at an airfield near Haeju. A few days later P'yongyang Radio announced that the defecting pilot had surrendered and had been interviewed. During night operations this L-19 could easily have been confused with the L-4.

Several propeller-driven aircraft were destroyed during the month of November, including a couple of LA-type fighters. These LA-9 or -11s were shot down by F-94s. A third propeller type was later destroyed by an F-94 but it could not be identified. Just before daylight on 30 January, a number of hostile flights were tracked by radar in the area below P'yongyang, but after unsuccessful attempts at contact by an F-94, the night fighters were called off and the task passed to an F-86 combat air patrol. They caught a Tu-2 flying low over the water about thirty miles northwest of Cho-do and destroyed it. This was the first confirmed sighting of a conventional type of enemy light bomber in many months.

The high point for the year 1952 for UN night fighters was marked by the destruction of an enemy jet fighter by an F3D Skyknight on 3 November. The aircraft was being flown by Marine Major William Stratton who was accompanied by radar operator Master Sergeant Hans Hoagland. The Skyknight was vectored into radar and visible contact with the jet, which the crew identified as a Yak-15 from the exhaust pattern, and in the ensuing pursuit at around 12,000 feet, the F3D scored hits on the Yak's port wing, fuselage and tailpipe before it was sent spinning earthward. Three explosions were observed as the Yak crashed in flames, the Skyknight flying through the debris. Russian records would later indicate that the target was actually a MiG-15 – the Yak-15 was not really suited for operational use and was not used in combat in Korea. Furthermore they claim that the MiG was only damaged and the pilot managed to get back to base where it was repaired within a few days.

The destruction of the Yak/MiG-15 was the first confirmed jet kill by a UN night fighter. It was followed by a second, five days later in the early morning of 8 November, when a Skyknight, flown by Captain Oliver R Davis and RO Warrant Officer 'Ding' Fessler from VMF(N)-513, caught a MiG-15 at 12,500 feet. After a burst of fire from the F3D's guns, the MiG's tailpipe exploded amid a cloud of dense black smoke. A second explosion occurred when the aircraft hit the deck. Soviet records do confirm this claim and state that the pilot Lieutenant Kovalyov ejected safely. This action was the first confirmed kill of a swept wing MiG-15 jet fighter during a night engagement. A third, unidentified, single-engine jet aircraft, was encountered and destroyed by an F3D somewhere in the vicinity of P'yongyang during the night of 15 January 1953.

A new danger to UN night fighters presented itself on the night of 17 January, when an F3D made contact with an enemy aircraft about twenty miles northeast of Sinanju. Immediately after starting its run on the enemy aircraft, the F3D was bracketed by between twelve and fifteen searchlights with accompanying anti-aircraft gunfire. The Skyknight pilot had to take evasive action and lost contact with the enemy airplane. During the following month, more encounters with searchlights were reported by UN pilots. On 7 February 1953, one F3D was bracketed by four of them and then became involved in a hornets' nest as its radar revealed an enemy fighter on its tail. After carrying out evasive turns, the pilot managed to lose the enemy and on returning to his original course was able to pick up the original contact. When he was six miles away and closing he lost contact with the bandit. This was followed by another warning from the tail radar at three miles at 22,000 feet. The enemy began closing rapidly, causing the F3D to pull away and break off the action.

The Final Year
On 13 January 1953, a dozen enemy fighters shot down a B-29 on a psychological warfare, leaflet-drop mission over North Korea. The crew included Colonel John K. Arnold Jr., commander of the 581st ARCW. Peking radio announced the capture of Arnold and his surviving crew members, less three who allegedly perished when the B-29 went down. The Communists would not release Arnold and his crew until 1956, minus the two radar experts who were probably passed on to the Soviets.

In January, aerial photographs revealed a new camouflaged yard at the Sui-ho hydroelectric dam and two of the four generators working. On 15 February, twenty-two F-84 Thunderjets from the 474th FBW returned to the area and while the eighty-two escorting F-86 Sabres drew off thirty MiGs they dropped their 1,000-pound bombs and escaped without loss. The attack halted power production at Sui-ho for several months.

On the night of 28 January, a 19th Bomb Group B-29 exploded over the target southwest of Sariwon. Enemy fighters apparently silhouetted the B-29 against a full moon and shot it down. This was the fourth B-29 loss since December but the last of the war. USMC Skyknight aircraft escorting the B-29s used new tactics to down an enemy night interceptor, the first enemy jet destroyed at night by a radar-equipped jet fighter. A 319th FIS F-94 tracked by radar and destroyed an La-9 aircraft late on the night of the 30th. This marked the first Starfire kill in Korea.

On 22 February things started moving at the Peace talks again. In a letter to Kim Il Sung, the North Korean premier, and Paeng Te-huai, CCF commander in Korea, the UN Command stated its readiness to repatriate immediately any seriously ill and wounded POWs who were fit to travel, and asked whether the North Korean and Chinese leaders were prepared to do the same. The North Korean truce negotiators agreed and hinted that the exchange might lead to a resolution of other issues hindering an armistice. On 30 March Chou En-lai, China's foreign minister, suggested that POWs not desiring repatriation might be placed in the temporary custody of a neutral nation until negotiations determined their final status. Prior to this proposal the Communists had insisted on the repatriation of all POWs. Their new flexibility on this issue provided an opportunity to resume truce negotiations and on 20 April Operation 'Little Switch' began and a number of sick and injured prisoners were exchanged.

On 12 April, an H-19 helicopter assigned to the 581st ARCW hoisted Captain Joseph C. McConnell Jr., an F-86 pilot with eight victory credits to date, from the Yellow Sea after he had ejected from his battle-damaged aircraft. On 18 May he downed three more MiG-15s to become the first triple jet ace and, with sixteen victories, the highest scoring ace of the Korean War. On the same day, an H-19 helicopter rescued two members of a B-26 crew twenty miles inside enemy territory by using tactics presaging those of later conflicts. The helicopter scrambled from its base and flew to a small island off the Haeju Peninsula to await fighters to clear the path to the downed airmen. Penetrating enemy territory at 5,000 feet, the helicopter followed the fighter pilots' directions until it located the survivors who were signaling with a mirror. After the survivors set off a flare to indicate wind direction, the helicopter landed and rescued them, staying on the ground for approximately thirty seconds.

The final four months before the ceasefire was agreed saw one crisis after another. In May the communists gave such indications of bad faith and evasiveness that General Clark was given authority from Washington to terminate the talks and continue with the war. All the while South Korean President Syngman Rhee was threatening to wreck the peace talks. One can understand his resentment: Korea was still divided in two, but now he had over a million Chinese facing him across the 38th Parallel.

On 13 May, a campaign began to destroy the dams which held the water to irrigate the rice fields in North Korea, thus reducing the supplies available in the north and for exporting to China. Rice was the Communist soldier's staple diet and approximately twenty dams held back the water used to irrigate the rice crops. Destroying these dams would release floods that could potentially destroy a year's rice planting. In the first raid, fifty-nine Thunderjets of the 58th FBW bombed the Toksan Dam holding the Potong River's water 20 miles north of P'yongyang. Floodwaters swirling from the breached dam washed out six miles of embankment and five bridges, destroyed two miles of the major north-south highway, rendered Sunan airfield inoperable, and ruined five square miles of prime rice crop.

On 16 May, ninety 58th FBW sorties breached the Chasan irrigation dam and the surging waters washed away three railroad bridges and destroyed the rice ripening in surrounding fields. On 21 May, using Shoran to aim the bombs, B-29s scored seven direct hits on the Kuwonga dam but failed to burst it because the North Koreans had lowered the water level by 12 feet, significantly reducing the pressure on the dam, but also the supply of water available for irrigation. From 13 to 18 June, in order to flood airfields at Namsi and Taechon, F-84s, B-29s, and Marine F4U Corsair fighter-bombers struck irrigation dams at Toksan and Kusong. However, the raids failed to breach the dams because the Communists had lowered the water levels to decrease water pressure. General Weyland later said these attacks were, 'perhaps the most spectacular of the war.' General Clark was also jubilant, telling the JCS that the breaching had been 'as effective as weeks of rail interdiction.'

The Arnold Shoot Down

Following a mass strike on the Sunhung hydroelectric power station on 12 January 1953, a lone RB-29 44-62217 from the 91st SRS was spotted over Antung. Russian Senior Lieutenant Khabiev intercepted the bomber and when the searchlights lit up the target, he made two passes firing for all he was worth. Slowly the bomber lost height and the crew bailed out over

Chinese airspace. According to Russian sources only eleven of the fourteen crew were captured alive, including the commander of the 581st Air Resupply and Communications Wing Colonel John Knox Arnold Jr and Major William Earl Baumer commander of the 91st SRS.

One of the crew that night was Radio Operator Steve Kiba and he has a different recollection of the survivors than the official Soviet record:

'On the night of 12 January 1953, while on a routine leaflet drop mission over North Korea, our "unarmed" B-29 was attacked and shot down. The 581st was tasked with unconventional and psychological warfare and our aircraft was definitely over North Korean territory, approximately forty miles south of the Yalu River. Colonel John K. Arnold was our wing commander. The crew members on our stripped-down, virtually unarmed B-29 were Captain Eugene Vaadi, aircraft commander; First Lieutenant Wallace Brown, pilot; First Lieutenant John Buck, bombardier; Captain Elmer Llewellyn, navigator; Second Lieutenant Henry Weese, radarman; Tech Sergeant Howard Brown, flight engineer; A/2C Daniel C. Schmidt, CFC gunner; A/2C Harry Benjamin, left scanner; A/2C John Thompson, right scanner; A/1C Alvin Hart, tail gunner; and A/1C Steve Kiba, radio operator.

'Our home base was Clark Field, Philippines, but two of our aircraft were on tour of duty to Yakota AFB, Japan and were attached to the 91st SRS. Our job was to fly leaflet drop missions over North Korea. Our first mission was on 12 January 1953. Because it was our first mission we had three extra men on board: Colonel John Arnold, the wing commander; Major William Baumer, instructor pilot; and First Lieutenant Paul Van Voohris, instructor radar man and Weese's friend.

'About 2245 hours we were attacked simultaneously by MiG-15s and radar-controlled ack-ack. Our B-29 sustained heavy damage: three engines were burning and the forward bomb-bay was engulfed in flames. Captain Vaadi gave the order to abandon the aircraft. We bailed out and were scattered all over the North Korean hillside.

'By late afternoon on 13 January most of the crew and "extras" had been captured. After we were captured we were taken to an old stone jail-house. About 1700 hours a young Chinese interpreter boasted to me that they had now captured thirteen airmen from our B-29 – two last night as they touched the ground. I asked him how everyone was, because I knew that Llewellyn and Baumer had been injured. He told me that only two men were wounded and all the others were in good shape. I now knew that thirteen of the fourteen were at least alive. Of the eleven of us who returned home, none of us was captured the night of the attack. The two captured that night had to be Weese and Van Voohris.

'About 1800 hours the Chinese put Benjamin and me in an American weapons' carrier. Tech Sergeant Brown, First Lieutenant Brown and Captain Vaadi were already in the carrier. There were also twelve heavily armed guards accompanying us. The weapons carrier drove us to a small town and stopped at a large U-shaped building. We were taken from the weapons carrier one by one and into the building and put into separate rooms. For about two hours we were on display for the townspeople. At 2100 hours I was blindfolded, handcuffed and placed in leg irons and put in a truck with other crew members. The truck took us to some old wooden barracks somewhere in the North Korean countryside.

'The next morning an English-speaking Chinese soldier came into my room to ask me a few questions. I enquired about the other crew members. He too, told me that two crew members were captured as soon as they hit the ground. He gave me some information about the other crew members. For example, Tech Sergeant Brown played football; Schmidt was worried about his wife; Baumer and Llewellyn were wounded, but not to worry because they would be treated well, and Benjamin was always singing and was in the room below mine. He apologized for the quality of the meagre food, the frigid room and the absence of toilet articles. He said because of the war many things were scarce and difficult to get here in North Korea.

'I was also questioned by a mean English-speaking Chinese soldier. On 16 January he asked me if I knew where I was. I told him I was in North Korea. He got upset and screamed that I was in the People's Republic of China. I insisted that I was in North Korea. This went on for about two hours. Later that same afternoon the friendly soldier came to my room. We chatted for a while and he informed me that shortly I would be taking a long train ride and my living conditions would improve greatly. He said that where I was going would be much better than a POW camp. I asked him if I was being taken to China and if he was also coming. He said I was going to China but he had to remain here in North Korea.

'That evening several Chinese soldiers came to my room. They blindfolded me, handcuffed me and placed leg irons around my ankles. They carried me downstairs and put me into an American jeep. They took me to another large U-shaped building where we (two guards and I) stayed until almost midnight. Then we walked to the train station, got on a passenger car loaded with Chinese soldiers and headed north. You see, we were taken into Red China by force on a train.

'We arrived in Mukden, Manchuria, about 1200 hours on 17 January. While in Mukden, from 17 January to 1 February I was held in two different prisons; the Hotbox and the Peanut Palace. At the Peanut Palace I underwent horrendous interrogations which lasted anywhere from six to twenty-four hours a day. Here, too, the interrogators arrogantly bragged about how the brave, heroic People's Volunteers shot our plane out of the sky and how two of our crew were captured as soon as they reached the ground.'

The war would be over for two years before Steve Kiba and ten of his comrades would regain their freedom. Weese and Van Hooris would never be released.

Aussie Meteors
Don Smith was one of the pilots destined to fly the Meteor over the closing months of the war. He recalled:

'I got my wings during National Service in May 1951 and moved on to a jet conversion course. I signed on for eight years and was destined for the day fighter/ground attack role. There was no two-seat Vampire in those days so this meant dual instruction in the Meteor Mk 7 and solo on the Vampire. After three months I went to the Vampire Operational Conversation Unit where we did battle formation, gunnery (air to air and air to ground) and rocketry. This was completed at the end of 1951 and I was posted to the Suez Canal Zone where I joined 32 Squadron, a Vampire Squadron based at Deversoir. Early in 1953 there was a call for volunteers to go to Korea on loan to the RAAF. I left Egypt on 19 March 1953 after fifteen months with some 330 hours on Vampires and sixty hours on the Meteor Mk 7. I arrived at Iwakuni in Japan in an RAF Hastings on 30 March 1953. This was the rear base for 77 Squadron and their location when the Korean War started in 1950.

'Within minutes of setting foot on Iwakuni airbase virtually the first aircraft I saw was a Meteor Mk 8 with over a hundred holes in it, the result of a near miss by a 37mm shell fired by a MiG-15. Each hole was covered with a canvas patch stuck on with a red substance so they showed up well! I had arrived with Flying Officer John Coleman, RAF and we were shown to the Mess where the 5 pm gathering of RAAF officers and nursing sisters greeted us with schooners of beer and the warmest of welcomes. Flying Officer Taffy Rosser, RAF had left the Canal Zone a few weeks before John and me. We learned that afternoon that he was already dead. If we were ever in doubt we now knew that we were becoming part of a serious business!

'Between 1 and 8 April I did a conversion course of fourteen trips and felt completely at home in the single seat Mk 8. Of particular value were three weapons sorties. On my Vampire squadron we each did one sortie a month firing four concrete-head single rockets with the impact being plotted by observers at two quadrants. We also did one air to ground gunnery sortie each month firing fifty rounds in a series of very short bursts at a 10 foot square canvas target with the hits being counted at the end of the session. All the rocket and gunnery accuracy was recorded for individual and squadron performance. It was all carried out in the classic 30-degree dive with no chance to experiment with angles of dive or firing long bursts, starting at longer range. The "range" at Iwakuni was a small island in the bay with a safety officer in a nearby boat. I soon realised that the Meteor was a far better ground attack aircraft than the Vampire. I made really good use of my three weapon sorties, each time firing four HE rockets as singles, followed by gun attacks using a full load of HE/SAP ammunition. I experimented with angles of dive and firing ranges, using a particular rock on the edge of the island as a target. After recovery from each rocket firing I could see the impact point, and see the cannon strikes while in the dive. Those three sorties were of tremendous value in broadening my experience after a year-and-a-half of rather academic weapon training.

'In the early fifties Glosters developed what became known as the Private Venture Meteor. It was based on the Mk 8 but was configured for ground attack. It had tip tanks and part of the design included rocket-rails and bomb-racks. They tried to market it, without success. The existence of the rocket-rail design made it relatively easy for 77 Squadron to move to a ground attack role. The bomb-racks were designed to carry a streamlined 1000-pound bomb. This weapon was not available in Korea but in 1953 a rack was designed to carry the type of bombs available to 77 Squadron. I believe that the design and prototype manufacture was carried out by a Flight Lieutenant Smith RAAF. I recall some test bombing taking place in Korea after the armistice. I was at K–14 for the last four months of the war and I am sure, contrary to at least one magazine article I have seen, that no bombs were dropped during hostilities.

'On 10 April, twelve days after arriving in Japan, I was on an RAAF Dakota destined for 77 Squadron's base at K-14, Kimpo which was between Inchon and Seoul and about fifteen miles south of the front line. Kimpo has become Gimpo and is now Seoul International Airport. The next day I did my first operational sortie, a "sector recce" and was shown round a lot of North Korea, flying as a pair with one of the flight commanders. In April 1953 the main activity for 77 was two pre-briefed rocket strikes a day. By this time the enemy aircraft had given up trying to operate out of North Korea and were using bases across the Yalu in Manchuria which the UN forces couldn't touch. Each morning and afternoon over one hundred Sabres were dispatched to "MiG Alley", i.e. the top 100 miles of North Korea. The Sabres operated in sections of four, sweeping the alley, and were there for about an hour-and-a-half to keep the MiGs occupied while the majority of the ground attack work took place.

'Accommodation at K-14 was tents with wooden floors and half walls. The one that John Coleman and I were allocated had a ceiling and the only canvas visible inside was the door. This was a lot better than the tent I had in the Canal Zone (that had a sand floor and just the canvas, resulting in an incredibly hot dwelling in the Egyptian summer). Another bonus was the food provided by the USAF mess hall. Most of the wartime rationing in UK was still in force when I left and the food in the Canal Zone was appalling because in 1951 the Egyptians had abrogated the treaty permitting UK forces to be there. They withdrew all the local labour and made obtaining fresh food difficult or impossible. I had never eaten steak until I reached Korea so life at Kimpo was a great improvement! Another benefit concerned laundry. We all retained a room in the Iwakuni mess and a bag of washing left in the orderly room on a Tuesday was flown there for the room girl to deal with, and was back on Thursday. I've never had such a service before or since!

'On my first strike, two days after arriving, I was wingman to the leader of the fourth section. We were all carrying napalm rockets and the scene that unfolded as I followed the thirteen aircraft in front of me has stayed with me ever since. I had seen grainy black-and-white news footage of flame throwers being used in WW2, but this was live and in colour! That day, and on many others, the target was a "troop concentration" – actually a mud hut village with straw roofs. There were a million North Korean and Chinese troops down there somewhere and we were assured that the description of these targets was correct.

'Each aircraft carried a gunsight camera. On a rocket attack the camera started running when the sight was uncaged (well before release) and stopped on release. Before dinner each evening we viewed the films, which were spliced in the order in which the aircraft had fired, and before each firing there was a title showing the pilot's name. When rockets were released, an immediate recovery was necessary so you never saw your own rockets hit. By viewing the film in this way we could individually see our release and hits in the film of following aircraft. For targets that had many small buildings, the photographs were divided so each section had an area allocated, and the section leader would then allocate each pilot one or several buildings. My second strike was with HE rockets and I was really chuffed to see a direct hit on my pair of huts! Those first two strikes left me with clear memories, as did a few others.

'I feel I must mention the ground crews who worked at K-14. The only covered work space available for Meteor servicing and repair was a three-sided structure where two aircraft could sit side-by-side, with the roof covering only the front half of each of the aircraft. Everything else was done in the open and conditions varied from freezing winter, hot summer and monsoon-type rain! This was the working environment and those servicing guys, all volunteers I believe, were magnificent. I remember doing an early morning air test after an overnight engine change. Serviceability was fantastic. Of the twenty-two Meteors kept at K-14 we often had as many as twenty available and regularly flew sixteen aircraft strikes twice a day.

'In late May I was one of a handful of pilots who did some night road recces. The enemy was expert at camouflage and very little movement was seen by day. At night, with few main roads, you could map read using the main roads which were lined with moving vehicles with headlights on. Four Meteors were used and we flew with fifteen-minute separation following the lines of vehicles. The roads were in valleys between rugged hills and mountains so the technique involved descending with throttles closed in line with the road. A single rocket was released at about one-thousand feet followed by a short cannon-burst and swift recovery and climb! The immediate effect was the extinguishing of all lights and the traffic obviously stopped. The fifteen-minute separation enabled the same effect just as they were lighting up and moving. Four aircraft could thus stop the progress of convoys for more than an hour and a half. I think we should have done more of it.

'We caused modest disruption to the enemy's reinforcement plans and they found a way to keep us out of our beds. I refer to the night raids by

"Bed-Check Charlie". These were light aircraft, even Po-2 biplanes, that lobbed mortar bombs over the side. Our airfields were not blacked out until the raiders were apparent, usually by an explosion! Everything was then switched off by some master switch, and the 77 Squadron management insisted that we all took shelter in slit trenches. Those of us who had experienced the Blitz in London and elsewhere were fairly relaxed about the need to take shelter but we were obliged to do it! We never received any bombs once all the lights were out as the raiders knew they had been rumbled. K-14 had impressive air defences. There were searchlights, many banks of machine guns and quite a few 40mm Bofors guns, with one close to our slit trenches. It was commanded by a huge black NCO called "Geronimo" who kept us informed about the situation. When the defences were given a "guns-free" the display of tracer snaking skywards was fantastic. We never saw an aircraft caught by the searchlights but that didn't deter the enthusiastic gunners!

'As I returned from my first night sortie I was advised that K-14 had a red alert and I was diverted to K-13 Suwon. They were also blacked out and I had the curious experience of doing a GCA into complete blackness until, at a few hundred feet, the lights were switched on for my landing and quickly off again before the landing run was complete. As I approached Suwon I was glad to find that their defences were aware that I was a "friendly"! I was able to return to K-14 later that night.

'The armistice was signed on 27 July and I took my two-week R and R in August, having chosen to delay it so as not to miss the last days of the war. I left the squadron in October and returned to complete my tour in the Canal Zone. John Coleman and I were given a month's leave, but no entitlement to RAF flights to the UK and we had no access to civil airlines in Egypt. Had it not been for an initiative by our station commander we would have spent our leave kicking our heels on the base! The CO fixed us both a ride in a Valetta transport which was off to UK for a major inspection. He also fixed the ride back, but when we met the crew at RAF Lyneham they knew nothing about us and every seat was taken! One of the passengers was an Air Commodore so they could not allow us to ride on the main spar. There was room for another double seat. Was there one lying about at Lyneham? Yes, and we were saved from becoming AWOL!'

Crossing the Line

A dozen Royal Air Force pilots from Fighter Command were seconded to the 4th Fighter Interceptor Wing of the US 5th Air Force to fly the F-86

Sabre. One of them was Colin Downes who had joined the RAF in 1942 and learned to fly in America. He flew Spitfires towards the end of the war and was flying Meteors with 41 Squadron at Biggin Hill before he joined the 335th Fighter Interceptor Squadron at K-14 Kimpo.

At 0600 hours on 18 June 1953, the yawning pilots gathered for a briefing for a full Group sweep of MiG Alley, along the Yalu River that formed the North Korean border with Manchuria. The weather conditions were discussed and noted, before the briefing staff got onto the next subject; emergency procedures. Everyone sat up and took notice as the islands of Cho-do and Paengnyong-do were pointed out on the map. Situated off the west coast of North Korea, the islands were occupied by South Korean forces. Cho-do was a rocky island with no beaches suitable for crash landings, but Paengnyong-do, forty miles south of Cho-do, had good beaches on the east side of the island and was a hundred miles from Kimpo. Luck would play a great part in a successful landing though, as the main beach could only be used as a runway if the tide was out. But if you could not achieve a landing, at least you could bail out over the islands and wait for the helicopters based on the islands to come and pluck you from the sea. They were ably assisted by patrolling Grumman SA-16 Albatross amphibian aircraft.

One last warning before the pilots left the briefing room; do not cross the Yalu River into Manchuria, the Chinese would not like it. A ridiculous prohibition really as the Chinese Army had crossed into North Korea and was fighting the UN Forces on a daily basis.

Downes took off from Kimpo, as wingman to four times MiG killer Captain Lonnie Moore, leading a flight of four F-86Es. As they climbed through 15,000 feet, they test-fired their guns and checked that their A-1 radar gunsights were working as advertised. As they approached MiG Alley at 45,000 feet they jettisoned their wing tanks and increased their speed to Mach 0.9.

The plan was for the Wing to fly along the south side of the border from Sinuiju at the mouth of the Yalu River to the Suiho Dam and lakes area, which was heavily defended by Soviet radar-controlled 88mm anti-aircraft artillery. The AAA defences also covered the two adjoining border cities of Antung on the Manchuria side of the river and Sinuiju on the south bank.

Moore had every intention of crossing into Manchuria, and in line with his orders the pilots changed their radio frequencies to the tower at Kimpo, two hundred miles away, which was too far for their radio chatter to be heard. He turned his fighter north and headed for the Kuan-Tien air base around twenty miles north-west of the Suiho Dam. Far below them they saw eight silver MiGs in pairs in line astern flying west towards Phen Chen, a large airbase twenty-five miles north of Antung.

Two of the four Sabres in Moore's flight called 'Bingo' fuel, whereby they now only had enough fuel left to reach home and headed back to the Yalu. Moore and Downes rolled over in a sonic dive and pulled out at 3,000 feet with the last pair of MiGs dead ahead of them. At 2,000 feet and 300 yards range Moore opened fire on the trailing MiG. Holes appeared in its fuselage and as Moore closed to 100 feet the stream of fire went straight up the jet pipe of the MiG and pieces of metal began to break away. The cockpit canopy opened straight away and the pilot ejected from the stricken aircraft.

In order not to overshoot the second MiG, Moore reduced power and deployed his airbrake and to avoid over-running him; Downes pulled up in a barrel-roll around him. While Downes was inverted above Moore he checked his Six and saw two MiGs closing in on them. He called to Moore to break left, but he was already firing at the second MiG now approaching the end of the Phen Chen runway. Downes repeated his call and this time Moore replied 'Roger, breaking left' and turned away. That was the last Downes heard from his flight leader as he passed over the airfield boundary and the whole airfield lit up like a Christmas tree as all the AAA guns on the airfield opened fire.

Downes was now down on the deck with a dark trail of smoke pouring from his engine exhaust, a poor operational characteristic of American jet aircraft at that time. He was an easy target but it was safer down in the weeds than back up at height where the AAA could find him and besides, there was another MiG a thousand feet ahead of him. Downes later recalled, 'In my anxiety to get out of the area before reinforcements arrived I opened fire too soon at 400 yards range. I saw strikes around his fuselage as the MiG broke to his left towards Phen Chen. I got the pipper back on the MiG and again opened fire. A red 'cricket ball' passed close to the top of my canopy and looking back I saw the underside of a MiG with flashes around the nose intake. I pulled left as hard as I could in a maximum turn lowering the nose to increase speed, and as I did so another red cricket ball passed behind the aircraft. I was probably lucky in two respects in that the MiG in front of me broke when he did; and the slow rate of fire of the 37mm cannon, around 400 rounds per minute placed a convenient distance between shells in a high-g turn.'

Downes was in trouble, with low fuel and no support and sandwiched between two MiGs. The first Mig had been hit and limped away, but the other stuck to Downes as he threw his Sabre around the sky trying to put him off his aim. Suddenly he saw the MiG slam into the side of a hill and explode in a ball of fire. Possibly he pulled too hard to get a deflection shot and overdid it, resulting in a high-speed stall that snap-rolled the MiG into the hillside.

Dropping to the deck at maximum power, Downes turned south towards the coast. Once clear of the Antung area he climbed to 10,000 feet and found himself totally alone. As he crossed the coast over the Korea Bay he felt more secure, although with 800 pounds of fuel remaining instead of the 1,500 pounds he needed to get back to Kimpo, he was running out of choices.

Downes discovered that his radio was not working, so he could not communicate with any of the airfields or the search and rescue forces on Cho-do where he was now heading. He switched on the Identification Friend or Foe (IFF) onto the emergency mode, as they had switched them off as they flew into Manchuria. There were two stark choices facing Downes now; either bail out over Cho-do or continue on to Paengnyong-do forty miles further on.

After making sure that he was below contrail height, Downes levelled off at 30,000 feet and cruised until his fuel gauges registered 400 pounds. He then switched off the engine and shut down all non-essential services. The windmilling engine provided enough hydraulic power for the gentle operation of the flying controls and he set up a glide angle of 160kt, giving a still-air distance covered of fourteen nautical miles per 5,000 feet of descent.

Eventually, Downes passed over Cho-do at a height of 15,000 feet, which he knew would allow him to make it to Paengnyong-do and land on the beach. It would be a close run thing though, as the tide would be halfway in as he arrived and so far, although many aircraft had crash landed with battle damage, no F-86s had actually landed on the beach.

The Sabre was down to 3,000 feet when Downes saw Paengnyong-do ahead of him and fired up the engine. The approach was from the south over sand dunes and the 400 pounds of remaining fuel allowed Downes to fly along the beach and check it out before landing. The north end of the beach was covered with people, together with the odd bullock cart, but when Downes pulled up in a climbing turn and dropped his undercarriage the civilians soon moved off elsewhere.

Downes touched down as close to the water as possible and taxied to the north end of the beach where a Republic F-84 was already parked. He shut down the engine with, as the saying goes, nothing showing on the gauges but the maker's name. There was about twenty US gallons left in the tanks as he switched off everything, put the safety pin in the ejection seat and closed the hood. Downes walked over to the Americans working on the F-84 and asked them to hand pump Avgas fuel from drums into his wing tanks. In the meantime he walked to the radar hut at the top of the cliff and asked them to inform the 4th FIW that he was OK and would return after refuelling his aircraft. They also confirmed to him that his radio and IFF was not working.

The Sabre carried 435 US gallons of fuel in its internal fuel tanks and Downes estimated that he would need 150 gallons to fly low level back to Kimpo. With his IFF not functioning his appearance on the Kimpo radar would result in the alert flight being launched to intercept him. It took two hours to pump the fuel in by hand and another three or four hours for the tide to retreat far enough to attempt a take off from the beach. Downes later recalled:

'I attempted to fire up the engine but got a wet start and shut it down. The start up power required was 1,000 amps, and if the starter generator was supplying insufficient power I had a big problem. I decided to risk a dry run to remove the excess fuel in the engine. After a short wait with some apprehension I carried out a second attempt to start the engine. The engine lit up and a loud bang came from the jetpipe; while ramming the throttle full open I stood up, prepared to abandon ship. The excess fuel ignited, sending a jet of flame torching twenty feet out of the jetpipe. The engine ran up to power and, waving away my temporary crew, I headed for the beach. The dramatic Roman candle effect scattered the Korean bystanders crowding in on the aircraft and helped to clear my way. As I lined up for my take-off run close to the water I saw people still wandering around on the beach despite a Jeep sent to clear them away. I opened up the throttle and, running close to the water, started my take-off run in the manner of my arrival, the people parting magically ahead of me. The southern half of the beach was unoccupied as I unstuck and cleared the sand dunes. I throttled back at 200 feet and headed for K-14.'

Downes flew south-east to avoid the enemy anti-aircraft artillery on the Haeju peninsular and then east towards the Han estuary. As he crossed the Han River he spotted the distinctive hill they called 'The Witch's Tit' in the distance to his right. The sun was low in the sky as he flew in over the paddy fields and lined up for a straight approach to the runway from the west. The runway was clear, so he selected airbrake, wheels, and flaps and touched down.

He taxied into the dispersal area to be greeted by his crew chief with the words, 'Gee, Captain, you're reported shot down and Captain Moore said you were dead!' He had been away from the base for ten hours.

⋇ The problems began when Downes walked to Group Operations and gave an edited debriefing to the intelligence officer, leaving out the details of his trip to Manchuria. Lonnie Moore then arrived and his first question was, 'Did you confirm my two MiGs?' Downes confirmed the MiG where the pilot ejected, but their two reports did not tally with the reports of the Group and the Group Commander, Colonel Johnson, then ordered Moore's gun-camera film to be shown. The film clearly showed Moore's attacks on the two MiGs, but unfortunately it also showed clearly the runway, hangar and revetments of Phen Chen airfield, 25 miles north of the Yalu River and the border with Manchuria. The Colonel collected the film and stormed out, saying to Moore; 'You know this means a court-martial.'

That evening, over drinks in the officers club Moore recalled that, although he had lost sight of Downes following the break, he observed his progress across Phen Chen by the intense AAA reception. There was nothing he could do to help Downes as he was low on fuel and just made it back to Kimpo, his engine flaming out as he landed on the runway.

Downes later reflected that they made a fundamental error in attacking the MiGs at the centre of the 8 plane formation, rather than the two right at the end in a hit and run attack before heading swiftly for home. Instead, they found themselves outnumbered four to one and in full view of the AAA on the airfield. Downes was indeed lucky to make it home in one piece.

In the end, there was no court-martial and Moore retained his four previous MiG claims and with the granting of a fifth destroyed over Phen Chen, he became the thirty-fourth Ace of the Korean War. Downes was not questioned again and believed that the Brass thought any proceedings against Moore, who received considerable publicity as a result of his ace status, would create too many problems and backfire to the detriment of the 4th FIW. Also, he did not think they cared to have a foreign pilot involved and decided to let sleeping dogs lie.

Downes continued to fly with Moore and occasionally crossed the border in search of prey, but never ventured near Phen Chen again. He considered the one-sided Rules of Engagement which allowed the enemy to cross the river to attack US forces, but prevented them from doing the same was absurd.

By the time the war came to an end, Captain Lonnie Moore was credited with ten confirmed MiG-15 kills and returned to the States to the Flight

Test Centre at Edwards AFB. Sadly he was killed while test-flying the McDonnell F-101 Voodoo on 10 January 1956.

Colin Downes later flew Hunters and Javelins with the Central Fighter Establishment, retiring from the RAF in 1961. At the time of writing, Wing Commander Downes was alive and well and living in Canada.

Marine Night Fighter Ace

Lieutenant Guy Bordelon joined Composite Squadron 3 (VC-3) at Moffet Field in California just before it was broken up into five-plane detachments and assigned to various aircraft carriers. They were flying the F4U–5N night fighter version of the Corsair and the pilots received specialist training in order to fly these hazardous missions. They not only had to contend with the risk of suffering an attack of vertigo as they manoeuvred in the dark, but they would be flying at low-level to engage targets whilst exposed to intense anti-aircraft fire.

Bordelon was with the detachment which joined the USS *Princeton* (CVA-37) for its second nine-month cruise off the east coast of Korea in the Sea of Japan. They began flying night time strikes against North Korean road and rail targets in late October 1952. At that time the North Koreans and Chinese moved most of their supplies at night, by ox cart, trucks and trains. If a night fighter caught a train in the open, the train driver would open the throttle and head for the nearest tunnel, hoping to reach the safety of its depths before the Corsairs bombs and rockets destroyed it. Sometimes the enemy would light smoky fires inside empty tunnels to try to lure the Corsairs down within reach of anti-aircraft guns hidden nearby.

In June 1953 Bordelon was sent to the Seoul area to try to help bring down the 'Bedcheck Charlie' bi-planes that were destroying precious stocks of fuel and ammunition during their nocturnal activities. On the night of 29 June, the Marine radar operator at K-16 at Pyongtaek picked up an intruder on his screen and Bordelon took off in pursuit. The ground controller vectored Bordelon onto the tail of the Yak-18 two-seat trainer and the bi-planes rear gunner opened up on the Corsair. Bordelon replied with a burst of high explosive incendiary shells from his four 20mm cannon and the intruder exploded in flames.

No sooner had Bordelon reported the kill, then the ground controller vectored him onto another bogey, a second Yak-18 and within minutes it too was diving towards the ground in flames. The next night he was flying CAP north of Inchon, when he was again vectored towards some intruders. He identified them as Lavochin La-11 fighters and later recalled, 'The La-11s were in a loose trail formation, so I pulled in right behind the rear aircraft and gave a "Tallyho!" on enemy bogeys. I was cleared to fire, and at once opened up on my targeted La-11. Two short bursts of cannon fire was all it took. This La-11 began to burn, and it dove straight down into the ground. The lead fighter started to follow the burning aircraft down, but I closed to point-blank range and immediately opened fire on it. This target turned left, then right, and started to climb as I gave him another burst. With that, he exploded in flames and fell apart. I followed the largest burning mass down to 500 feet and saw it crash near my first kill. "Over so fast?" I thought.'

For the next two weeks the North Koreans did not send any more 'Bedcheck Charlies', but one night Bordelon found himself closing in on two Tupolev Tu-2 bombers heading for Inchon. He could not fire on them because of a disconnected wire in his direction finding gear, so he accelerated past them, turned around, dropped his landing gear and turned on his landing light. He was almost on them when they took evasive action, one diving towards the ocean and the other pulling upwards. They abandoned their bombing run and fled northwards.

On the night of 16 July 1953, Bordelon went aloft after another intruder. As he closed in on the La-11 he requested, and was given, permission to fire but immediately the La-11 began violent evasive manoeuvres which suggested that his frequency was being monitored. It did not do him any good though, as Bordelon stayed with him and fired a long burst from his four cannon. The enemy plane exploded, briefly blinding the American pilot, but he switched on his Corsair's autopilot, which promptly righted the aircraft.

Bordelon had become the navy's first prop ace in Korea and when he returned to the USS *Princeton* he was welcomed by the ship's band, banners, Marine sideboys and a personal greeting by the Commanding Officer, Captain O. C. Gregg. His Corsair 'Annie Mo' was wrecked shortly afterwards in an accident whilst being flown by an Air Force Reservist, a point that Bordelon enjoyed making at later Fighter Ace's Association gatherings. He was the Navy's only ace in Korea and the only night ace in Korea. He stayed in the Navy for twenty-seven years and passed away in December 2002.

Armistice at Last
There were 170,000 North Korean and Chinese prisoners in the UN POW camps and around 20,000 UN and US soldiers were either missing in action or languishing in Chinese run prisoner of war camps along the Yalu River. The main issue blocking the signing of the armistice was the Communists'

insistence that all prisoners of war be exchanged, whether they wanted to return home or not. It was becoming clear that not all Chinese or North Koreans wanted to return home, with a consequent loss of face for their governments. Should the UN force them to go back? At the end of the Second World War the Allies forcibly repatriated tens of thousands of Russian soldiers who had been captured by the Nazis. Stalin wanted them back, but they knew he planned to punish them for being captured in the first place – a bullet in the head for the officers and ten years in a Siberian labour camp for other ranks. The ill-feeling that this created behind the Iron Curtain caused the supply of enemy defectors to dry up for some years after the end of the war. Why defect or surrender to the Americans if they only send you back, they asked?

Eventually it was agreed that any prisoners who did not want to return home would be handed over to representatives from a neutral country – in this case India – where they would remain for ninety days while their governments subjected them to 'explanations' and tried to persuade them to come home. Thereafter, they would revert to civilian status and the Neutral Commission would help them relocate to a new home. President Rhee did not agree with this, though. As far as he was concerned, on the day the armistice was to be signed, any North Korean who did not want to return home would be set free to live in the south.

Just after midnight on 18 June, the ROK guards at the four main POW camps threw open the gates and the first of 25,000 North Koreans who did not want to be repatriated walked out into the night. Outside the gates they were met by ROK soldiers and police, and given civilian clothes and directions to hiding places in private homes. By the time US troops took over the camps, the North Korean POW population had dropped from 34,500 to less than 9,000.

The Chinese response was not slow in coming. They launched their most violent offensive in two years and fired so much artillery at the UN lines that they appeared to be using up all the shells they had stockpiled during the two years since the front had stabilized. They threw three armies totalling almost 100,000 men against five ROK divisions of half that number and pushed them back several miles until UN artillery stalled the offensive. The fighting continued into the early days of July and clearly shook President Rhee's determination to continue the war without the UN if necessary.

On 11 July, South Korean President Syngman Rhee agreed to accept a cease-fire agreement in return for promises of a mutual security pact with the United States. On the same day Major John Bolt, USMC, flying with the

39th FIS of the 51st FIW, shot down his fifth and sixth MiGs to become the Marines' only Korean War ace. On 16 July, Commander Guy Bordelon, flying with 5th Air Force, became the war's thirty-eighth Ace and the only ace for the US Navy.

On 27 July at 1000 hours. Lieutenant General William K. Harrison, USA, the senior delegate for the UN Command, and General Nam Il, the senior delegate for the North Korean Army and the Chinese Volunteers, signed the armistice agreement to produce a cease-fire in the Korean War.

In the final hours before the cease-fire, 5th Air Force fighter-bombers hammered the North Korean airfields. Post-strike photography from 67th TRW aircraft confirmed that every airfield in North Korea was unserviceable for jet aircraft landings, indicating the successful conclusion of the airfield neutralization program. Captain Ralph S. Parr Jr. became a double ace with the last air-to-air victory of the war by shooting down an IL-12 transport.

Flying a 91st SRS RB-29, Lieutenant Denver S. Cook piloted the last Bomber Command sortie, dropping leaflets over North Korea. An 8th Bomb Squadron B-26 dropped the last bombs of the Korean War in a night, radar-directed close support mission. Aircraft from the same squadron had flown the first combat strike into North Korea. An RB-26 of the 67th TRW made the last combat sortie of the war over North Korea. As the Korean War formally ended, by 1001 hours, all FEAF's aircraft were located either south of the front line or more than three miles from North Korea's coast.

On 5 August, Operation 'Big Switch' began with the first exchange of prisoners of war 'desiring repatriation' by both sides. The United Nations Command began the transfer of 75,823 enemy POWs (70,183 North Koreans and 5,640 Chinese) directly to the communists in the de-militarized zone (DMZ) and the communists began the transfer of 12,773 Allied POWs, including 7,862 South Koreans, 3,597 Americans and 1,000 British, in return. This 'limited' war had been exceedingly bloody but a full accounting of the casualties will never be known. It has been estimated that military casualties on both sides were approximately 2.4 million, while another two million civilians were casualties. These civilian figures actually may be conservative. The United States suffered 36,686 men killed and another 103,284 wounded.

The war in the air was also bloody. FEAF lost 1,466 planes out of a total of 1,986 UN aircraft destroyed. Of these total losses, 1,041 were in combat. The always dangerous flak claimed the most aircraft, 816 (most of these on ground attack missions), while 147 were lost in air-to-air combat. FEAF also had 1,841 casualties, including 1,180 dead. In the process of sustaining these losses, FEAF units flew almost 721,000 sorties and delivered 476,000 tons of ordnance. Among the equipment claimed destroyed by UN aircraft were 976 planes (including 792 MiG-15s), 1,327 tanks, and 89,920 vehicles. Some 184,800 enemy troops were also claimed killed. On the other side, the Soviets claimed 510 UN aircraft shot down in just the first year of the war and a total of 1,300 during the entire war. They acknowledge the loss of 345 MiG-15s.

Whatever the cost of the war in aircraft, the cost was even higher for the loved ones trying to lead a normal life while their fathers, husbands and sons were serving their country. The former prisoners of war who returned home under Big Switch had a chance to rebuild their lives. The pilots who were listed as Killed in Action would be remembered with honour, but what about those carried on the rolls as Missing in Action? Were any of them still alive and if so, where were they?

Chapter 5

The Lost Pilots

Chapter Contents

A LTOGETHER, 1,690 US Air Force personnel were brought down behind enemy lines – 1,180 as a result of direct enemy action. Of these, 175 were rescued immediately by helicopter or flying boat. It is known that 155 were killed when their planes crashed. Of the rest, 263 are known to have been captured; 248 were returned during the prisoner exchanges Big and Little Switch, and fifteen were still held by the communists in China, in violation of the armistice agreements. In addition 999 were carried as missing in action and eventually declared dead.

Only three Air Force pilots managed to return to friendly lines after being captured. Captain William D. Locke escaped during the confusion of a North Korean retreat early in the war. He hid under the floor of a schoolhouse in P'yongyang, where he had been temporarily interned, and waited there until UN troops had advanced to his position. Another pilot, Captain Ward Millar, walked out of an enemy hospital where he had been kept for three months and, with the help of a North Korean Army sergeant who had defected, managed to signal a UN plane, which later directed a helicopter in to pick them both up. First Lieutenant Melvin J. Shadduck was shot down, captured and then, entirely unaided, planned and successfully executed an escape from behind enemy lines.

There were almost a hundred Air Force officers who fell into a special category; after they were shot down they were neither rescued nor captured. Most of these men landed in no-man's-land and eventually found their way back to friendly lines. A dozen or so landed deep in enemy territory and some sneaked back through the Communist lines, completely unaided. Others made their way to the sea and eventually made contact with friendly naval forces or with the Air Rescue Service. A few were assisted by Christians, or by North Koreans who wanted to collect the 'blood chit' reward, the equivalent of a years pay.

But what happened to the 999 Air Force pilots who were listed as missing in action at the end of the war, as well as the US Navy, Marine, Army and UN pilots also carried as missing in action? Men like Wing Commander Johnny Baldwin, RAF, a British pilot who was shot down while flying an F-86 with the USAF? One intelligence report claimed that he was being held in a North Korean tungsten mine together with thirty-five American officers; none of whom came home. Canadian Squadron Leader Andrew MacKenzie was held by the Chinese until 1955 and on his release confirmed that the Chinese had told him that they also held 'Johnny Baldwin'.

The Corso Report

During the Korean War Colonel Philip Corso was head of the Special Projects Division in the G-2 Section of Far East Command. One of his primary duties was to keep track of enemy prisoner of war camps in North Korea – their locations, the conditions in the camps, estimated numbers of American and allied prisoners of war in each camp and the treatment that the prisoners received at the hands of the enemy. He also served as a member of the UN truce delegation at Panmunjom during the closing days of the war, and participated in the discussions on Operation Little Switch, the exchange of sick and wounded prisoners of war. He stayed on for Big Switch and was present at the time when the prisoners were brought in.

At the end of Little Switch, he prepared a document showing that not all the sick and wounded were returned. Intelligence reports indicated that there were between 1,700 and 2,000 sick, seriously ill or wounded men in the camps. Around 1,200 were eventually repatriated and Corso estimated that another 500 would not survive unless they were handed over for treatment. Four more months would pass before any more prisoners were handed over.

After Big Switch Colonel Corso went back to the United States and was assigned to President Eisenhower's National Security Council's operations coordinating board as a member of the staff. His primary duties were prisoner of war matters on the National Security Council level, because he had compiled and worked on this data in the Far East Command and in Korea. Following the end of Big Switch, Colonel Corso and his colleagues concluded that around 8,000 prisoners of war had not been returned. He was directed to prepare a statement on the subject for Henry Cabot Lodge to read out at the meeting of the United Nations in New York. At the same time, it was discovered that the Chinese, under Russian tutelage, were conducting detailed and scientific Pavlovian-type experiments on UN prisoners. Although they knew about the information, they were hindered from sending agents to the north to find out more because it was being handled by OPC, which was a unit of the Central Intelligence Agency.

While the war was still going on, Colonel Corso received evidence daily that prisoners had been sent to the Soviet Union. It came from the interrogation of North Korean and Chinese prisoners, defectors, and photographs from reconnaissance aircraft. He received between 300 and 400 reports indicating that UN prisoners of war had been sent up through Manchuria to Manchouli where they changed trains because of the difference in the rail line gauges and continued on to the Soviet Union. At least two train loads of prisoners, and possibly a third, were involved.

One day Colonel Corso was called to brief President Eisenhower on the reports of prisoners being transferred to the Soviet Union. He told him that between 900 and 1,200 American prisoners had been transferred from North Korea to the Soviet Union. The President had a very serious look on his face and he asked Corso for his recommendations. Corso said, 'These men will never come back alive because they will get into the hands of the NKVD (later the KGB) who will use them for their purposes; espionage, playbacks or whatever. This is not uncommon in the intelligence business. Once they fall into their hands there is little hope of them coming back. My recommendation is to not make it public in order to protect the families.'

Almost sixty years later the families are still waiting to hear the fate of their loved ones, and only Russia can provide the answers.

With the benefit of hindsight, it is pretty clear that the United Nations were not going to get all of their prisoners of war back, even if every single North Korean and Chinese POW was handed back during Big Switch. Throughout the war the CIA had been receiving reports of US and South Korean POWs being shipped by train into Russia, as well as sightings of US and British POWs at various locations inside China. Years after the war ended there were many reports of sightings of US prisoners in the hundreds of concentration camps comprising the Gulag in Siberia. It is not unreasonable to assume that once the prisoners were interrogated and bled dry of information, they were given Soviet names and shipped to various camps in the Gulag. Over time they would have succumbed to the extreme weather, harsh working conditions, poor diet and absence of medical assistance. Some may have been deliberately killed or worked to death. A small number, sympathetic to the Communist cause or brainwashed by their rhetoric, or maybe considered useful to the Soviet authorities, may have survived a while longer. Not one came home to tell their story.

Where Did All the Sabre Pilots Go?

According to US Government figures, fifty-six F-86 Sabres were shot down during the war and fifteen live pilots and one set of remains were handed back at the end of hostilities. Of the forty others it was estimated that nine of the pilots could not have survived. The other thirty-one or fifty-five per cent of those shot down were listed as missing in action. This is unusually high when compared to the MIA rates for pilots flying other types of aircraft. But is it really surprising? The Sabre was the latest jet fighter in the US inventory and the Soviets would have wanted live pilots to go with the wreckage of one Sabre already recovered after ditching in shallow water. They would have been at the top of the Soviets list for interrogation.

Proof that Soviet intelligence was targeting F-86 pilots came when Marine Corporal Nick Flores was recaptured after escaping from POW Camp 1 at Chongsong in July 1952. Before he left the camp the other prisoners gave him various articles of clothing including a US Air Force flight jacket to help ensure his survival in the harsh terrain. After ten days on the run he walked into a camouflaged anti-aircraft position near Sinuiju, which was manned by Soviet gunners. An officer said in English; 'You are the American pilot' and ordered him to be bound and blindfolded. Flores expected to be returned to his POW camp, but he was bundled into a truck and driven across the twin bridges at Sinuiju to Antung in Manchuria.

He was taken into a building where he was handed over to a Soviet Colonel with the words, 'Here is the American F-86 pilot' and four hours of interrogation began. Flores continued to insist that he was an enlisted Marine and an escaped prisoner of war. He was unaware that at 0920 hours that morning Major Felix Asla had been shot down flying his Sabre in the vicinity of Sinuiju and the Russians must have thought he was the missing pilot.

The Russian interrogator demanded to know which squadron he flew with and the location of their airfield. He also repeatedly asked Flores about his knowledge of germ warfare, adding ominously that, 'All the other pilots have confessed' and he should do so as well. Eventually, another officer entered the room and spoke to the Colonel who then halted the interrogation. After eighteen hours Flores was helped aboard another truck, still blindfolded. Once on the truck he removed his blindfold and could see that he had been held in an earth-covered bunker on a major airfield with rows of MiGs parked nearby. He was driven across the Yalu River and back to Camp 1.

The treatment of Corporal Flores was proof that the Soviets had a special handling procedure for pilots, especially Sabre pilots. They would be taken directly to a Soviet interrogation site, completely bypassing the normal prisoner of war camps. This was confirmed in 1993 in a report from the Pentagon entitled *The Transfer of US Korean War POWs to the Soviet Union*. It came to the following conclusions:

- The Soviets had a programme of the highest priority to capture F-86 aircraft and pilots for technical exploitation.
- The Soviet forces in North Korea had seventy teams whose mission was the recovery of US pilots.
- The Chinese turned pilots over to Soviet officers as a matter of policy.
- Soviet policy was to establish a veil of deniability over the transfer of prisoners by taking them directly after capture to the Soviet Union. Such prisoners never mixed with the general POW population in North Korean or Chinese hands.
- There is no record of repatriated US POWs who were transported to the Soviet Union for technical exploitation and then repatriated.
- The Soviet forces in Korea devised and executed a plan to force down at least one intact F-86.
- Intact F-86 aircraft and at least one pilot were delivered to the Sukhoi and Mikoyan Design Bureaux for exploitation.
- A number of POWs, notably including F-86 pilots, were transferred by air to the Soviet Union for exploitation of their technical knowledge.
- The evidence suggests that the Soviets had a special interest in the MIAs shown on Table One (in the report), and specifically Captain Albert Tenney and First Lieutenant Robert Neimann. There is a good chance that Captain Tenney and his aircraft were transferred to the Soviet Union for exploitation.

It is now believed that Captain Albert G. Tenney, USAFR, was captured alive and taken, together with his aircraft, to Moscow. Tenney's flight was making a high-speed descent over North Korea when it was attacked by enemy aircraft. The aircraft was seen to dive away from an enemy MiG fighter and execute evasive manoeuvres at an extremely low altitude. He was informed of his low altitude and was instructed to pull up. Immediately thereafter, he levelled the wings of his F-86, which then struck the surface of the water in a low-angle, high-speed glide approximately three miles offshore near the mouth of the Yalu River. Enemy aircraft forced the leader to leave the area and he did not see whether the aircraft sank into the water or not. When search aircraft returned to the scene later that day they could find no trace of the aircraft or pilot. In recent years, information has been received from the Sukhoi and MiG Design Bureaux that at least two examples of the F-86 were sent to Moscow and one of these was full of sand. The pilot is believed to have accompanied the aircraft.

Other pilots had a good chance of surviving the loss of their plane, including Captain Robert H. Laier, USAF, who was declared missing in action on 18 June 1951. He was participating in a four-ship fighter sweep in the area of Sinuiju when he came under attack from enemy aircraft. When last seen his aircraft was seriously damaged, trailing smoke and in a steep dive at approximately 10,000 feet, thirty kilometres southeast of Sinuiju. An aerial search for his aircraft wreckage was unsuccessful. A subsequent unofficial Chinese propaganda broadcast supports a belief that he survived the shoot-down and was captured.

First Lieutenant Laurence C. Layton, USAFR, was also declared missing in action on 2 September 1951. A few minutes after arriving in the target area the flight engaged in combat with a number of enemy fighters. During the mêlée Layton's F-86 was hit. He radioed that he was going to try to reach the northwest coast of Korea and bail out. Another member of the flight accompanied Layton and observed him parachute from the damaged aircraft near the mouth of the Chongchon-Gang River, roughly six miles off the coast. Subsequent information reveals that Layton is believed to have been rescued by a large enemy powerboat.

First Lieutenant Charles W. Rhinehart, USAFR, was declared missing in action too, on 29 January 1952. During a combat mission over North Korea Rhinehart's F-86 experienced a flameout and all attempts to restart the engine were unsuccessful. At an altitude of 4,000 feet he was seen to successfully parachute from the plane and land in water off the mainland amid an area of numerous sand and mudflats some twenty-five miles south of Chongju, North Korea. A subsequent aerial search of the area failed to locate any trace of the pilot. He would have been an ideal candidate for MGB (later KGB) interrogation as he had studied aeronautical engineering at Iowa State College, had gone through USAF All-Weather Interceptor Aircrew Training, and conversion training on the F-86-4 model, the newest variant of the Sabre at that time.

Some pilots were kept for propaganda purposes, such as the crew of a B-29 and a handful of Sabre pilots brought down in Chinese airspace. The men would eventually be tried by Chinese courts before being released in 1955. The main purpose of this was to embarrass the United States at the behest of Stalin himself. On the night of 12 January 1953, an RB-29 from the 581st Air Resupply and Communication Wing was shot down while on a leaflet-drop mission over North Korea. On board were Colonel John K. Arnold, the Wing Commander and eleven other crew members, plus an instructor pilot and First Lieutenant Paul Van Voohris, a radar instructor. The men were shipped to Mukden, Manchuria, where they were questioned anywhere from six to twenty-four hours a day. In February they were sent to a jail in Peking and the interrogations continued, with the crew spending months in solitary confinement. Eventually, they were all sentenced to between four and ten years' imprisonment for 'espionage'.

In December 1954, they found themselves sharing a cell with two CIA agents who had been shot down in November 1952. They never saw their two pilots again, but John Downey and Richard Fecteau were sentenced to twenty years in jail. They would not be released until President Nixon visited China in 1972. It became clear to the Arnold crew that there were other Caucasians in the jail; they saw them taking exercise and in the washroom and most had been treated badly. Most of the Arnold crew was released by the Chinese in August 1955, two years after the war. Two of the crew, Second Lieutenant Henry Weese and First Lieutenant Paul Van Voohris, both radarman, were not released and were probably passed on to the Russians.

Sabre Pilots in China

It was 4 September 1952, 1630 hours. The lone F-86 was in trouble. Four enemy MiGs were after him and his buddies were nowhere to be seen. One of the MiGs began his attack just as Lieutenant Roland Parks came on the scene. Separated from his flight leader in a dogfight in the clouds, he was heading south to rendezvous near Cho-do Island, a friendly island off North Korea. He immediately opened fire on the MiG and saw pieces fly off as he pressed his attack:

'Then some of the other MiGs moved in on me and I felt some hits on my plane, so I broke off. I had made about a 180-degree turn in attacking the MiG, so I turned back and picked up on my compass a general heading of south. I had to keep zigzagging. I was keeping my eye on the compass, flying through soup. Some of my other instruments already had been knocked out, I could see. Soon I found out that my compass had also been damaged. When I broke out of the overcast and could see the coastline, I realised that I had been flying west into the sun and must be considerably west of Korea.

'Shortly after breaking out of the overcast, at an altitude of about 42,000 feet, my engine quit. I knew from this altitude I could easily glide a hundred miles and planned to glide back southeast as far as I could and then bail out over the water. At this point, though, I ran into more MiGs and got bounced again. With my engine dead, my only alternative was to get out. I had the choice of bailing out over the sea or over the land in the vicinity of Port Arthur. I elected to bail out over the land, with the hope, ridiculous though it may sound, of hiking my way back. I thought I could walk further than I could swim. So I just rolled my plane over on to its back and went down as fast as I could. During this time I had got into radio contact with one of our own craft, briefly explained the situation, and said I was bailing out.

'I tried to pick a place that was thinly populated, but every place was thickly populated. At about 10,000 feet I headed the plane for the water and ejected. Everything was going perfectly, just like I'd been told to do. But after my parachute opened I saw the plane starting to circle back, heading right towards me. It went underneath me by about 200 feet.

'While I floated down the plane circled again and hit the side of a mountain. I could see people watching me from the ground. I lit on a rock-covered side of a mountain and rolled a good way down it, but fortunately I was not even bruised. I headed for some trees, hunting cover, climbing this mountain like a goat. Finally I made it to a valley on the other side and hid in some woods until dark. I still had my pistol and some emergency rations, but had lost my knife and my escape kit. After dark I headed for the highest point of land in the vicinity to get my bearings. I could see water on three sides, and I was between Port Arthur and Darien.

'I wanted to get back to where I had lost my escape kit and recover it, and set out in that direction. But I ran into a bunch of Chinese and turned back before they spotted me. It was just about midnight when I ran into these Chinese and started to sneak around them. While trying to circle them, I ran smack into another Chinaman. He was so scared he shook. I tried to make him understand that I wouldn't hurt him, and only wanted him to help me. I was just grasping at straws, hoping I might have found one Chinese friendly to us. I followed him into a small village, and then, just as we reached the village square, he grabbed me and started yelling. Chinese came from everywhere. They were armed with iron spears that must have been four-feet long. Here I was with just one pistol, surrounded by all these Chinese.

'I just said to myself, "Parks, you've had it." I threw my forty-five on the ground and put my hands up. One kid tried to run me through with his spear, and they all converged on me. I think they would have killed me right there if one old man hadn't driven them off. He brought me a drink of water that I really needed badly. Pretty soon two Russian soldiers walked up, just sightseeing apparently. Then came several Russian officers, one of whom could speak English, and several armed Russian soldiers. They put me in the back of an old truck and drove about thirty minutes. We stopped in the middle of a cornfield and I began to sweat. I was expecting a bullet in the back of the head. But apparently this was a camouflaged airfield, for a MiG flew in and landed nearby. We went through a gate into a camouflaged area of tents, occupied by Russian soldiers. The Russians seemed friendly and treated me well. They fed me. Then they questioned me, but only generally, and gave me back the watch and pen from my escape kit that had been found. I gave them the general information that we were permitted to give, but gave them the wrong air base that I had flown from. I explained that I had got lost, and that's how I came to be near Port Arthur.

'In the morning a Russian Army doctor came to examine me. He was accompanied by a beautiful young Russian woman who spoke perfect English. They brought in a bottle of lemonade. They were surprised to find that I, a jet pilot, was only twenty-two-years-old. The real questioning got under way later in the day. It was done by Russian officers. They seemed especially interested in our radar equipment, but I told them I didn't know anything about it. The place we were in was a military compound in a residential area of Port Arthur. I spent the next thirteen days in this compound. Between 6 and 9 September, they questioned me about everything, especially equipment, and wanted me to draw maps of our airfields. On 11 September, a Russian officer questioned me about American politics and asked what party I belonged to. Sometimes I was embarrassed, because he asked me some questions about the details of the American governmental system that I just couldn't answer.

'On 17 September the Russians told me they were taking me to Russia where I would be with other Americans. I had told them I did not want to be turned over to the Chinese and that's probably why they told me they were taking me to Russia. I thought they were taking me to the Siberian salt mines. I had made up my mind that if we kept going north towards Siberia I was going to go over the hill at all costs. We stopped in Darien for food and supplies for the trip. My Russian guards on this trip were dressed in civilian clothes until we crossed the border between the Russian zone of Port Arthur and China proper. Then they put on uniforms. We drove until late that night.

'I saw a number of American GIs riding in American six-by-six GI trucks on my way from Port Arthur to Antung. They appeared to be hauling firewood. There were two Americans in the back of one truck and one in another. I was rather shocked; they were heading west and moving right along. When I recovered I said to myself, "Did you really see that?" The GIs were well dressed in typical winter garb: GI field jackets, wool sweaters and typical GI winter hats with flaps. I did not see any guards, although I do not know who was driving or who was riding in the cab. Also where I was held in or outside of Antung, I was aware of other Americans held there. Who they were I will probably never know.

'We finally arrived in Antung about 1500 hours and stopped near the airfield. A Russian officer went away and came back in about an hour with some Chinese officers. Then I was blindfolded while we drove about thirty minutes more, stopping at what I learned later was a Chinese military base, where I was taken into a room and the blindfold was removed. The Russians took away everything Russian they had given me, destroying the evidence that I had been in Russian hands.

'The Chinese immediately started questioning me, with the interpreting being done by a Chinese named Lue who spoke perfect English and who said he had taken pilot training in the United States during World War II. Lue turned out later to be the man they used as a sort of "pacifier" to soothe you and to try to trick you into telling something when things didn't suit them in their long interrogations. Lieutenant-Colonel Edwin L. Heller and Captain E. Fischer (who were later imprisoned) also encountered this character Lue. I really learned to hate him. He thought he was such a slick operator. Finally it became so obvious that I disliked him that they kept him away from me. On 21 September another American was brought into the room next to mine, under guard. He moaned constantly for the day-and-a-half he was there, apparently wounded. During the last half of 21 September I was questioned repeatedly, hour after hour, sometimes nine hours at a stretch. They tried to get me to say that I had flown into Manchuria many times. They showed me a pamphlet accusing the Americans of atrocities and I wouldn't look at it. Some guards gave me apples, candy, nuts and butter and some clothing. They tried to get me to write a description of American air-to-air combat tactics. When I refused they kept questioning me far into the night. They always held out the promise that if I cooperated I would go to a North Korean prison camp, and threatened that if I didn't cooperate things would be very bad for me.'

On 4 October, Parks was taken by train from Antung to Mukden. The journey, which lasted almost seven hours, took the American further into China to a town where the occupying Japanese had housed American and British prisoners during the Second World War. His cell was cold and damp and the food was pretty inadequate. On 30 October he received three meals instead of two. He later learned that this was the day Lieutenant Lyle W. Cameron arrived at the prison. Eighteen days later Cameron joined his fellow pilot in his cell.

One day Cameron jokingly told the guard that for a drink of whisky and some apples he would give him his watch. That night the guard came in and woke them up and offered some Chinese wine and two apples. They drank the wine, ate the apples and then demanded two more bottles of wine and more apples before they gave him the watch. During the next few nights the guard paid up and got his watch. The Chinese were really strict about guards taking prisoners' watches and if he had been caught he would have been in trouble.

In February 1953 the pair found themselves in trouble with their jailers. All the food they were served was bad, but the least bad was the cold Chinese sausage called 'chong char'. They decided the sausage would taste better if it was hot and started heating it with their candles. One of the guards intervened and tried to take their candles, but Lyle just pushed him out of the cell. The guard called for reinforcements and then they took away the candles. After a while they found a new way to heat their food. They started hoarding toilet paper and would build a small fire in the latrine, where one would cook the sausage while the other stood watch for the guards. They got by with this method for weeks.

In April 1953, while the Little Switch prisoner exchange was taking place in Korea, Parks and Cameron were moved to a new jail and put in separate cells. Within a few days they realised there were other Americans in the prison after hearing them talking to the guards. One of them was Captain Harold E. Fischer, who was two cells away from Parks. Another 'resident' was Andy MacKenzie, the Canadian F-86 pilot. August 1953 came and went, with the interrogators insisting that the prisoners write confessions that they had repeatedly flown across the Yalu River into Chinese territory. Across the border in Korea Operation Big Switch began and the repatriation of prisoners of war commenced. However, there was to be no going home for the prisoners in Mukden jail. Their solitary confinement did come to an end, though, and Parks, Fischer and Cameron were all put in the same cell.

The months dragged on until June 1954. It was almost a year since the guns had fallen silent in Korea. On 28 June Parks received a cablegram from his family; the first news from home in twenty-two months. That month one of the interpreters returned to the prison and mentioned that he had been spending time with Lieutenant-Colonel Edwin L. Heller in a hospital in Mukden. He had been in the hospital for almost two years and had had four operations on his injured leg. During the winter of 1953/54 the pilots were separated following some infraction of the rules. Captain Fischer was blamed and sent to another wing of the prison. After a week or two he had had enough. He dug a hole through the wall and went out into the night in freezing weather. He had no plan and no provisions. He walked for several hours, wading across a small stream on his journey. With wet feet and becoming colder by the hour, he saw a guard shack on a bridge. He decided to turn himself in and was soon brought back to the prison.

In January 1955, United Nations representative Dag Hammarskjold visited China to try to obtain their release, but the wheels of diplomacy turn slowly. In May 1955, the men were taken to Peking and put on trial on charges of violating Chinese territory. After a show trial they were pronounced 'guilty' and ordered to be deported immediately. On the afternoon of 31 May they crossed the border into Hong Kong.

After thirty-three months of imprisonment – twenty-one of them after the war in Korea had ended – Roland Parks was free.

Strategic Reconnaissance

The North American B-45 Tornado was the first operational American jet bomber and it first flew in 1947. Although it dropped Atomic bombs twice, in atmospheric nuclear tests in 1951 and 1952, it was not a great success and the decision was made to change its role from bombing to reconnaissance.

Three RB-45Cs from Detachment A, 84th Bomb Squadron, 91st Strategic Reconnaissance Wing arrived at Yokota Air Base, Japan in September 1950. Powered by four General Electric J47-GE-13/15 turbojet engines, they had a top speed of 570mph and were armed with two 0.50-caliber machine guns in a tail turret. They were tasked with risky night-photography missions, often flying out to a radius of 500 miles to search out targets.

They had to avoid the enemy radar-directed anti-aircraft guns as well as the new MiG-15 fighters that appeared in the theatre a few weeks after the RB-45C. Tragically, on 4 December an RB-45C piloted by Captain Charles E. McDonough disappeared, believed to have been shot down by a MiG. Also on board were Colonel John R. Lovell, a Pentagon intelligence officer, Captain Jules E. Young, the co-pilot, and First Lieutenant James J. Picucci, the navigator. There was no crew seat for Colonel Lovell and his role on the mission has never been explained. He was the highest ranking intelligence officer lost during the war. Apparently he worked directly for the head of Air Force intelligence, Major General Charles P. Cabell, who recommended in October 1950 that the RB-45 be used for reconnaissance over the Soviet Union. Usually officers with as much knowledge of secret US war plans as Lovell would never be allowed to fly over enemy held territory, but perhaps he was under orders to report back to his boss on the success of the spy plane's role?

It was a highly-classified aircraft full of the latest reconnaissance and intelligence-gathering equipment. Not only was it used to fly missions over North Korea, but it carried out intelligence-gathering flights over China and the Russian port of Vladivostok as well. There is no doubt that the Soviets dearly wanted to shoot down an RB-45C in order to examine its wreckage and interrogate the crew.

Lovell's name was mentioned in an enemy broadcast from China picked up by US intelligence on 21 May 1951, which suggested he had been captured in Korea. His name also appeared on a December 1954 list of seventy-one names of men positively identified by Far East Command as 'men positively identified as remaining in the hands of the communists' after the final exchange of Allied and Communist POWs in September 1953. The fact is however, that he was dead within a day or two of being captured. The story goes that he angered a North Korean General when he refused to stand up when he entered the room and the irate officer ordered a sign to be hung on him saying 'US War Criminal.' Thereafter he was taken to the nearby village where he was beaten to death by angry villagers.

The fate of the crew would remain a mystery for forty years until the Iron Curtain was briefly opened to allow researchers into some of the Russian archives. There they found a one page report dated 18 December 1950 which stated that pilot McDonough parachuted from his plane after it was hit by MiGs near the Yalu River but died two weeks later. His burial location was not mentioned, nor the cause of death. The note stated, 'I am informing you that the pilot from the shot-down RB-45 aircraft died en route and the interrogation was not finished.' It was signed by Marshal Stepan Krasovskii, the senior Soviet military adviser to China, and addressed to Marshal Pavel Batitskii, chief of the General Staff in Moscow.

The note corroborated the report from the only American to have talked to McDonough after he was shot down. Air Force pilot Hamilton B. Shawe, Jr. spent about three days with McDonough as a prisoner of war in a bombed-out prison in Sinuiju, North Korea, starting around 14 December. He said he last saw McDonough being taken away from the prison on an ox cart and that he was in such bad condition that it seemed unlikely he could live much longer. Shawe said McDonough told him he had parachuted from the burning RB-45, but later suffered severe frostbite while trying to evade capture in the frozen wilds. When he sought food at an isolated Korean house, the occupants turned him in to the military.

A second report dated 17 December 1950 was later found by the researcher which stated that the RB-45 was shot down about forty-five miles east of Antung, China, just across the border from Sinuiju, North Korea. The report summarized what McDonough told his Chinese and Soviet interrogators and asks that Russian 'advisers' in Korea help retrieve downed American aircraft. The report was signed by the Soviet commander of the 64th Fighter Aviation Corps, which headed the Soviet air operations in Korea.

Voices from the Gulag

There were two main prison systems in Russia that absorbed the US and UN prisoners received from North Korea and China. The Sharashka system comprised small, unnoticed camps or sites where Soviet and foreign professionals, either sentenced and confined or kidnapped off the streets, were forced to carry out research and development work on defence associated projects. Engineers, Phds, scientists and technicians were sentenced to imprisonment in the Sharashkas. Usually located near the more notorious forced labour camps, the Sharashkas were able to draw individuals from the prison population who would then work as assistants in areas such as bacteriology (for germ warfare), rockets, atomic energy, radar, etc. The USSR documented the vast acceleration in their defense design programs as a result of the exploitation of such men.

Most POWs were destined for the Gulag System. The brainchild of Joseph Stalin, this was the cruellest and most severe of the Russian prison systems. Thousands of camps with millions of inmates were situated in Siberia and other inhospitable areas of the Soviet Union. The prisoners were used for forced labour by brutal guards, endured poor accommodation and food, and almost non-existent medical care. Hundreds of thousands, if not millions, died in these remote camps and that included American and other UN prisoners of war.

A CIA report dated 2 September 1952, reported on the location of Soviet transit camps for prisoners of war from Korea:

- Since July 1951, several transports of Korean POWs passed through the ports of Bukhta (near Vladivostok), Okhotsk and Magadan. Each ship contained 1,000 or more prisoners. Between the end of November 1951 and April 1952, transports of POWs were sent by rail from the Poset railway junction on the Chinese-Soviet frontier. Some were directed to Chita in Eastern Siberia and some to Molotov, European Soviet Russia, west of the Ural Mountains. It is most probable that POWs are undergoing some sort of investigation and selection process while in the MVD prison in Chita. Some of them are retained in prison in Chita for a long time, while others are sent directly by rail to Molotov and other industrial regions in the Ural Mountains.
- In some camps situated near the Gubakha railway, about a hundred-and-fifty Americans were kept, probably soldiers and NCOs. From these camps one to three POWs were taken every few days by officers of the MVD for transportation to Gubakha or Molotov. They never returned to their camps and their fate remained unknown. According to the supposition of persons acquainted with MVD methods, these POWs had been observed in the camps by specially-assigned agents of the MVD, who knew the English language and were able to identify those individuals who were very hostile to the Communist regime and ideology and those who could be considered sympathetic. Those belonging to the first group were most probably either sent to prison or to especially hard labour camps for extermination. The others were probably sent to special political courses in Molotov.

Following remarks by Russian Premier Boris Yeltsin that Americans were imprisoned in the Russian camps system, Task Force Russia was formed in 1990 to try to track down any survivors and discover the fate of those who died inside the Soviet Union. There was enormous resistance by the KGB and GRU to the work of the joint American–Soviet commission, and most of their records remain out of reach to this day. However, the commission advertised their search for information in newspapers and in radio broadcasts and people started to come forward.

In a series of interviews in 1996, a Soviet veteran who lived in Minsk claimed to have seen a US POW in May or June 1953. He was reportedly a US F-86D pilot whose plane had been forced to land in North Korea in the late spring of 1953. The witness who served in An Dun, China, from December 1952 to February 1954 said that the pilot was sent to Moscow the day after his forced landing. The witness claimed that the pilot later became an instructor and taught at the Monino Air Force Academy between 1953 and 1958. Apparently he taught air battle techniques and tactics and assisted the Soviets in figuring out a US radar gun sight.

During an interview in 1993, a witness in Lithuania described an encounter with Americans at the Novosibirsk Transit Prison around June 1952. The witness stated there were two American pilots in the group of prisoners brought into his small room. The other two or three prisoners were German. The Americans reportedly told him that they had been shot down in Korea. They were dressed in khaki shirts and trousers with no belts. The first American was tall with a red beard and he told the source that he was a Captain in the Air Force.

A Polish former inmate waiting for release from the Gulag recalled that an American arrived at Coal Mine Number Six in Vorkuta in June of 1953. Other prisoners told the witness that the American was a pilot from a spy plane downed by the Soviets. He was approximately six-feet tall and about forty years-old, of medium height and thickset with dark or auburn hair.

A former German POW detained in labour camp OLP-9 in Vorkuta in 1952 heard from a driver that approximately nineteen miles north of Vorkuta was a 'Camp of Silence' where the inmates did not have to work and were not eligible for mail privileges. According to the driver who was an ex-prisoner engaged in hauling supplies to various camps, this Camp of Silence held Americans and British captured in Korea.

One thing that puzzled the author while he wrote the last chapter of this book is why the subject of US and UN POWs in Russia was not included in the Armistice talks in 1953. The CIA knew very well that prisoners had been shipped to Russia since 1951, so why was the signing not subject to the return of these men as well as those known to be in North Korean and Chinese hands? Was it really a surprise to the negotiators that 8,000 missing men did not come home during Big Switch?

The Korean War was a very brutal affair against a cruel and merciless enemy and almost sixty years later both sides still face each other across the most fortified strip of land in the world. In recent years, dozens of former South Korean POWs have escaped into China and back to South Korea, after fifty years of slavery in North Korean coal mines. Is it possible that there are still American or British prisoners of war surviving in the far flung corners of North Korea, China or the former Soviet Union? It is possible, but it is more likely that most are lying in unmarked graves outside long ago abandoned labour camps in Siberia. We can only learn the lessons of history and make sure that such things do not happen again. We can also remember the brave men who flew their fighters and bombers in the skies over Korea and gave their lives to ensure the freedom of the people of South Korea. Wherever their bones lie, may they rest in peace.

In the months before the manuscript for this book was completed, a North Korean submarine torpedoed a South Korean Navy ship killing dozens of sailors. Then, possibly in response to US and South Korean military exercises, the north unleashed a prolonged artillery barrage against a village on a South Korean island, causing extensive damage and a handful of casualties. No one can read the minds of the unstable rulers of the Stalinist regime in the north, so it is difficult to assess whether or not war will come to the peninsula again. This time however, conflict on their borders is the last thing Russia and China desire. North Korea does possess nuclear weapons and if they decide to use them, who knows what retaliation may rain down on North Korea and across the frontiers of the neighboring countries. One thing for sure is that American and Allied pilots will be flying in the skies over North Korea again one day and some will probably be captured.

Let us hope that their governments will make greater efforts to bring them all home than they did the first time.

END

Index

MILITARY UNITS

United States Air Force –

MILITARY UNITS